Alexander Hamilton's Religion

Stephen J. Vicchio, Ph.D.

Wisdom Editions

Minneapolis, Minnesota

Minneapolis
FIRST EDITION August 2021

Printed in the United States of America.
10 9 8 7 6 5 4 3 2 1

Cover and interior design: Gary Lindberg

ISBN: 978-1-950743-61-2

This book is dedicated to my oldest and dearest friend,
Joseph Cieslowski, who saved my life.

Contents

Also by Stephen J. Vicchio

Muslim Slaves in the Chesapeake: 1634 to 1865
Mala'ika: Angels in Islam
Evil and Suffering in the Bible
The Akedah or Sacrifice of Isaac
Evil in World Religions

Alexander Hamilton's Religion

Introduction

The work that is to follow is a study of American statesman Alexander Hamilton. The First chapter will begin with a short summary of the biography of Mr. Hamilton, followed by some comments of the statesman's earliest religious life in his childhood and early adulthood on the island of Nevis in the Caribbean. This will be followed in the second half of Chapter One with a summary and a discussion of Mr. Hamilton's earliest religious life and the religious sources of the same.

In Chapter Two of this study regarding Alexander Hamilton's religion, we will speak and write specifically about what the statesman said and wrote about God, Jesus Christ and the Christian religion. This will be followed in Chapter Three with what Alexander Hamilton wrote and said publicly about Holy Scripture or the Bible.

The focus of Chapter Four shall be what the statesman wrote and said about other religions, specifically Judaism, Catholicism and the faith of Islam.

Chapter Five will be taken up with three principal goals. These will be the statesman's views on ethics, or the nature of the Moral Good; what Hamilton had to say about the nature and extent of Moral Responsibility; and what Hamilton believed, wrote and said about specific moral issues.

The chief focus of Chapter Six shall be to introduce and discuss what the statesman wrote and said about the issues of religious freedom and religious toleration. As we shall see, some of the material in Chapter Six will overlap and extend the views presented in Chapter Four.

Chapter Seven will explore specifically what the statesman said and wrote about the phenomenon of prayer. As we shall see in this chapter, Mr. Hamilton was a firm believer in the idea of the efficacy of prayer in his life and the lives of his family.

In the eighth chapter, the main focus will be what appears at times to have been the contradictory perspectives on what the statesman said and wrote about the idea of slavery in the United States and elsewhere in the eighteenth century.

The main focus of Chapter Nine will be the notion of American Nationalism and ultimately will ask and answer the question in the affirmative, "Was Alexander Hamilton an American Nationalist?" This question will be raised after a discussion of the nature of Nationalism, as well as how that phenomenon developed in the United States in the late eighteenth century.

Throughout this study on Alexander Hamilton's religion, we will periodically call him the "American statesman," or even the "great American statesman," in many places when we refer to Mr. Hamilton.

Finally, the tenth chapter should be seen as a conclusive chapter, or a general summary of the major conclusions that we have made about American statesman Alexander Hamilton. This brings us to Chapter One that will include a short biography and an analysis of Alexander Hamilton's earliest religious life.

Chapter One
Short Biography and Earliest Religious Life

The boy's exceptional skills and endless learning capacity soon
saw him running the firm upon his owner's absence.
—**John T. Sullivan, "Alexander Hamilton"**

Hamilton said, "A promise should never be broken." This
shows he knew the importance of honesty in government.
—**Nathan Bierle, "Alexander Hamilton: Founding Father"**

Why has government been instituted at all? Because the pas-
sions of man will not conform to the dictates of reason and
justice without constraint.
—**Alexander Hamilton, *The Federalist Papers***

Introduction

There are two major purposes in this first chapter of this study of
Alexander Hamilton's religion. The first of these is to give a short
summary or biography of the life of Alexander Hamilton. The second
goal of Chapter One is to describe and to discuss what we know of
the earliest religious life of American statesman Alexander Hamilton,
including his most important early religious influences on his faith
from the Academy in Elizabethtown, New Jersey, as well as in his
time at King's College in New York City. We move, then, to the short
biography of Alexander Hamilton.

A Short Biography of Alexander Hamilton

In this short biography of the life of American statesman Alexander Hamilton, we will divide the life of the Founding Father into the following ten parts:

1. Birth and Childhood in the Caribbean
2. Hamilton's Education
3. Hamilton and the Revolutionary War
4. Hamilton, the Constitution, and *The Federalist Papers*
5. Hamilton and Congress of the Confederation
6. Hamilton as Secretary of the Treasury
7. Hamilton's Post-Secretary Years
8. Death of Philip Hamilton in a Duel
9. Hamilton's Duel with Aaron Burr
10. Alexander Hamilton's Death and Influence

In this opening section of Chapter One, we will make some observations about each of these ten sections of the life and times of American statesman Alexander Hamilton beginning with his birth on January 11, 1757, and childhood until 1772 when Hamilton left Saint Croix, arrived in Boston and then traveled to New York.

Alexander Hamilton was born on the island of Nevis in the British West Indies in 1755 or 1757; the exact date is in some dispute.[1] His parents were Rachel Fawcett Lavine (or Lavien), who was of British and French Huguenot descent, and James Hamilton, a Scottish trader. At the time of Hamilton's birth, Rachel was already married to John Lavine (or Lavien), a much older merchant whom she had been pressured into marrying by her parents when she was only sixteen.[2] John and Rachel had one son named Peter.

There is evidence that Mr. Lavine was abusive to his wife, and he had spent nearly all of her inheritance which she received when her father died in 1745. During this tumultuous relationship, following Danish Law, he even had her imprisoned for several months on charges of adultery. When she was released, instead of returning to her husband, the independent-minded Rachel fled the troubled marriage and moved to the island of St. Kitts.[3] It was there that she met and moved in with

James Hamilton, with whom she soon had another son, James, the statesman's older brother who was born in 1753.[4]

Either two, or four, years later, Alexander Hamilton was born. What came next was a series of tragedies, adversities and hardships that would seem to make it impossible that the American statesman would ever become prominent in any way. First, when Alexander was ten years old, his father left the family with no explanation.[5] A year later, in 1768, when her sons were eleven and thirteen, Rachel died at the age of thirty-eight. The boys were left penniless and placed in the guardianship of an older cousin who committed suicide when the statesman was twelve years old. All of these facts went into the making of John Adams referring to Hamilton as "The bastard brat of a Scottish peddler."[6]

Determined to make a good way for himself in life, the bright and ambitious young Alexander began to work as an accounting clerk in a mercantile establishment on St. Croix. The young lad quickly impressed his employers of the firm of Beekman & Cruger. The statesman's supervisor at that time was the firm's partner, Nicholas Cruger, whose firm traded throughout the Caribbean, as well as with the British colonies that would later become the United States.

Mr. Cruger quickly recognized the talents of Mr. Hamilton. Even though the boy was only fifteen, it was clear that he had a knack for mathematics and business. He kept track of expenses and profit ledgers and was able to communicate with local officials and sea captains about the business. It was also with Beekman & Cruger that we begin to see the first flares of Alexander Hamilton's writing abilities.[7]

In fact, at the age of fifteen, the young Mr. Hamilton published several letters and small collections of poetry in the local newspapers that at least gave him some notoriety on the island of St. Croix. When Mr. Cruger left the island for business purposes, he usually left the young Alexander in charge of the company.

Nicholas Cruger was so impressed with Hamilton that the businessman gathered together a group of other merchants who pooled their resources with a Presbyterian minister on the island, a man named the Reverend Hugh Knox, who also edited a newspaper on St. Croix. We will say more about Rev. Knox in the second section of this first chapter. The purpose of the group of businessmen was to find a way to send the young Hamilton to America for a university education.

So, in the fall of 1773, Hamilton arrived in New York City, where he enrolled in what was then called King's College that was later renamed Columbia University. Despite his gratitude to his benefactors, the statesman only attended the school from the end of 1773 to the middle of 1776, not long enough to meet the requirements for graduation.[8]

As it was at most other colonial colleges, the curriculum of King's College was dominated by the study of the Greek and Roman classics. In addition, however, Hamilton hired a private tutor to help him continue his work in mathematics. During his time at King's College, Hamilton also started a literary club and a debating society to discuss the issues of the day, mostly the American colonies' relationship with Great Britain.[9]

The Revolutionary War began in 1775. In 1776, Hamilton left King's College to join the army as part of the New York Provincial Artillery Company. The future statesman went on to fight in the Battles of Long Island, White Plains and Trenton.[10] The following year, Hamilton also fought at the Battles of Brandywine Creek, Germantown and Princeton. After these battles, he was promoted to the rank of lieutenant colonel of what was then the Continental Army.

It was also in this period that Alexander Hamilton caught the attention of General George Washington, who made Hamilton his assistant and trusted confidant. For the next five years, from 1776 to 1783, Hamilton put his writing skills to work. He wrote many of Washington's most important letters and composed even his most critical reports on the goings-on of the war. Hamilton was also responsible for a restructuring of the Continental Army.[11]

Alexander Hamilton was appointed the aide-de-camp to George Washington in 1777. Hamilton was only twenty years old at the time and was already beginning to pile up many impressive accomplishments. He held the post of aide-de-camp until resigning on April 30, 1781. Three months later, the statesman was given the command to lead a light-infantry battalion from New York and Connecticut and afterward was ordered to Virginia. In Virginia, Hamilton commanded a battalion of light-infantry troops of the Continental Army at the Battle of Yorktown, also known as the Siege of Yorktown, which lasted from September 28 until October 19, 1781.[12]

The statesman was also with General Washington at Valley Forge in the winter months of 1777 and 1778. It was also during this winter that General Horatio Gates accused Hamilton unsuccessfully to incriminate Hamilton in what was known as the "Conway Cabal," a plot among senior Continental Army officers who wished to have George Washington replaced in late 1777 and early 1778.[13]

On December 14, 1780, Alexander Hamilton married Elizabeth Schuyler, daughter of Philip Schuyler, a Revolutionary War general. Elizabeth's mother was a member of the Rensselaer family. Both the Schuyler and the Rensselaer families were very wealthy and prominent New York families. By all accounts, the Hamilton marriage was a good one and produced eight children.[14]

One final note about the Washington-Hamilton relationship involves an episode on February 16, 1781, in which the statesman quarreled with the first president, and the friendship was forever soured. In a letter to his father-in-law dated February 18, 1791, Hamilton wrote of the incident,

> Two days ago, the General and I passed each other on the stairs. He told me he wanted to speak with me. I told him that I would wait upon him immediately. I went below, and delivered to Mr. Tilghman a letter to be sent to the commissary containing an order of a pressing and interesting nature.[15]

Hamilton goes on in the letter to speak of being stopped by the Marquis de la Fayette with whom he conversed for a few minutes, and afterward, met General Washington again at the head of the stairs, where Hamilton says, "He accosted me in an angry tone." This was followed by Hamilton relating that General Washington said:

> You have kept me waiting at the head of the stairs these ten minutes. I must tell you, sir, you treat me with disrespect.

In the letter to his father-in-law, the statesman related, "I replied without petulancy but with decision, 'I am not conscious of it, sir, but since you have thought it necessary to tell me so, we part.'" "Very well," said General Washington, "if it be your choice."[16]

Later, Hamilton led the successful attack on Yorktown in Virginia; the statesman continued in the army for a couple more years. He was made a colonel on September 30, 1783, and by the end of the year, he left the service and refused to collect a pension.[17] The year 1782–1783 also marked the beginning of Alexander Hamilton's political career, item number four on our biographical outline. This brings us to Hamilton and the Congress of the Confederation, item number five of the outline.

After Yorktown, Alexander Hamilton returned to New York. After a short apprenticeship, he passed the Bar in October of 1782 after only six months of self-study, although he did not practice law right away. He accepted an invitation from Robert Morris to become the collector of continental taxes for the State of New York. In July of 1782, the statesman was also appointed to the Congress of the Confederation as the representative of New York.

While Hamilton was in Congress, he perceived that disenchanted soldiers in the army were beginning to pose a danger to the now young United States. In May of 1778, the government promised soldiers that they would receive a pension of 50 percent of their pay when they were discharged from the service. Among other things, this is what made soldiers disgruntled about the government, for this money never found its way to the pockets of the retired soldiers.[18]

The top priority of Alexander Hamilton's political agenda was to establish a stronger federal government under a new constitution. In 1787, while serving as a New York delegate, Hamilton traveled to Philadelphia to discuss, among other items, how to fix the Articles of Confederation, which by now had become a very weak document. During the meetings, Hamilton expressed his view that a reliable, ongoing source of revenue was necessary to developing a more powerful and resilient central government.[19]

Although Hamilton did not have a strong hand in the writing of the US Constitution, he did have a good bit of sway in its ratification. So, in collaboration with John Jay and James Madison, these three Founding

Fathers developed what came to be called *The Federalist Papers*, a series of eighty-five essays pertaining to the national government. Of the eighty-five essays, Hamilton wrote fifty-one of them.[20]

In these political essays, the statesman craftily and artfully explained and defended the new US Constitution prior to its eventual approval a year later in 1788. Hamilton was also an important figure in the New York State ratification convention held in Poughkeepsie, where two-thirds of the delegates opposed the national Constitution. Hamilton effectively argued for ratification, arguing against the anti-Federalist sentiments growing in New York. In the end, Hamilton was successful, for New York agreed to ratify the US Constitution.[21] This brings us to item number six of our outline—Alexander Hamilton as secretary of the Treasury.

When George Washington was elected the first president of the United States in 1789, he appointed Alexander Hamilton as the first secretary of the US Treasury. At the time, the United States was facing great foreign and domestic debts due to expenses incurred during the Revolutionary War.[22]

During his years as Treasury secretary, the statesman often butted heads with other members of the Washington cabinet, those who were often fearful of a centralized government holding so much power over American citizens. Hamilton firmly believed that the US Constitution gave him the authority to create economic policies that made the central American government stronger. He proposed, for example, the idea of federal war bonds, suggested that the federal government assume some of the debts of states, and, perhaps most importantly, he instituted a federal system for tax collection.[23] Among other things, this would help the United States establish credit with other nations.

During a dinner conversation between Hamilton and James Madison on June 20, 1790, the two Founding Fathers met to discuss economic and other federal issues. At the dinner, Hamilton agreed that a site near the Potomac would be established as the nation's capital, and Madison, in turn, agreed that he would no longer block Congress—particularly the Virginian contingent—from the approval of federal policies that promoted a more powerful centralized government in regard to states' rights.[24]

Alexander Hamilton stepped down from his appointment as secretary of the US Treasury in 1795, leaving behind a far more secure US economy than it had been when he assumed the position six years earlier. This brings us to an analysis of Alexander Hamilton's post-secretary years, item number seven on our outline.

After his time in politics, Hamilton went back to his home in New York, where he continued to practice law. He also wrote a series of articles under two different pseudonyms named Camillus and Philo Camillus.[25] Hamilton was also appointed inspector general of the army with a rank of major general in 1798, an appointment from which he resigned two years later in 1800.[26] At that time, along with some friends, Hamilton also founded the *New York Evening Post* in 1801.[27]

Another significant event at the end of Alexander Hamilton's life was the death of his eldest son, Philip Hamilton (1782-1801), who ironically died at the age of nineteen when he was fatally shot in a duel with George Eacker in a field in Weehawken, New Jersey. When Philip was born, Alexander Hamilton wrote of his birth, "It was attended with all the omens of future greatness."[28] The death of Philip affected Alexander Hamilton in many ways. Perhaps the most important of these was the great American statesman's return to his Christian faith at the end of his life. Another effect was that following Philip's death, his seventeen-year-old sister, Angelica, suffered a mental breakdown. Her mental state continued to deteriorate, and she never recovered.

During the 1800 presidential election, Thomas Jefferson, a Democratic-Republican, and John Adams, a Federalist, were vying for the presidency. At the time, presidents and vice-presidents were voted for separately, and Aaron Burr intended to be Mr. Jefferson's vice-president.

Alexander Hamilton also chose Mr. Jefferson in the statesman's view, "the lesser of two evils." Ultimately, the House of Representatives chose Jefferson as president, with Burr as his vice-president. But the standoff soured the relationship of Hamilton and Aaron Burr. Indeed, when Burr read a newspaper account in which Hamilton was quoted as saying that Burr was "the most unfit and dangerous man of the community," Aaron Burr became infuriated.[29] Burr was also now convinced that Hamilton had ruined a second election for him. Mr. Burr demanded from Hamilton an explanation, or what at the time was referred to as "Satisfaction."[30]

When Mr. Hamilton refused to comply, Aaron Burr, even more enraged, challenged the statesman to a duel. Mr. Hamilton grudgingly accepted. On July 11, 1804, at dawn, the two Founding Fathers met in a field in Weehawken, New Jersey. Both men drew their pistols and shot. Hamilton's bullet missed Mr. Burr completely, while Mr. Burr's shot hit its intended mark, severely wounding Hamilton, who was brought back to his home in New York City.

Alexander Hamilton died the next day at his home on July 12, 1804. The statesman is buried in the church cemetery of the Trinity Church in downtown Manhattan, at Wall Street and Broadway. Hamilton was forty-seven years old when he died.[31] The Corporation of Trinity Church in Manhattan has erected a monument in memory of Alexander Hamilton. It says:

> In Testimony of their Respect for
> The PATRIOT OF incorruptible INTEGRITY
> The SOLDIER of approved VALOUR
> The STATESMAN of Consummate WISDOM
> Whose TALENTS and VIRTUES will be Admired
> Grateful Posterity
> Long after this MARBLE shall have mouldered into
> DUST
> He died July 12, 1804, Aged 47.

The political philosophy espoused by Alexander Hamilton in *The Federalist Papers* continues to be an important and powerful influence over the roles of government in American life. In addition to the many statues, place names and memorials dedicated to Hamilton throughout the United States, he has also recently been immortalized in the hit Broadway musical *Hamilton,* written, directed and playing the part of the central character Lin-Manuel Miranda.

This brings us to the second section of Chapter One, in which we will identify and discuss the major sources of the earliest religious life of American statesman Alexander Hamilton.

Hamilton' Earliest Religious Life

There are three main sources to be considered to ascertain the earliest religious life of American statesman Alexander Hamilton. First, there is the mentorship of the Rev. Hugh Knox, Presbyterian minister, editor and sometimes physician whom Hamilton met on the island of St. Croix in 1772.[32] The second source is a collection of religious poems completed by Mr. Hamilton that he more or less wrote in his youth until the time of his withdrawal from King's College.[33] The third source is the religious education he received in school in Nevis, as well as in the Academy in Elizabethtown, New Jersey, and at King's College in New York City.

The Rev. Hugh Knox provided the statesman with a strong spiritual and intellectual grounding. Knox took Hamilton under his wing shortly after Rachel's death. He was a Scottish Presbyterian at odds with the mainstream of his denomination chiefly over the problem of the Providence of God, or the doctrine of predestination, and human free will. Calvin, as well as most of his followers, were believers in double predestination. That ism that some souls are predestined to salvation while others are determined to reprobation.[34]

For someone like Mr. Hamilton, who otherwise would have been predestined to obscurity given his family background and tragedy, it is clear that the Rev. Knox's views on free will would have acted as an impetus for the idea of dreaming bigger dreams. Following Knox's philosophy, a Christian individual, by the power of his own free choices, was able to make something of himself. And he did just that as soon as he left the Caribbean.

The Rev. Knox was a brilliant sermon writer and preacher, and occasional editor who took the young Hamilton under his wing and tutored the boy in the humanities and the sciences of the day. When the American statesman was able to get away from his office of Beekman & Cruger, Mr. Hamilton furthered his intellectual horizons by his perusals of the books in Rev. Knox's personal library that included many volumes of Greek and Roman classics, literature, and Western history.[35]

The time that Hamilton and Knox had together was little more than several months, long enough for Knox, Cruger and other merchants to raise the cash to send this young man to America for a university education. There are, however, several letters in the *Hamilton Papers*, going both ways, including one dated October 27, 1783, from the Rev. Knox to "Colonel Hamilton."

In this missive, Knox is worried that he has not heard from his charge. "It hath puzzled me," Knox says, "very much to account for your silence." It is understandable Knox says when Hamilton was at war, "but now in a time of profound Peace & Tranquility, you cannot, it seems, find two minutes for this kind office." Nevertheless, it appears that the Rev. Knox was also instrumental in tutoring the young Hamilton in the French language and particularly in aiding the American statesman in his ability to write letters in French.[36]

The Rev. Hugh Knox was also instrumental in the arranging of an interview for Alexander Hamilton at what was then known as the "College of New Jersey," which later changed its name to Princeton University in 1746. As we have seen, however, the statesman chose instead to matriculate at King's College, the original name of Columbia University, after he had been rejected for studying at the College of New Jersey.

We do not know, however, whether the young Alexander Hamilton attended the services and the lively sermons of the Rev. Hugh Knox. If he did, he certainly would have become familiar with many of the Calvinist and Presbyterian theological ideas preached in the sermons of by the reverend.

As indicated earlier in this second section of Chapter One, another source for understanding the American statesman's early religious life is in a series of poems, often with religious themes, published from 1771 to 1773 in the *Royal Danish American Gazette*, the first known newspaper published in the Danish West Indies, what today would be the Virgin Islands. The newspaper was published on the island of St. Croix, where Hamilton's family had moved in 1765 when the American statesman was ten years old.[37]

One of these youthful poems of Hamilton's published on April 6, 1771, begins with a preface by the author. In this preface, the young Hamilton related, "I am a youth of seventeen and consequently such an attempt as this must be presumptuous; but if, upon perusal, you think the following piece worthy of a place in your paper, by inserting it you'll much oblige. Your obedient servant."

The opening stanza of the poem followed next:

> In yonder mead my love I found
> Besides a murmuring brook reclined
> Her pretty lambkins dancing round
> Secure in harmful Bliss.
> I bad the waters gently glide
> And vainly hushed the heedless wind.
> Then softly kneeling by her side
> I stole a silent kiss.[38]

Many of these youthful poems were similar love poems such as "Celia's an Artful Little Slut," which begins:

> Celia's an artful slut;
> Be fond, she'll kiss et cetera—but
> She must have all her will;
> For do but rub her against the grain
> Behold a storm blow winds and rain
> Go bid the waves be still.[39]

Another of these poems, published in the *Gazette* on October 14, 1772, is a theological response to a recent hurricane that had devastated the island of St. Croix. In the poem, the young Hamilton described the storm as an instrument of Divine retribution. The hurricane was sent by God to chastise "guilty nations" and whose fury was eased only upon the "penitential cry" of those in its path.[40]

In the poem, Hamilton employs two different theological views to explain the meaning of the hurricane. These are what theologians sometimes referred to as Retributive Justice Theory and the Moral Qualities or Test Approach. The former suggests that God employs evil and suffering to punish people for past sins. The latter view argues that the Divine sometimes employs evil and suffering to "test" the moral characters of believers or to improve these moral characters.

On October 17, 1772, three days later than the first poem, the *Gazette* published a second poem entitled, "The Soul Ascending into

Bliss." It is a straightforward imitation of Alexander Pope's "Dying Christian to His Soul." Like Pope, the young Hamilton sings the praises of God who rewards a soul's "constant virtue" by "unlocking the Gates of Bliss," an obvious reference to Heaven.

Among the stanzas of the "Soul Ascending," we find the following:

> Let reason silence nature's strife.
> And weep Maria's fate no more.
> She's safe from all the storms of life,
> And wafted to a peaceful Shore.

"Soul Ascending" was published with the pseudonym "Omicron." This was the first time, but not the last time, that Hamilton employed false authorship to express his ideas. Another stanza of this poem also contains theological themes. It tells us this:

> O Lamb of God! Thrice gracious Lord
> Now, now I feel how true Thy word:
> Translated to this happy place,
> This blessed vision of Thy face;
> My soul shall all Thy steps attend
> In songs of triumph without end.

In this stanza, the youthful Hamilton assents to a host of theological beliefs, including the existence of the soul, the singing of praises to God, the idea of a beatific vision, or seeing the face of God, and, most importantly, to "attend" to the Will of God in whatever way one's "steps" may lead one.

Another early Hamilton poem also captures the pangs of a young man separated by a distance from his lover. It is entitled, "Answer to the Inquiry Why I Sighed." It is a furtive poem that again has theological overtones. Consider these two stanzas:

> Before no mortal ever knew
> A love like mine so tender true—
> Completely wretched—you away—
> And but half blessed e'en while you stay.

> If present love [illegible] face
> Deny you to my fond embrace
> No joy unmixed my bosom warms
> But when my angel's in my arms.[41]

Another youthful poem of his, written in October of 1772, was entitled "Christiansted: A Character." The poem begins this way:

> Eugenio blessed with every pleasing power
> To sweeten life and gild the social hour
> A sprightly wit, a judgment well refined
> And better still an honest generous mind.
> With all those means to gain, fearce owns a friend
> Those very means defeat their proper end.
> Wit not well governed rankles into vice
> He to his jest his friends will sacrifice.[42]

Finally, two other of Hamilton's youth poems, one called "Thoughts of Seeing a Five Grove of Trees Destroyed by the late Hurricane," and the other entitled "The Melancholy Hours," were also written and published in the *Gazette* in October of 1772. Neither of these poems, however, is published in the *Hamilton Papers*.[43]

In these eight poems written by the American statesman from 1771 to 1773, we may make the following conclusions about the earliest religious life of the first secretary of the treasury of the United States.

1. Hamilton, as a youth, was a firm believer in God.
2. He was influenced in his poetry by the Rev. Hugh Knox, Presbyterian cleric.
3. The young Hamilton had a firm belief in the soul and its ability to survive death.
4. When it came to evil and suffering, the young Alexander Hamilton relied on what we have called Retributive Justice, as well as the Test or Moral Qualities theological responses.
5. In this youthful poetry of Alexander Hamilton, he appears to assent to a whole host of theological ideas that were common in the second half of the eighteenth century.

Among these ideas were: that it is possible to have a beatific vision, that it is important to sing the praises of God, and, most importantly, that God has a Divine Plan by which "All will be Well" in the words of Alexander Pope, Hamilton's favorite English poet.

This brings us to the third and final source of the earliest religious life of the early American statesman, his attendance at the Presbyterian Church-run academy in Elizabethtown, New Jersey, when the young Hamilton arrived there in the winter of 1772. Since Hamilton had little or no formal education, he attended the academy in preparation for his college studies at King's College.

Hamilton at the Elizabethtown Academy and King's College in New York City

The Academy at Elizabethtown, New Jersey, was run by the First Presbyterian Church. The building in which the young Alexander Hamilton attended classes was located across the courtyard from the church. Among the subjects we know that Hamilton studied were English, mathematics, geography, Latin and Greek.[44]

The Elizabethtown Academy was "one of the most celebrated schools in the colonies."[45] The academy's other alumni—and somewhat ironic—include Aaron Burr, future vice president and the man who shot Hamilton to death; Jonathan Dayton, the youngest signer of the US Constitution and future speaker of the House; and Brockholst Livingston, future justice of the US Supreme Court.[46] The Livingston family lived at Liberty Hall on campus, while the Boudinot family resided in Boxwood Hall.

At the time, the minister at the First Presbyterian Church was the Rev. James Caldwell, a friend of the Rev. Hugh Knox and a patriot later killed during the Revolutionary War.[47] The headmaster of the academy was Mr. Francis Barber, who also fought in the war and, again ironically, served under Alexander Hamilton at the Battle of Yorktown in Virginia.

The young Hamilton attended two semesters at the academy in the winter of 1772 and spring of 1773. While there, he lodged with the family of William Livingston, who soon later became New Jersey's governor. During that time, Hamilton also became friendly with Elias Boudinot, who later was the president of the Continental Congress. In the following autumn, Alexander Hamilton attended King's College in New York City but continued his friendships with the people he met at the Elizabethtown Academy.

While Hamilton was a student at the academy, he was required to attend Sunday services at the church across the courtyard, as well as the Sunday school catechism classes that were mandatory for all students. With Hamilton's interests in Latin and Greek, and classical Greco-Roman literature, he must have been impressed with the scholars he met at the church and academy, including the Calvinistic sermons he must have heard from the Rev. Caldwell.[48]

The building at the academy where Hamilton attended classes was later destroyed by fire by the British in 1780 during the Revolutionary War. It was replaced, however, in 1917 with an academic building that still stands on the same site. That building is now known as the Parish House. The academy was reopened under the name The Snyder Academy of Elizabethtown at 42 Broad Street in Elizabeth, New Jersey.

John C. Hamilton, the American statesman's son, reflected on the two semesters that his father spent in Elizabethtown. He said, "In that winter, he was accustomed to labor until midnight, and in the summer when it was his habit to retire at dawn to the quiet of the neighboring cemetery preparing his lessons of the day."[49]

The young Mr. Hamilton appears to have studied long and hard in the two semesters in Elizabethtown, and the fact that he kept up with his New Jersey friends for the rest of his life suggests that his time there was another formative period in the early religious life of this American statesman.

It was in the following autumn of 1773, Mr. Hamilton applied for admission into the College of New Jersey but was denied admittance because the college would not agree to the accelerated plan submitted and suggested by the future American statesman. He, therefore, entered King's College as a "private student" and then was officially admitted in May of 1774 at the next commencement of the college.[50]

Alexander Hamilton studied at King's College until "The American Revolution supervened," but "never graduated; the college having been broken up before his course of studies was completed."[51] There is little information about what Hamilton studied beyond the fact that he had courses in mathematics, Latin and anatomy, and had an interest in forming a debating club, as well as a writing and literature group among the undergraduates.

One final point about early intellectual sources in the early religious life of Alexander Hamilton is that when he was growing up on the island of Nevis, he was tutored by a Jewish schoolmistress who taught the future American statesman classical Hebrew, so that he could read the Ten Commandments, among other things, in the original text. We will say more about this in a section of Chapter Four devoted to Hamilton and the Jewish faith. For the moment, however, it is important to point out that in addition to writing in French and studying Greek and Latin, he also learned how to read Hebrew at a very tender age.

We know that when Hamilton was at the college, his friends were impressed with his religious devotion, but this may have stemmed from the school's religious requirements that the future American statesman was quite willing to oblige. These included attendance at chapel before breakfast, a ceremony of bells that chimed after dinner at evening prayers, and two separate services on Sundays.[52]

Robert Troup, one of Hamilton's classmates, suggested that Hamilton's religious devotion came from more than religious duty. Troup related in an interview, "He was attentive in public worship and in the habit of praying on his knees both night and morning. I had often been powerfully affected by the fervor and eloquence of his prayers."[53] Mr. Troup adds, "He had read many of the polemical writers on religious subjects and he was a zealous believer in the fundamental doctrines of Christianity."[54]

One might well argue, however, that Alexander's devotion to the Christian religion was instilled in him as a boy long before his time at King's College, in his time with the Rev. Hugh Knox, his time studying Hebrew on Nevis, and in the Academy in Elizabethtown, New Jersey, where religion was a central part of the curriculum.

This brings us to the major conclusions we have made in this first chapter of this study of Alexander Hamilton's religion. The principal content of Chapter Two shall be what the American statesman believed, said and wrote about Christianity.

Conclusions to Chapter One

In the introduction to this first chapter, we indicated that it was to have three goals and three sections. The first of these was to provide a short summary or biography of the life of Mr. Hamilton. We went on to fulfill this first goal by dividing the life of the American statesman into nine separate parts and a short discussion of each of those parts.

These parts of Mr. Hamilton's life included his birth and childhood in the Caribbean, his early education, Hamilton's career in the army, his work on the ratifying of the US Constitution and the writing of most of *The Federalist Papers*, Hamilton's service at the first secretary of the Treasury, his post-Treasury years, his duel with Vice President Aaron Burr, and Hamilton's death and influence.

The second goal of this chapter has been to explore eight poems with many religious themes that Alexander Hamilton wrote in his youth. After describing and quoting from those poems, we indicated in section two that we could make four conclusions about these poems written in Hamilton's teenage years.

The first of these conclusions was that, in his early years, Hamilton was a firm believer in God. Secondly, that his early theological views were influenced by the Rev. Hugh Knox, as well as the Minister's library. Thirdly, the youth poems of Hamilton referred to his belief in the existence of the soul and its survival of death. And finally, that the early poems of Hamilton suggest beliefs in a whole host of Christian theological ideas that included: the possibility of a beatific vision; that one ought to sing the praises of the Lord; beliefs in Retributive Justice and the Moral Qualities or Test View in responding to the phenomena of evil and suffering in the world; and finally, that God has a Divine Plan in which in the end, "All Will be Well," as his favorite English poet, Alexander Pope, put the matter in his poem the "Essay on Man."

The third goal of this opening chapter was to catalog and discuss many of the ways in which Hamilton's early education appears to have been instrumental in the American statesman's early religious life.

More specifically, we pointed out that three different school experiences contributed to the early religious life of Alexander Hamilton. First, while attending grammar school on the island of Nevis, the future statesman was taught Hebrew by a Jewish schoolmistress so the young Hamilton could read the Ten Commandments in the original classical Hebrew language.

Secondly, we pointed out that when Mr. Hamilton left the Caribbean, he studied for two semesters at the Academy in Elizabethtown, New Jersey, and where he made many life-long friends such as the Livingston and Boudinot families. We also indicated that in that time, Mr. Hamilton also refined his study of Greek and Latin.

We have also shown that, at the academy, the students were required to attend Sunday services at the Presbyterian church across the square from the college, as well as the Sunday catechetical classes also required of every student.

Finally, we indicated that, although he did not graduate, Alexander Hamilton's time at King's College was filled with religious services and religious events that surely went into the making of the earliest religious life of the American statesman.

Again, at King's College, Hamilton studied both classical Greek and Latin, refined his fluency in the writing of French, and enlisted the help of a private tutor to continue his work in mathematics.

Finally, we indicated that Robert Troup, one of Hamilton's classmates and roommate at King's College, in an interview later in life, spoke of the fervent attitude that the young college student Alexander Hamilton had, and that the future American statesman was in the habit of praying in his room "on his knees in both the morning and at night."

This brings us to Chapter Two, where we will describe and discuss what the American statesman believed, said and wrote about God, Jesus Christ and the Christian religion.

Chapter Two
Hamilton and Christianity

Alexander Hamilton was as reliable as was Benjamin Franklin
for a good quote.
—Goodreads.com

He later became one of the strongest proponents for a Federal Form of a national Government.
—Flavia Medrut, "25 Alexander Hamilton Quotes"

You should have taken advantage of my sensibility to steal
into my affections but you chose not to.
—Alexander Hamilton, *Letters*

Introduction

The chief purpose of this second chapter is to explore what American
statesman Alexander Hamilton believed, said and wrote about the
religion of Christianity. We already in this study indicated that Mr.
Hamilton, even early on, professed a deep faith in Jesus Christ and the
religion associated with him. In the first section of Chapter Two, we
will discuss the end of Hamilton's life on July 11 and 12, 1804, where
it can be shown that Hamilton continued in his faith, even to the very
end. The first section of Chapter Two, then, will be about his duel with
Aaron Burr and his death.

In the second section of Chapter Two, we will turn the conversation
to a number of very general comments that Mr. Hamilton made about
God and his religious views that often look very much like what many
of the other Founding Fathers have also said about these subjects.

The third section shall be specifically about what Alexander Hamilton believed, said and wrote about Jesus of Nazareth. As we shall see, the statesman made various comments over the years, but very few, interestingly enough, in his many essays of *The Federalist Papers*. In point of fact, God is only mentioned three times in the entire corpus of *The Federalist Papers*.[55]

In the fourth and final section of Chapter Two, we will introduce and discuss an idea of Alexander Hamilton to form what he proposed to be a "Christian Constitutional Society," an idea that never came to fruition in reality. But we will bring Chapter Two to a close by discussing the idea that he had in mind to form with his friend, James A. Bayard, as we shall see in the final section on Alexander Hamilton's religion.

Hamilton and Christianity at the End of His Life

In Chapter One, we indicated the Christian beliefs of Alexander Hamilton up to and including his time at King's College in New York City. After a violent hurricane struck St. Croix in 1772 when Hamilton was fifteen years old, he wrote the following text about the events that had just transpired:

> Where now. Oh vile worm, is all thy boasted fortitude and resolution? What has become of thy arrogance and self-sufficiency? Why does thou tremble and stand aghast. How humble, how helpless, how contemptible you now appear… Oh impotent, presumptuous fool!

After berating others on the island, the fifteen-year-old Alexander Hamilton continued:

> How darest thou offend that Omnipotence, whose nod alone is sufficient to quell the destruction that hovers over thee or crush thee to atoms…He who gave the winds to blow and the lightning to rage even him have I always loved and served his commandments have I obeyed and his perfection I have adored. He will snatch

> me from ruin. He will exult me to the fellowship
> of Angels and Seraphs, and to the fullness of
> never-ending joy.[56]

It should be clear that the young Hamilton was a firm believer in many of the traditional beliefs of Christianity, like the view that God is Omnipotent, that He created all things, that He is to be adored, that He has prescribed Commandments, that God possesses perfection, and that humans after death may some day be exalted along with the "Angels and Seraphs." In short, the future American statesman was clearly an avowed Christian.

However, the same truth can also be made at the end of Alexander Hamilton's life, which is what we hope to show in this section of Chapter Two.

After Mr. Hamilton was fatally wounded in the duel with Aaron Burr, he called for the Episcopal minister Dr. John Mason and requested that the statesman participate in the Lord's Supper, Holy Communion. Dr. Mason declined to do so because his church had a principle "never to administer the Lord's Supper privately to any person under any circumstances."[57]

Dr. Mason also took the opportunity to inform Mr. Hamilton that the Lord's Supper "is not a requirement for salvation," and the minister proceeded to explain the plan for salvation in very clear details. Mr. Hamilton reportedly assured Dr. Mason that he had not requested communion as a means of obtaining Heaven, and he gave the following testimony about his salvation, "I have a tender reliance on the mercy of the Almighty, through the merits of the Lord, Jesus Christ."[58]

The Rev. Mason's account on his meeting with Hamilton at his home in New York City after the stateman returned from the duel said that General Hamilton said:

> I went to the field determined not to take his life.
> He repeated his disavowal of all intentions not
> to hurt Mr. Burr and the anguish that was there
> in recollecting what had passed; and his humble
> hope of forgiveness from his God.[59]

Dr. Mason goes on to say that the two began a conversation about Divine Compassion, the freedom of pardon in the Redeemer Jesus to perishing sinners, "That grace, my dear general, which brings salvation is rich, rich. Then he interrupted me and said, 'Yes, it is rich grace.' And on that grace, said I, a sinner has the highest encouragement to repose his confidence because it is tendered to him upon the surest foundation."[60]

Dr. Mason tells us that the conversation turned to the Holy Scriptures that "testify that we have redemption through the blood of Jesus and the forgiveness of sins according to the richness of his grace." At this point, the minister tells us, "The General let go of my hand and now clasped his hands together, and, looking up toward Heaven said with some emphasis, 'I have a tender reliance of the mercy of the Almighty God through the merits of His Son, the Lord Jesus Christ.'"[61]

Dr. Mason also related that Hamilton admitted that "I am a sinner. I have a tender reliance on the mercy of the Almighty through the merits of Jesus Christ." Another sign that the dying statesman believed in the saving work of Jesus Christ for the rest of humanity.

Rebuffed by Dr. Mason, Hamilton redirected his hopes of communion from the Rev. Benjamin Moore, the Presbyterian minister of a Calvinist church on Cedar Street in New York near Hamilton's home and a friend of Hamilton's. But as luck would have it, the Rev. Moore refused Hamilton's request for communion, as well. Mr. Hamilton is said to have roused himself with one final burst of plaintiff persuasion in which he said, "My dear Sir, you perceive my unfortunate situation and no doubt have been acquainted with the circumstances that led to it. It is my desire to receive communion at your hands. I hope you will not conceive there is any impropriety in my request."[62]

The Rev. Moore reportedly gave several reasons for his refusal of the sacrament to Mr. Hamilton. One of those was that the Calvinist preacher was morally against the idea of dueling. Nevertheless. Moore returned to the home of Mr. Hamilton a few hours later, and the Presbyterian relented and administered the sacrament to the great American statesman, after which Mr. Hamilton died a short time later.[63]

The Rev. Moore recorded a question that he would have asked Mr. Hamilton, "Do you sincerely repent of your sins of the past? Have you a lively faith in God's mercy through Christ, with a thankful remembrance of the death of Christ. And are you disposed to live in love and charity with all men?"[64]

The Rev. Moore even went so far as recording that he asked Hamilton to renounce dueling. The minister records that he asked the statesman, "Should it please God to restore your health, Sir, will you never again be engaged in a similar transaction?"[65] There is nothing in the Rev. Moore's record, however, about how the great American statesman responded to that question if he did respond.

We relate these episodes here on the final two days of Alexander Hamilton's life so we may see and establish that the great American statesman, and first secretary of the US Treasury, appears to have held his fervent beliefs in God and Jesus Christ as his Savior until the very end.

This brings us to the second section of Chapter Two, in which we will identify and discuss a number of general comments that Mr. Hamilton made about God and Christianity over the course of his lifetime, the topic of the next section of this chapter.

Hamilton's General Comments on God

In the life of statesman Alexander Hamilton, four different kinds of general comments about the Christian religion may be detected in his writings and speeches. These can be summarized this way:

1. General comments like other Founding Fathers
2. God and the Constitution
3. Religion and politics
4. The value of the Christian religion

In this second section of Chapter Two, we will analyze and discuss examples of each of these four very general categories of statements about the Christian religion, beginning with Hamilton's use of the word "God" and its relation to the other Founding Fathers. Such as George Washington and Thomas Jefferson, for example, Alexander Hamilton rarely used the English word "God" to indicate the deity.

Instead, he more often preferred vague, Enlightenment-tinged language to speak of the Creator of the Universe. For example, in *Federalist* number thirty-seven, Hamilton related,

> It is impossible for the man of pious reflection, not to perceive
> in the Constitutional Convention a finger of the Almighty
> Hand, which has been so frequently and signally extended.

In *Federalist* number two, as well, Alexander Hamilton employed the word "Providence" to indicate God no less than three times.

Shortly before his death, Hamilton wrote to an unknown recipient encouraging him or her to "Arraign not the dispensations of Providence."[66] The Declaration of Independence, a document in which Hamilton had a hand, refers to the "Laws of Nature" and to "Nature's God."[67] In other places, Alexander Hamilton referred to "Creator," "Supreme Judge" and the "Supreme King of All the World."[68]

None of this is surprising if we consider that George Washington employed nearly a hundred terms to indicate the deity in the course of his military and political careers, many of these references actually written by Alexander Hamilton when he was the aide-de-camp of the general, such as Washington's "Farewell Address" to the people of the United States on September 19, 1796. In that address, the pen of Alexander Hamilton was behind the three mentions of the Divine, including the claim that the new nation has been chosen by God, a great "Sympathy," as it is called.

In his Camillus number twenty-two dated in 1795, Alexander Hamilton again used the vague language of the Enlightenment when he wrote,

> Let me add as a truth—which perhaps has no exception, however uncongenial with the fashionable patriotic creed—that in the wise order of Providence, nations, in a temporal sense, may safely trust the maxim, that the observance of justice carries with it its own and full reward.[69]

In a number of places in his corpus of work, Alexander Hamilton also made general comments about the relation of God to the founding documents of the nation. When the statesman was asked, for example, about putting God in the Constitution, he exclaimed, "Absolutely not! No Gods or set of laws claimed to be written by such gods are so special that I would give it any weight over human laws."[70] On another occasion, Hamilton was asked the same question, and his response was this: "Keep God completely away from the Constitution."[71]

In point of fact, the US Constitution makes no reference to God. The omission was too obvious to have been anything but intentional. When asked about it on a third occasion, however, Mr. Hamilton, according to one account, said, "The new nation is not in need of any foreign aid," while according to another source, the statesman was reported to have said, "We forgot."[72]

Alexander Hamilton also made many comments about the Christian religion when discussing the place of religion in politics. In an undated "Fragment on the French Revolution," for example, he related:

> As a corollary from these premises, it is a favorite tenet of the sect that religious opinion of any sort is unnecessary to society; that the maxims of a general morality and the authority of the magistracy and the laws are sufficient and ought to be the only security for civil rights and private happiness.[73]

On another occasion, Alexander Hamilton again turned his attention to the relation of religion to civil authority when he wrote, "An established religion is a religion in which the established authority engages not only to protect but to support… the characteristic differences between a tolerated and an established religion consist in this way."[74]

Mr. Hamilton made similar remarks in his essay entitled "On the Quebec Bill," number eleven from 1775, at the beginning of the Revolutionary War. Regarding the exercise of religion in the new nation, Hamilton wrote:

> They are allowed to exercise their religion without molestation, and to maintain their clergy as they think proper. These are wholly dependent upon their congregations and can exact no more than they can stipulate and are satisfied to contribute. But with respect to the support for the latter, the law is active and provident.

Mr. Hamilton in this observation makes the following points. First, he is in favor of all religions and sects to exercise their religious freedoms any way they see fit. Secondly, neither believers nor their clergy should be molested about those religious freedoms. And finally, the statesman again voices his belief in a Divine Law that is "active and provident."

Finally, the American statesman also frequently made several general comments about the value of the Christian religion, such as in his 1796 essay called "The War in Europe," in which he observed:

> How clearly it is proved by this that the praise
> of a civilized world is justly due to Christianity;
> war, by the influence of the humane principles
> of that religion, have been stripped of half its
> horrors. The French renounce Christianity, and
> they relapse into barbarism; war resumes the
> same hideous and savage form which it wore in
> in the ages of Gothic and Roma violence.

In his work entitled The *History of the Republic of the United States*, edited by Hamilton's son, J. C. Hamilton, the American statesman gave us another endorsement of the Christian faith. He told us:

> I have examined carefully the evidence of the
> Christian Religion; and if I was sitting as a juror
> upon its authenticity, I should unhesitatingly
> give my verdict in its favor. I have studied it and
> I can prove its truth as clearly as any proposition
> ever submitted to the mind of man.[75]

In *The Federalist Papers* number eighty-five, shortly after the Constitutional Convention in 1787, Hamilton made this statement about Christianity, "For my own part, I sincerely esteem it a system which without the finger of God, never could have been suggested and agreed upon by such a diversity of interests."

Although, for the most part, Alexander Hamilton had this positive evaluation of the Christian religion, he nevertheless had many negative judgments about organized religion, particularly Christianity. In his *A Memorial and Remonstrance* from 1785, for example, Mr. Hamilton told us this:

> During the almost fifteen centuries has the legal
> establishment of Christianity been on trial, what
> has been its fruits? More or less, in all places,
> pride and indolence in the Clergy; ignorance and
> servility in the laity; in both superstition, bigotry
> and persecution.

Mr. Hamilton made the same point in a letter to William Bradford on November 9, 1803, where he speaks of the separation of church and state and its importance in America. The statesman related, "The purpose of separation of church and state is to keep forever from these shores the ceaseless strife that has soaked the soil of Europe in blood for centuries."

Then Hamilton again spoke of the damage that he believed organized Christianity had on what he considered the true Christian religion mostly related to the ethical teachings of Jesus. In a letter to William Bradford from April 1, 1774, Hamilton observed, "Religious bondage shackles and debilitates the mind and unfits it for every noble enterprise."

In *The Federalist Papers* number ten, "Fragment on the French Revolution," Alexander Hamilton made another general comment about politics and religion when comparing the two. The great American statesman told us this:

> For in politics, as in religion, it is equally
> absurd to aim at making proselytes by fire and
> sword. Heresies in either can rarely be cured by
> persecution.

In the same essay on the French Revolution mentioned earlier, Hamilton remarked, "The praise of a civilized world is justly due to Christianity." This comment, again, is most likely related to a belief held by many of the American Founding Fathers, like Franklin, Washington, and Jefferson, for examples, that the organized Christian sects in the late eighteenth century in America were only a shadow of the true "Natural Religion" that Jesus Christ brought to the world.

The home where Alexander Hamilton died at number 82 Jane Street in Manhattan has survived. There is now a plaque on the wall of the house that speaks about the statesman's duel and death. The house is not far from the Trinity Church graveyard where Mr. Hamilton is buried at Wall Street and Broadway and where his wife Eliza is interred as well.

A building and a lawn were named after Alexander Hamilton on the campus of Columbia University. There is also a commemorative statue of the great American statesman erected outside the building.

This brings us to the third section of Chapter Two in which we will identify and explore what the great American statesman, Alexander Hamilton believed, said, and wrote about the person of Jesus Christ.

Alexander Hamilton on Jesus Christ

Already in this chapter, we made some observations about what Alexander Hamilton believed about the person of Jesus of Nazareth, including the conversations that Mr. Hamilton had on his deathbed with the two Christian ministers he had asked them to administer Holy Communion to him. Dr. Mason asked the statesman, "Do you sincerely repent your sins past? Have you a lively faith in God's mercy through Christ?" And Hamilton answered in the affirmative.[76]

With the Rev. Moore, as well, Hamilton discussed the "merits of the Lord Jesus Christ," and the statesman is reported to have said, "I have a tender reliance on the mercy of the Almighty through the merits of the Lord Jesus Christ."[77] Even with his wife Eliza, who was much more religious than her husband, it is reported that in times of family troubles—like when their son too died in a duel—the American statesman frequently told his wife, "Remember Betsey, we are still Christians."[78]

When the Rev. Moore returned to Alexander Hamilton the second time, the minister later reported that the two spoke of the "confidence in the mercy of God through the intercession of the Redeemer, Jesus Christ."[79] After administering the sacrament to the statesman, the Rev. Moore commented, "I remained with him until two o'clock this afternoon when death closed the awful scene. He expired without a struggle and almost without a groan."[80]

One important theological question that may be raised about Alexander Hamilton's death is why the American statesman was so insistent on receiving the Eucharist on his deathbed. The answer may well be the account of the Last Supper and the instituting of the sacrament in the twenty-second chapter of the Gospel of Luke, in which Jesus ultimately says, "Do this in remembrance of me."[81]

Surely, Mr. Hamilton must have remembered these words from the preaching of the Rev. Hugh Knox and from the 1662 edition of the Anglican *Book of Common Prayer* that was used at the Trinity Church, as well as at home with his children. We can only imagine that Mr. Hamilton prepared himself to receive the sacrament and thus remain a member of the mystical body of Christ. For Hamilton, the receiving of Holy Communion was a way to enter the hope of God's everlasting community by the merits of the most precious blood, death, and resurrection of His dear Son.

For the American statesman, Alexander Hamilton, the receiving of the sacrament provided for him another truth of the Gospel message, as well as a belief in the grace of God that could strengthen one's faith in this time of great need. This is why Jesus said to his disciples, "Do this in remembrance of me."[82]

This brings us to the fourth section of Chapter Two, in which we will discuss the idea that Alexander Hamilton had of forming something he referred to as the "Christian Constitutional Society."

Hamilton and the Christian Constitutional Society

Around the turn of the nineteenth century, Alexander Hamilton began to envision an organization he wished to call "The Christian Constitutional Society." The statesman wrote a letter to his friend James A. Bayard on April 16, 1802, who was the co-founder of the proposed society. Hamilton begins the letter in question this way:

> I now offer you the outline of the plan they have suggested. Let an association be formed to be denominated the "Christian Constitutional Society," whose object is to be the support of the Christian religion. And second, the support of the United States.

Hamilton goes on in the letter to Mr. Bayard to describe more about the nature of the proposed society. At this time, Hamilton was quite concerned about the state of religion in the French Revolution. The American statesman hoped to publish a number of pamphlets promoting charities and establishing immigrant aid services and vocational schools. And all of these services would come under the umbrella of the Christian Constitutional Society, as well as the Federalist Party, though not necessarily in that order.

At the same time, Hamilton and some friends began to circulate some salacious pamphlets stating that Thomas Jefferson was an atheist, and Hamilton wished to make some political profit from the rumor about the third president. If true about Mr. Jefferson, he would have totally breached the supposed separation of church and state.

Mr. Hamilton did not want to exploit his religion for political purposes but rather to establish a Christian society in which some of the society's ills could be treated under the purview of the Christian Constitutional Society.

The atheism of the French Revolution and Mr. Jefferson's embrace of it while ambassador to France helped to restore Alexander Hamilton's renewed interests in the Christian religion. For Hamilton, religion was the basis of all law and morality, and he believed the world would be a hellish place without it.

The establishment of the Christian Constitutional Society would have been another response in this war against atheism, but the organization never came to fruition, for Mr. Hamilton was murdered before it could be put into place in America.

One interesting fact about the religious life at the end of Alexander Hamilton's life is that, although his wife Eliza rented a pew at the Trinity Church in downtown Manhattan, her husband showed no interest in attending services with his spouse. The old views of Mr. Hamilton regarding organized religion had not really vanished. On the other hand, Eliza was said to be so fervent that some called her the "Little Saint."[83]

The papers of John Church Hamilton, the statesman's son, shed more light on his father's late religiosity. John Hamilton points to the annotated copy of William Paley's book *A View of the Evidence of Christianity* in his father's personal library.[84] From Alexander Hamilton's notations in his copy of the book, as well as other volumes written by William Paley, the great American statesman found in these texts an "irrefutable proof" of the Christian religion that he will later speak about in his final letter to his wife Eliza on his deathbed.

In the final letter to his wife Eliza dated July 4, 1804, Alexander Hamilton wrote about Christianity, "I have studied it and I can prove its truth as clearly as any proposition ever submitted to the mind of man." In another letter, Mr. Hamilton related to a friend, "I have examined carefully the evidence of the Christian religion and if I were sitting as a juror upon its authenticity, I should rather abruptly give my verdict in its favor."[85]

Among the other books of William Paley's that so much affected Mr. Hamilton were *Natural Theology: Evidences of the Existence and Attributes of the Deity and Evidences of Christianity*[86] and *The Principles of Moral and Political Philosophy*, most recently published in Washington by the Liberty Fund in 2002.[87] *Natural Theology*, on the other hand, was most recently published by Benedictine Classics in 2017.[88]

Another book in Hamilton's library that the statesman relied upon when it came to theological matters was Voltaire's "Reflections on Religion." Hamilton found a section of this text in which the French philosopher comments that "There are no Sects in Geometry. When the truth is clear," the Frenchman wrote, "then it is impossible for parties and factions to arise."[89] Alexander Hamilton was fond of this passage because it gave him guidance on the contradictory claims of the various Christian sects and religions in his own day.

Alexander Hamilton's copies of these three books, as well, in his personal library at the Grange, are all heavily annotated, particularly in sections that highlight Paley's version of the Argument for Design, or what philosophers call the Teleological Argument for God's Existence. Like Benjamin Franklin, Mr. Hamilton espoused the Paley version of the existence and the attributes of the God of Christianity, or in Voltaire's case, the idea of objective truth in religion.

John Hamilton also spoke of his father strolling the grounds of the family property known as the "Grange," and that one day he said to his wife, "I may yet have another twenty years, please God and I will one day build for them [his children] a chapel in the grove."[90] The desire to build a chapel at the Grange in his later years is another example of Alexander Hamilton's commitment to Christianity late in his life.

In the April 16–21, 1802, letter to Mr. Bayard, Mr. Hamilton spoke of the organization of the Christian Constitution Society, as well. It was to consist of:

1. A directing council consisting of a president and twelve members, of whom four members and the president shall be a quorum.
2. An additional directing council consisting of a vice-president and twelve members, four of whom and the vice-president shall be a quorum.
3. There should be as many state societies as the local circumstances will permit.[91]

In another section of the same letter, Mr. Hamilton spoke of what he told Mr. Bayard would be the "Means" of the new society. It was to include:

1. The diffusion of information.
2. The use of all legal means to elect fit men.
3. The promotion of institutions of a charitable & useful nature.

The Hamilton letter to Mr. Bayard about the nature and extent of the Christian Constitutional Society also included a warning about "Jacobin influences that might give impulses in America." This was an obvious warning that the leftist revolutionaries in France might also establish a footing in the New World. As indicated earlier, Alexander Hamilton, at the turn of the nineteenth century, was deeply concerned about the atheism that existed in France at the time, as well as elsewhere in Europe.

Among other reasons the idea of the Christian Constitutional Society was put forth by the great American statesman was to counteract the effects the French might bring to America. Something he and James Bayard were worried about. When Hamilton suggested with Mr. Bayard the Christian Constitutional Society in 1802, he told his friend it would be "to take hold of some strong feelings of the mind," and it would advocate "Christian welfare societies" for the poor. Unfortunately, one of the consequences of Mr. Hamilton's untimely death was that the Christian Constitutional Society would never come to fruition.

Alexander Hamilton closes the letter to James Bayard with his belief that "The forgoing is to be the principal engine that members should now be adopted as soon as possible and the repeal of the judiciary law before the Supreme Court." Mr. Hamilton refers to another concern he had in the late eighteenth and early nineteenth centuries that the 1789 judiciary law that established the federal court system was taking away many of the rights that were meant to be in the states.[92]

The atheism of the French Revolution and Thomas Jefferson's apparent embrace of the Jacobin ideas were two of the major causes of Alexander Hamilton's movement to, or return to, religion in his later years. In his 1796 *Phocion Essays*, Mr. Hamilton wrote, "Mr. Jefferson has been heard to say since his return from France that the men of letters and philosophers he had met in that country were generally atheists."[93]

James Monroe, another Virginian, was also in France when Jefferson was ambassador there. Hamilton believed that Monroe had become infected by the French *Philosophes*, as well. As Ron Chernow puts the matter in his monumental book, *Alexander Hamiton*, "He pictured the two Virginians dining together to 'fraternize' and 'philosophize' against the Christian religion and the absurdity of religious worship."[94]

For Alexander Hamilton, the enemy was Jacobinism of the French Enlightenment, a brand of thought that the "atheistic" Jefferson had utilized to establish the doctrine of the separation of church and state. In the words of the great American statesman, the first principle of the new society was "the support of the Christian religion." This is what Mr. Hamilton told Mr. Bayard in the April 16–21, 1802, missive on the nature and function of the proposed Christian Constitutional Society.[95]

Meantime, in America, a clear rift began to develop between Mr. Jefferson and his vice-president, Mr. Aaron Burr, who firmly believed that the cause of that rift was Alexander Hamilton. In a letter to his son-in-law, while Burr was vice-president, he wrote, "I now and then meet cabinet ministers in the streets."[96] Ron Chernow relates that the vice-president's contact with the president "were confined to fortnightly dinners and he met with the cabinet once a year."

Theodore Sedgwick (1811–1859), American attorney, politician and jurist, declared Mr. Burr to be "wholly without any personal influence."[97] And this was the accepted view at the time in Washington when Aaron Burr was vice-president.

This estrangement of Mr. Burr from Mr. Jefferson, of course, will ultimately have grave consequences when the man who the vice-president thought was responsible for his rift with the president, Alexander Hamilton, would meet Mr. Burr in the duel that would take Mr. Hamilton's life. In this sense, we end this second chapter in precisely the same place where it began.

This brings us to the major conclusions we have made in this chapter of this study on Alexander Hamilton's religion. The major focus of Chapter Three shall be about what Hamilton believed, wrote and said about Holy Scripture or the Bible in his public and private lives.

Conclusions to Chapter Two

In the introduction to Chapter Two, we indicated that the chapter about the statesman and Christianity would unfold in four parts and thus four sections of the chapter.

In the first of these sections, we examined the roles Christianity played at the end of Hamilton's life, including the statesman's overall wish to receive the sacrament of Holy Communion at the end and the initial refusals of both Dr. Mason and the Rev. Moore to administer the sacrament. We also indicated that in the end, just before Hamilton's death, the Rev. Moore agreed to the task.

We also indicated in the opening section of Chapter Two that his conversations at the end of his life with the two Christian ministers expressed clear assent to a whole host of Christian doctrines, including the existence and attributes of God, a belief in the soul's immortality after death, and in the saving grace of the death and resurrection of Jesus Christ, through his body and blood.

In the second section of Chapter Two, we turned our attention to a number of general comments that Alexander Hamilton made about God. In the beginning of section two, we indicated that Mr. Hamilton made four separate kinds of general comments regarding the Divine. These were summarized this way:

1. Very general comments like other Founding Fathers.
2. God and the Constitution.
3. God and American politics.
4. The value of the Christian faith for Mr. Hamilton.

Next, in section two, we provided examples of each of these four general types of Alexander Hamilton's mentions and comments about God. In the first of these categories, we mentioned that, like many of the other Founding Fathers, Hamilton avoided the actual use of the English word "God" in favor of much more Enlightenment theological terms like "Nature's God" and the "Almighty Hand."

In the second type of general comments Hamilton made about God, we indicated that he was firmly against the idea of including any language about the Divine in the US Constitution, as well as in the other founding documents in America.

Still, in section two of Chapter Two, we went on to say more about the role of God in American politics, at least from the perspective of Alexander Hamilton. We indicated the statesman's views on established religion, separation of church and state, as well as other theological ideas in the birth of the nation.

The value of the Christian religion regarding the opinions of American statesman Alexander Hamilton on the value of the faith, we made three important points. First, Mr. Hamilton believed Christianity was the finest religion and system of ethics that humanity has ever created. Secondly, we indicated that Hamilton believed that there is empirical evidence that the truths of the Christian faith are objectively true. And thirdly, he believed that organized religion and the division of Christianity into sects were often harmful to humanity, and this was chiefly because the natural religion of Jesus of Nazareth has been obscured or changed by organized religion.

In the third section of Chapter Two, we turned our attention to what Alexander Hamilton specifically believed, said, or wrote about the person of Jesus Christ. In that section, we relied on what Mr. Hamilton said in the conversations with the Reverends Mason and Moore on the statesman's deathbed, several essays of Hamilton's in *The Federalist Papers*, as well as other material like the farewell letter that the great American statesman wrote to his wife, Eliza.

In the fourth and final section of Chapter Two, we turned our focus to an idea of Alexander Hamilton's and James A. Bayard's proposal to establish something the pair of Founding Fathers wished to call the "Christian Constitutional Society."

In that fourth section, we focused on an April 1802 letter that Mr. Hamilton wrote to Mr. Bayard that sets out an outline of what the society was proposed to be, including the make-up of its officers, the idea of a quorum in the organization, the society's goals, and the "means" or purposes of the society.

We also related in the fourth section that at the end of Alexander Hamilton's life, he experienced a return of sorts to the childhood religion of his in the Caribbean and that of his religious mentor there, the Rev. Hugh Knox. In this theological return of Alexander Hamilton to the Christian faith at the end of his life, we also pointed to a number of sources for this theological shift.

As indicated in section four, two of the main impetuses for Alexander Hamilton's return to Christianity were the blatant atheism of many of the proponents of the French Revolution, as well as the time that Thomas Jefferson spent in Paris as ambassador to France and Hamilton's belief that the third president now was also enamored with French philosophers.

Alexander Hamilton was horrified by the excesses of the French Revolution and wrote several essays that were critical of the Jacobins. He was concerned that they wanted to overthrow the Christian religion in France. He thought that would be "Robbing mankind of its best consolations and most animating hopes and to make a gloomy desert of the Universe."[98] Mr. Hamilton added, "The praise of a civilized world is justly due to Christianity."[99] Indeed, he thought Christianity formed the basis of all law and morality, "and the world would be a Hellish place without it."[100]

Two years before he died, Alexander Hamilton proposed his Christian Constitutional Society to counteract the Jacobinism in the United States. Perhaps he was simply acting as a politician, but many on the right in American politics today in the twenty-first century suggest that even early on, Mr. Hamilton recognized the attraction, as well as the danger that Leftist Progressivism can bring to America.

In fact, we have shown that Mr. Hamilton believed that when Mr. Jefferson had returned home from France, Alexander Hamilton thought of him as an atheist. The great American statesman, as we also have shown in the final section of Chapter Two, that he had his doubts about the faith of Virginian James Monroe, as well that he may also have been influenced by the Jacobins at the turn of the century.

As indicated in our analysis at the end of Chapter Two, at the close of Alexander Hamilton's life, an impassable rift had developed between Vice President Aaron Burr, President Thomas Jefferson, and the great American statesman Alexander Hamilton. Ultimately, of course, one of those rifts will be responsible for the death of Hamilton.

In the end, as we have argued, Alexander Hamilton returned to his Christin faith at the end of his life. This became very clear in his conversations on his deathbed with the Reverends Mason and Moore, as well as in the final letter that the great American statesman wrote to his wife Eliza on July 4, 1804. As indicated, the letter was only to be given to his wife if he did not survive the duel with Vice President Burr a week later on July 11, 1804.

In the letter he wrote to his wife on July 4, 1804, a week before his duel with Mr. Burr, Alexander Hamilton told his spouse, "Fly to the bosom of your God and be comforted, with my last idea, I shall cherish the sweet hope of meeting you in a better world. Adieu, best of wives and best of women. Embrace all of my darling children for me. Ever yours, A. H."

The bottom line on great American statesman Alexander Hamilton on the Christian faith should now be clear. In the final week of his life, he expressed to his spouse his belief in God, in the afterlife and a "better world" in which they might meet someday, as well as the fundamental importance of love for his wife and his "darling children."

This brings us to Chapter Three, the central concern of which shall be what great American statesman Alexander Hamilton believed, said and wrote about the Bible.

Chapter Three
Hamilton and the Bible

Elias Boudinot and his family undoubtedly exerted strong Christian and Biblical influences on Alexander Hamilton. Moreover, Christianity and the Bible saturated King's College at the time. Morning chapel was obligatory before breakfast and students were required to attend church twice on Sundays.
—**Mark Ellis, "Alexander Hamilton"**

This statement makes two claims. First, that words or concepts that appear in the Bible or that are the words of Jesus Christ are off limits to the government even if, as you say in this case the words or concepts appear in multiple religious and non-religious texts.
—**William P. Marshall, "The Concept of Offensiveness"**

Give all power to the many and they will oppress the few. Give all the power to the few, and they will oppress the many.
—**Alexander Hamilton, *Letters***

Introduction

The main focus of this third chapter is to identify, describe and discuss what great American statesman Alexander Hamilton believed, wrote and had to say about the Holy Scriptures, or the Bible, of the Judeo-Christian tradition.

We will achieve this central goal of Chapter Three by including the following parts, and thus sections, of the chapter. These parts or sections are the following:

1. General comments about the Bible throughout Hamilton's life.
2. Passages of the Old Testament quoted or employed by Mr. Hamilton.
3. Passages of the New Testament quoted or used by Mr. Hamilton.
4. References in *The Federalist Papers* where the Bible is discussed.

We move next, then, to relevant, general comments and experiences of Alexander Hamilton related to the idea of Holy Scripture, the first section of Chapter Three, followed by passages of the Old Testament, the New Testament, and relevant sections of *The Federalist Papers* for this third chapter on God, ethics and Holy Scriptures.

The Bible in the Life of Alexander Hamilton

Earlier in this study, we pointed out that, as a boy on the island of Nevis, Alexander Hamilton's mother enrolled him in a Jewish school where he studied the Torah and learned to read in the original classical Hebrew language. We know little else about this experience, but certainly it must have had an effect on the boy who could have been no older than eight to ten years old.[101] We know that the Jewish school on Nevis was housed in the only synagogue on the island in the capital Charleston. Mr. Hamilton was a student at the Jewish school in the academic year 1763 to 1764, but beyond that, we know nothing else.

Mr. Hamilton would not have been allowed to attend the local Anglican school of Nevis because he was a bastard in the eyes of the church. His mother Rachel never divorced her first husband, Johann Lavien, so her union with James Hamilton was therefore not a marriage, at least in the eyes of the law at the time. This, of course, made Alexander Hamilton illegitimate in the eyes of both Danish and British law.

We can also be sure that Mr. Hamilton heard the Presbyterian sermons of his theological mentor on the island, the Rev. Hugh Knox. The statesman also shared the philosophical response to the hurricane discussed earlier that also included some theological themes. In fact, he first shared his letter on the hurricane with the Rev. Knox, who helped him publish the essay.[102] We also indicated earlier in this study that Alexander Hamilton used books about the Bible from the personal library of the Rev. Hugh Knox.

We also know that religion and the study of the Bible were parts of the curriculum at the New Jersey Elizabethtown Academy when Alexander Hamilton was matriculating there. In fact, Elias Boudinot, a life-long friend of Mr. Hamilton, was the president of the American Bible Society, as well as being president of the New Jersey Academy and the president of the Continental Congress.[103]

While Mr. Boudinot was president of the American Bible Society, he gave a number of speeches that spoke of the Holy Scriptures, including the comment, "Were you to ask me to remember the most valuable book in the world, I should fix on the Bible as the most instructive both to the wise and the ignorant."[104]

On another occasion, and speaking in the same context, Mr. Boudinot related:

> For nearly half a century, I have anxiously and
> critically studied that invaluable treasure of the
> Bible; and I still now rarely pick it up that I do
> not find something new in it.[105]

It is most likely that in Alexander Hamilton's time in New Jersey in his late teens, and at King's College in New York City, in his early twenties, the statesman received instructions on the Bible. At the end of his life, as well, there is more evidence that the statesman returned to his study of the Holy Scriptures.

On Sunday mornings since the death of his son Philip in 1801, Alexander Hamilton gathered in the garden to sing Biblical hymns and read the Bible aloud to his family.[106] In this time, Hamilton grew increasingly more religious, returning to active participation in the liturgy at Trinity Church in Manhattan. The American statesman observed at the time:

> I take the children to Church on Sunday/a sign
> of the cross at the door/and pray/that never used
> to happen before.[107]

Eliza Hamilton indicated that both before and after Philip's death, she instructed one of the older boys (Philip, Alexander, James or John Church) to read from the scriptures before breakfast, along with making a theological reflection about the text of the day.

Even in his conversations with Dr. Mason and Bishop Moore on his deathbed, the subject of the Holy Scriptures came up several times on July 11 and 12, 1804, the time of the statesman's death. Dr. Mason reported that Mr. Hamilton told him, "The scriptures testify that we have redemption through the blood of Jesus Christ."[108] Clearly, at the end of Alexander Hamilton's life, he believed in the saving power of the crucifixion and the resurrection of Jesus Christ for all of humanity.

In one of his letters in the same period, after the death of Philip, Mr. Hamilton agreed with John Adams and John Dickinson that, "The Bible is the most Republican of all books in the world."[109]

On another occasion in the same period, from 1801 to 1804, the great American statesman commented again about his genius and the Bible. He wrote this at the time:

> Men give me credit for some genius. All the genius I have is in this: When I have a subject at hand, I study it, profoundly, and I do not move on quickly, like the Bible, for example. When I read the Book of Job or one of the Proverbs, I study it and contemplate its deepest meanings.[110]

Thus, there is ample evidence that Mr. Hamilton had a deep and life-long reverence for the Biblical text, but particularly in his first twenty years of life, as well as his last three years, from 1801 to 1804. This brings us to passages in the Old Testament with which Alexander Hamilton was familiar or employed in his written or spoken words, section two of this chapter on Alexander Hamilton and the Bible.

Hamilton and the Old Testament

In the first section of Chapter Three, we have shown that Alexander Hamilton had a familiarity with certain books of the Old Testament, such as the Books of Job and Proverbs, for example. He was also familiar, however, with certain phrases or themes from the Old Testament, like one frequently employed by another of his mentors, General George Washington.

The text in question contains a phrase that appears three times in the Old Testament at Micah 4:4, Zechariah 3:10 and First Kings 4:25. It also appears in Isaiah 36:16 and First Maccabees 14:12. The phrase in question is "the vine and the fig tree," such as at Micah 4:4 that tells us:

> But they shall sit every man under his vine and under his fig tree, and none shall make them afraid; for the mouth of the Lord of Hosts hath spoken it.[111]

At the Prophet Zechariah's 3:10, he relates,

> In that day, saith the Lord of Hosts, shall ye call every man his neighbor under the vine and under the fig tree.[112]

At First Kings 4:25, the writer speaks of,

> And Judah and Israel dwelt safely, every man under his vine and under his fig tree, from Dan to Beersheba, all the days of Solomon.[113]

At Isaiah 36:16, the Prophet speaks of,

> Eat ye every one of his vine and every one of his fig tree, and drink ye every one the waters of his own cistern.[114]

And First Maccabees 14:12 tells us:

> For every man sat under his vine and his fig tree and there was none to fray him.

This Hebrew phrase in question, "the vine and fig tree," was employed over fifty times in George Washington's letters, including in his "Farewell Address." The first president used this picture of "the vine and fig tree" not only as a shorthand for his beloved home at Mount Vernon but also as a metaphor for economic freedom.

Scholar Daniel Dreisbach puts the matter of the vine and fig tree this way:

The first president looked to the Hebrew Scriptures for a favored blessing and made it his own. The ancient blessing of Micah 4:4 embraced the multiple facets of Washington's life. It encapsulated enduring political principles of civility, rule of law, limited government, and property rights.[115]

In the opening chapters of the book of the prophet Micah, he paints a picture of the New Jerusalem in a New World, in much the same way as George Washington employed the idea of every man cultivating his own "vine and fig tree" and thus helping in the establishment of economic freedom for his family, as well as that of other Americans.

Alexander Hamilton was fully aware of General/President Washington's uses of the phrase, so much so that the phrase is employed in a song called "One Last Time" in the Broadway musical *Hamilton*. Not surprisingly, in the show, the phrase is sung by the character who plays George Washington.

Indeed, in the musical *Hamilton*, there are at least seventeen other Old Testament references in the songs of the show. We will cite three more examples here and speak about their relevance for this Chapter Three.

In another song of *Hamilton* named "My Shot," the lyrics include the words, "We roll like Moses, claimin' our Promised Land." This is another reference, of course, to the Old Testament patriarch Moses who led his people out of bondage in Egypt and took them to the "Promised Land" in the Land of Canaan. Moses did this in the Book of Exodus after he had met the God Yahweh face to face on Mount Sinai. One reason that this text was significant to Alexander Hamilton, we will remember, is that the statesman was able to read the text in the original classical Hebrew he had learned at a Jewish school on the island of Nevis.[116]

Moses is not only revered in the Jewish and, by extension, the Christian faith in the New Testament, he is also the most often mentioned prophet in the Muslim Holy Book, *Al Qur'an*, where his classical Arabic name is *Musa*.[117]

Another song of *Hamilton* called "A Winter's Ball" includes:

Watch this obnoxious, arrogant, loudmouthed
brother be seated at the right hand of the Father.

In more than a hundred verses of the New Testament, Jesus is described as being at the right hand of the Father of God. This is another way of saying that Jesus is "God's right-hand man." In other words, God and Jesus work together for their people and rule over the Heavens and the Earth. To be seated at the right hand of God to these ancient people meant that you were a crucial—and central—figure. The idea of being at "the right hand of the Father" can be seen in the New Testament at Acts of the Apostles 7:55 and 56, Romans 8:34, Ephesians 1:20, and Colossians 3:1, among many other places.

In the musical, it is Hamilton who is the one seated at the right hand of George Washington, the Father of the Nation. Thus, Alexander Hamilton was attempting to gain favor with the Father, and thus he was deemed necessary and crucial to the cause of the American Revolution.

Another song in the musical is the "Ten Duel Commandments." It is the fifteenth song from Act One. As with most of its songs, Lin-Manuel Miranda wrote both the music and lyrics. Miranda gives credit to the eponymous ten commandments at Exodus 20:1–17 and Deuteronomy 5:4–21. Miranda also said, however, that the idea of the song stemmed from the "Ten Crack Commandments" by the Notorious B.I.G. that served as a guide to what constituted illegal acts in rap culture in America in the 1990s.

The "Ten Duel Commandments" are a fictionalized list of rules for a duel. They are mentioned several times during *Hamilton*, mostly in connection with three separate duels that appear in the musical. These are Lee v. Laurens, Philip Hamilton v. Eacker, and Aaron Burr v. Alexander Hamilton. We already mentioned the second two duels listed here, in which both Philip Hamilton and his father were mortally wounded.

The Lee-Laurens duel took place between Colonel John Laurens and General Charles Lee on December 24, 1778. Lee was challenged by Laurens in the event that he failed his command given to him by George Washington when Lee abandoned his army and instead sought the company of prostitutes. Alexander Hamilton was originally to be Lee's opponent, but Washington would not permit it, so Laurens took his place, as we learn in the *Hamilton* song, "Stay Alive."

In the Lee-Laurens duel, General Lee was wounded in the side, and Laurens was declared the victor. In the musical, Mr. Miranda puts forth "Ten Duel Commandments." These are the following:

1. Agree to the duel
2. Assign seconds
3. Have seconds meet
4. Organize weapons and medical assistance
5. The duel before dawn
6. Leave messages for family members
7. Pray
8. Have the seconds meet again
9. Take your places
10. Fire your weapon

The Irish *Code Duello*, formalized in 1777 and followed in the English-speaking world in the eighteenth and nineteenth centuries, originally consisted of twenty-five rules, the rules of ruling etiquette in Europe. Mr. Miranda shortened this list to these ten mentioned above. Throughout the musical, they are continually referred to and sung, particularly in relation to the three duels mentioned earlier in this section of Chapter Three.

Dueling with firearms grew in popularity in the eighteenth century, especially after the adoption of the Irish Code Duello at the Clonmel Summer Assizes in 1777 for the government of duelists by the gentlemen of the counties of Tipperary, Galway, Mayo, Sligo, and County Roscommon.

The Code Duello consisted of twenty-five rules, including several footnotes. Rule sixteen, for example, gives the choice of weapons to the challenged party, but the choice of swords can be avoided if the challenger swears on his honor that he "is not a swordsman."[118]

The Irish Code Duello banned the practice of what was called "deloping," the deliberate discharging of one's weapon into the ground or over the opponent's head. The word comes from a French term that means "to feign," to "to fake."

Of course, it is important to remember is that these ten commandments put forward by Mr. Miranda have nothing to do with those in chapter twenty of the Book of Exodus or Deuteronomy 5:4 to 21. For one thing, the Hebrew Decalogue are universal moral prescriptions with no exceptions, while Miranda's list is more like cultural norms or what Aristotle would call "Non-Moral Virtues."[119]

At any rate, other Old Testament passages about which Alexander Hamilton was fond, or employed in his work and letters, included Exodus 21:23–25 and 24:19–21; the Book of Job 1:1, 14:14, 19:25–27 and 42:5–6; Proverbs 3:16; 8:18 and 11:3; and Psalms 41:12, 112:3 and 112:7.

Mr. Hamilton liked the verses from Exodus listed above because they call for "An eye for the eye and a tooth for a tooth." He was attracted to the verses suggested from the Book of Job because he was a "blameless and upright man" who nevertheless went through great suffering—something with which Alexander Hamilton could surely identify.

He also favored Job 19:25 to 27 for its Redeemer passage that seems to promise resurrection of the body at the end of time.[120] Alexander Hamilton was also fond of Job 14:14 because the text asks, "If a man shall die, shall he live again?" And the great American statesman saw this verse as a confirmation of immortality of the soul.

All the verses listed from the Book of Proverbs are connected in one way or another to the idea of moral virtue, something Alexander Hamilton was fond of discussing when engaging in conversation. The same can be said for Psalm 41:12, which Hamilton would have read in the King James Version, tells us this, "And as for me, Thou upholdest me in mine integrity, and settest me before Thy face forever."[121] Hamilton liked this verse mostly for its emphasis on the idea of integrity, something he valued over any other attribute.

Alexander Hamilton was attracted to Psalm 112:3 and 7 because the former speaks of "righteousness that endures forever," while the latter tells one "not to be afraid of evil tidings while trusting in the Lord."[122] Again, the Psalms most liked by Alexander Hamilton were those that feature moral virtues like integrity and honesty that he valued in himself and his friends and family.

In summary, then, at least in regard to the Old Testament, Alexander Hamilton appeared to have been very familiar with the Biblical texts and was often attracted to certain passages of the Old Testament, chiefly because of their moral content. Among his favorite Old Testament passages, we have identified verses from:

> The Book of Micah
> First Kings
> Zechariah
> The Book of Job
> The Book of Proverbs
> Psalms
> Exodus
> Deuteronomy[123]

This brings us to the third section of this chapter on the study of Alexander Hamilton's religion, in which we will speak of the great American statesman and the New Testament.

Hamilton and the New Testament

In *The Federalist Papers* of Alexander Hamilton, the great American statesman quotes or mentions several New Testament passages as well as in his letters and written works. Among these passages from the New Testament, we have chosen the following eight as a representative example or sample:

> Matthew 22:24
> Romans 8:34
> Ephesians 1:20
> Colossians 3:1
> Philippians 4:8
> 1 Peter 2:16–17
> 1 Peter 3:22
> 2 Peter 1:1–9

Already in this study and in this third chapter, we indicated that the idea of "sitting at the right hand of the Father" is an image employed by Lin-Manual Miranda in his writing of the musical *Hamilton*. This image can be seen throughout the New Testament, including Romans 8:34; Luke 22:69; Colossians 3:1; Matthew 26:64; Hebrews 1:3, 8:1, 10:12 and 12:2; Acts of the Apostles 2:33 and 5:31; Matthew 28:18; and the Gospel of Mark 14:62.[124]

Like Benjamin Franklin, one of Alexander Hamilton's keen interests in the New Testament—particularly at the beginning and end of the statesman's life—was in virtue, ethics, and what could only be called integrity. Thus, Hamilton quoted the "Beatitudes and Woes" recorded at Luke 6:20 to 26, for example.[125]

Similarly, Mr. Hamilton admired Paul's letter to the Romans 12:9–21, which speaks of genuine love and real hate.[126] The great American statesman also quoted the third chapter of Colossians because of its provisions to "imitate God" and to "live as children of God."[127] First Corinthians 13:4–8 and 13 was also admired by Alexander Hamilton mostly because of the text's concentration on the nature and extent of *agape*, or Christian love.[128]

Alexander Hamilton also quoted directly from Ephesians 4:25–32 and 5:1–10 because of the former's "putting away of falsehood" and the latter text's provision to be "imitators of God."[129]

Alexander Hamilton also admired several passages in First and Second Peter, again mostly for the moral value and mentions of Christian virtues. As suggested above, these passages included:

> 1 Peter 2:16–17
> 1 Peter 3:8, 9 and 22
> 2 Peter 1:1–9

In his letters, Alexander Hamilton frequently quoted 1 Peter 2:16 and 17 and the remainder of the chapter because of its discussion of "false prophets" and "false teachers" among you, particularly when dealing with Thomas Jefferson and Aaron Burr at the end of his life. Chapter 3 of First Peter was also admired by the great American statesman because it speaks of "compassion" and "love" in verse 8 and "inheriting a blessing" in verse 9, and Jesus "sitting at the right hand of God" in verse 22 of First Peter 3.

However, there were also many passages in the New Testament that, like the other Founding Fathers, were not admired by the great American statesman. Chief among these was the final book of the New Testament—the Book of Revelation. Like George Washington, Benjamin Franklin and Thomas Jefferson, Alexander Hamilton had serious doubts that the Book of Revelation was indeed divinely inspired. The main reason for this judgment was the apocalyptic imagery contained in the book, as well as what sense to make of those images and their meaning.

Benjamin Franklin preferred that many of the explicit murders recorded in the Old Testament that purportedly came from the "Angel of the Lord" could not have originally been of divine origin, such as the killing of the Canaanite general Sisera by Jael in chapters 4 and 5 of the Book of Judges.[130] Many of the other Founding Fathers, including Alexander Hamilton, had similar misgivings about certain narratives in the Old Testament.

Like the Deists, many of the Founding Fathers of America, like Benjamin Franklin, for example, eschewed the idea of Biblical revelation and relied almost entirely on the idea of Reason when it came to scriptural matters. Alexander Hamilton should be included in that group of Founding Fathers, as well.

However, unlike Thomas Jefferson, who skillfully removed all the references to survival after death in the "Jefferson Bible," Alexander Hamilton—particularly at the beginning and at the end of his life—expressed a devout and firm belief in the idea of the immortality of the soul.[131] In his final letter to his wife Eliza, for example, on July 4, 1814, just a week before his duel with Mr. Aaron Burr, the great American statesman mentioned seeing his wife again in a greater and more peaceful place, suggesting that he meant Heaven and survival after death.

This brings us to the fourth and final section of Chapter Three on Alexander Hamilton's views on the Bible or those places in *The Federalist Papers* where the American statesman spoke of God, ethics and Biblical text.

Hamilton and the Bible in *The Federalist Papers*

The Federalist Papers were a series of essays written by Alexander Hamilton, James Madison and John Jay, under the pen name "Publius," to promote the ratification of the US Constitution. These three statesmen crafted this series of eighty-five essays in the wake of the Philadelphia Convention in 1787. These essays were first published in a period that spanned from October of 1787 until May of 1788. The bulk of *The Federalist Papers* were written by Alexander Hamilton, most likely fifty-one or fifty-two of the total eighty-five.[132]

These essays addressed very broad Republican ideas, like the separation of powers, the nature of Federalism, and the built-in safeguards against majority oppression. While the US Constitution set forth a series of rules, *The Federalist Papers* provided an exposition and reasons for those rules. It is difficult to overstate the importance of *The Federalist Papers*. Thomas Jefferson called them "The best commentary on the principles of government which has ever been written."[133]

Federalist number 2 is important because Mr. Hamilton mentions "Providence" three separate times in the letter. In the first mention of Providence, Mr. Hamilton speaks of the value of the soil that God has given to the new nation," the United States.[134] In the second of these, Hamilton points out that he has noticed that "Providence has been pleased to give in one connected country to one united people."[135]

And in the final reference to Providence in *Federalist* 2, Alexander Hamilton suggested that the "plan by which all of this came about must have been designed by Providence," an indication of Alexander Hamilton's belief in the teleological argument for God's existence or the "argument from design," mentioned in Chapter Two of this study.[136]

Alexander Hamilton originally published *Federalist* 15 on December 1, 1787, also under the pseudonym, Publius. This essay mostly addresses the failures of what Mr. Hamilton believed could be found in the Articles of Confederation. Ultimately, Mr. Hamilton suggests that "Government implies the power to make laws in the same way that God gave power to Moses to do the same thing."[137] If "there is no force behind government, then there can be no force in its laws."

And again, the statesman mentioned the relationship between Yahweh and Moses and the force that the Divine showed in the Torah when his laws were not followed.[138]

In Essay 37, Alexander Hamilton again points to how "Nature has been arranged and assorted" and that they are "perfectly accurate," other references to the argument from design. When it comes to human government, however, things are not as nearly ordered and designed. Again, in Essay 37, the great American statesman speaks of the Biblical model of God and Moses in which the former gave to the latter the "rules by which a government shall appear to be ordered in the Book of Exodus," though it now cannot be that simple as back then.

The Federalist Papers 78 by Alexander Hamilton was also published by Publius. It is entitled "The Judiciary Department," and its aim was to speak of the role of the judiciary under the proposed Constitution of the United States. Mr. Hamilton indicated in Essay 78 that the judiciary would be the weakest of the three branches of government because, "It had no influence over either the sword or the purse." It would have "neither Force nor Will, but mere Judgment."

The mention of the Divine also entered into Essay 78 in the context of Alexander Hamilton quoting from Montesquieu who said of the judiciary, "Of the three powers above mentioned, the judiciary is next to nothing." This is followed by a discussion of how, in the relationship of Yahweh giving Moses the Ten Commandments, it involved "nothing that would resemble the judiciary."

God also comes up in Alexander Hamilton's discussion of the moral behavior of judges if they were to be given lifetime appointments. Hamilton remarked that "good behavior" should be a requirement for tenure in the judicial system. And if it were not a requirement, then the system would be defective.[139]

Again, in Alexander Hamilton's view, the character of the judges of the American Supreme Court should be imitations of the moral character of the figure of Moses in his role in the bringing of the decalogue to the people from Mount Sinai. Hamilton points out that the most heroic virtue of Moses in the Book of Exodus is his "steadfast obedience" and that this is a quality that should be found in every member of the Supreme Court. But for Moses, the obedience was to God. Whereas,

Alexander Hamilton suggested that for the nine judges, the steadfast obedience should not be to God, but to the US Constitution that also would require the notion of being "fit and moral men."[140]

There are also several other observations about God, religion and ethics in Alexander Hamilton's essays in *The Federalist Papers*. Among these are the following:

> In Essay 20, Hamilton urges Americans to let their praise of gratitude for auspicious amity distinguishing political counsels rise to Heaven.

> Essay 37 tells us that any person of pious reflection must perceive that in drafting the Constitution, there is to be found in it a finger of that Almighty Hand.

> Essay 43 asserts that nothing is more repugnant than intolerance in political parties, and Hamilton stresses the importance of moderation. He also maintains that one cannot avoid a belief that the greater principle of self-preservation is a transcendent law of both nature and God.

> In the very first essay, Hamilton expresses the view that in politics, as in religion, it is absurd to try and make proselytes by fire and sword. He also points out that heresies in either are rarely cured by persecution.

> In Essay 31, Hamilton tells us that theorems may sometimes conflict with common sense, but at times common sense is much like the sense of "religious mysteries."

> Essay 37 also relates that it is sometimes difficult to express ideas and words clearly without ambiguity. Hamilton says, "The Almighty

sometimes condescends to address mankind in their own language. His meaning, luminous as it must be, is rendered dim and doubtful by the cloudy medium through which it is communicated."

In Essay 44, Hamilton suggests that there must be safeguards against the misuse of religion in that no religious test should ever be required as a qualification for any office or public trust under the United States.

Essay 51 tells us that in a free government, the security for civil rights may be the same as for religious rights.

And finally, in Essay 57, we find the claim that no qualification of wealth, birth, religious faith, or civil profession should be permitted to "fetter the judgment or disappoint the inclination of the people.

The importance of *The Federalist Papers* in helping to lay the foundations of the government of the United States cannot be over-estimated, and that mostly comes because of the thought and writing of great American statesman Alexander Hamilton who wrote over fifty-one of the eighty-five essays of *The Federalist Papers*.[141]

Mr. Hamilton saw the tension regarding religion in the new nation. On the one hand, he forged ahead in making certain that religious liberty and toleration would be central in the new government. On the other hand, religion would not be permitted to divide the new nation or otherwise tyrannize any individual, sect or religion.

The writers of *The Federalist Papers* made it clear that there should be no established religion; but they also made it clear that faith-based beliefs are natural and free expressions and should be respected and tolerated in what will become the new United States.

This brings us to the major conclusions of this third chapter on Alexander Hamilton and the Bible of this study of Alexander Hamilton's religion. The subject matter of Chapter Four of this study shall be what Alexander Hamilton believed, wrote and said about other religions, particularly Judaism, Catholicism and Islam.

Conclusions to Chapter Three

We began this third chapter on Alexander Hamilton and the Holy Scriptures by suggesting in the introduction of the chapter that it was to unfold in four principal sections. These were to be general comments about the Bible in the life of Alexander Hamilton. Secondly, passages within the Old Testament that the great American statesman was particularly fond, as well as expressions in the Hebrew Bible to which he found a liking.

In the introduction to Chapter Three, we also indicated that the third section of the chapter was to be devoted to passages from the New Testament that Alexander Hamilton used in his letters and other written works, as well as others that he generally admired from their moral value.

Finally, in the fourth and final section of Chapter Three, we set out to identify and discuss the places in *The Federalist Papers* where Alexander Hamilton makes particular references to God, ethics and the Bible.

In the first of these four sections outlined here, we began by pointing out the many places in Alexander Hamilton's life where the American statesman appears to have studied the Bible. These include the Hebrew School on the island of Nevis, where his mother enrolled him and learned classical Hebrew and was able to read and write the Ten Commandments in their original language.

We also indicated that it is likely that the then teenage Alexander Hamilton heard many of the sermons given by his theological mentor on the island, the Presbyterian minister, the Rev. Hugh Knox. We also related that Mr. Hamilton had the use of the Rev. Knox's personal library, which undoubtedly contained works about the Bible.

In the first section of Chapter Three, we indicated that Bible studies were on the curriculum of the New Jersey Academy when

Mr. Hamilton matriculate there, as well as at King's College in New York City when he was a student there, as well.

Additionally, in the first section of Chapter Three, we spoke of several other times in the life of Alexander Hamilton when the subject matter of the Bible came to the fore in his life. Some of these experiences included when his New Jersey mentor, Elias Boudinot, became the president of the American Bible Society, and when Eliza Hamilton had one of her eldest sons read Bible passages before breakfast, followed by short meditations on these texts, as well as Mr. Hamilton reading to his family from the scriptures in the garden in the final few years of his life in the family home of the Grange.[142]

Mr. Boudinot and his family undoubtedly exerted a strong Christian and Biblical influence on the life of Alexander Hamilton. Moreover, as we have shown, Christianity and the Bible saturated King's College at the time. Morning chapel with Bible readings was obligatory at the time before breakfast, and King's students were required to attend two separate services on Sunday, the first of which included a reading and a sermon on a Biblical text.[143]

As we indicated, Mr. Boudinot (1740–1800) was president of the American Bible Society and was a life-long reader and studier of the Holy Scriptures. One of Boudinot's French ancestors was a French Protestant who fled France when King Louis XIV took protection and religious rights away from the Huguenots.

Elias Boudinot also wrote a reply to Thomas Paine's *Age of Reason* entitled the *Age of Revelation*. Boudinot also wrote a biography of preacher William Tennent, a man who started a "Log College" to train "Biblical Preachers." In short, the influence of Elias Boudinot on Alexander Hamilton's early views on the Bible cannot be underestimated.

We also pointed out that, after the death of his eldest son Philip, Alexander Hamilton became considerably more religious than he had been in the years before Philip's death. This fact can be seen in at least two separate ways. First, Alexander Hamilton began again to attend Sunday services at Trinity Church, the Anglican Church near his home, taking his other children along with him, making a sign of the cross and praying and pointing out, "that never used to happen before."[144]

In the second section of Chapter Three, we turned our attention to the Old Testament and passages and language and phrases that the American statesman was particularly fond of. In that section, we indicated that Hamilton quoted from, or in some way employed verses, from ten different books of the Old Testament, including the apocryphal book of First Maccabees.

These include the books of Micah, Zechariah, First Kings, Isaiah, First Maccabees, Exodus, Deuteronomy, Proverbs, Psalms, and the Book of Job, one of Mr. Hamilton's favorites, as we have shown, because of the subject of innocent suffering and survival after death. He found immortality of the soul at Job 14:14 and resurrection of the body at Job 19:25–27.

We also pointed out that the verses and passages in the Books of Proverbs and Psalms that Alexander Hamilton favored were mostly about those that speak of moral virtues, such as Psalms 41:12 and 112:3 and 7.

In the third section of Chapter Three, we turned our attention to passages in the New Testament that Alexander Hamilton was either fond of or quoted directly in his letters and other writings. We began the section by pointing out nine separate New Testament portions that Mr. Hamilton was fond of. This included two from the Gospels (Matthew 22:24 and Luke 22), four from Saint Paul (Romans 8:34, Ephesians 1:20, Colossians 3:1, and Philippians 4:8) and three from the letters of Peter (1 Peter 2:16 and 17 and 3:22; and 2Peter 1:1–9).

After an analysis of these nine New Testament passages, we turned our attention to why Alexander Hamilton was so interested in these passages. Next, we turn our attention to why the great American statesman was so interested in the New Testament passages that he was, and we made the suggestion that he was principally attracted to them because of the moral virtues that are discussed in them—moral virtues that Mr. Hamilton saw in himself, his wife, Eliza, and in a number of his friends.

We also indicated that like some of the other American Founding Fathers, there were also some passages and books of the New Testament, which Hamilton either saw as having little value, or he simply admitted that he did not understand them. And chief at the top of his list, along with Thomas Jefferson, is the New Testament Book of Revelation that both men believed is a mystery.

In the fourth and final section of Chapter Three, we turned our attention to an examination of places in *The Federalist Papers* where Alexander Hamilton commented upon issues related to God, ethics and the Bible. Indeed, in this section, after an introduction to *The Federalist Papers*, we then turned our attention to Essays 2, 15, 37, and 78.

We have shown that in each of these four essays of *The Federalist Papers*, Alexander Hamilton, through his pseudonym Publius, made comments and observations about Providence or God, ethics and the Bible, both Old and New Testaments. We also pointed out at the close of section four that *The Federalist Papers* also make a host of other observations about God, ethics and religion, and that these additional observations may be found in *The Federalist Papers* Essay 1, 20, 31, 37, 43, 44, 51 and 57.

Along the way, in the fourth and final section of Chapter Three, we also have shown that Hamilton believed that the federal court system and the Supreme Court were the weakest of the three branches of government, an idea that he borrowed from French nobleman and philosopher Montesquieu.[145]

Finally, we showed that Alexander Hamilton believed that Supreme Court justices were to have a lifetime appointment, and, at least in Mr. Hamilton's view, there should be some guarantee that these justices be of the highest of moral character at all times.[146]

This brings us to Chapter Four of this study. As we shall see next, the subject matter of this chapter is what the great American statesman Alexander Hamilton believed, said and wrote about religious faiths other than his own Christianity. More specifically, we will explore what Alexander Hamilton thought and wrote about Judaism, Catholicism and the faith of Islam. It is to comparative religion, then, to which we turn next.

Chapter Four
Hamilton and Other Faiths—Judaism, Catholicism and Islam

May the children of the Stock of Abraham, who dwell in the land, continue to merit and enjoy the good will of the other inhabitants; while everyone shall sit safely under his own vine and fig tree and there should be none to make him afraid.
—**George Washington, Letter to Newport Hebrew Congregation**

True freedom should embrace the Mahometan and the Gentoo [Hindu], as well as the Christian religion.
—**Richard Henry Lee, Letter to Congress (June 7, 1776)**

If they had been friends to the Protestant cause, they never would have provided such a nursery for its greatest enemy.
—**Alexander Hamilton, "On the Quebec Act"**

Introduction

The main focus of Chapter Four is to explore what great American statesman Alexander Hamilton believed, said and wrote about other religions other than his own Christian faith. We will achieve this main focus by devoting one section apiece in this chapter to Hamilton and Judaism, Hamilton and Roman Catholicism, and Hamilton and the Islamic faith.

Alexander Hamilton and Judaism

In this study of Alexander Hamilton's religion, we already made a few comments about his brushes with the Jewish faith. For example, his mother's first husband, Johann Lavine, was a Danish merchant and, as we shall see later in this section, may have required Rachel to join his Jewish religion. We have also seen that Alexander Hamilton's mother, Rachel, sent her son to a Jewish school since he could not have enrolled in the Anglican school on the island of Nevis because he was a bastard child.

We also indicated that at the Jewish school, Alexander Hamilton studied classical Hebrew and, at the ages of eight and nine, he could read the Ten Commandments in their original language, as well as reciting them.

We do know that the Nevis synagogue and Jewish school was on the outer edge of the capital of Charleston. Today one can see the ruins of a one-story stone structure on the main highway leading to the famous mineral baths on the island where there was a "bath house." The natives now call the structure "The Jews' School," although it clearly was the synagogue that also housed the Hebrew school, where, in the early 1760s, Mr. Hamilton received his earliest elementary education.

By the year 1723, the Nevis Jewish community had grown to about seventy-five people, at least according to a rather derogatory account written by the local Anglican minister at that time to the bishop of London.[147] We know that some civil rights were extended to Jews on the island, chiefly because Solomon Israel, a Jewish resident, served as a jury foreman, as well as a witness to the wills for some of his Christian friends on the island. Mr. Israel also served as the executor of one of these estates.[148]

There are several incidents in the life of Alexander Hamilton in which the Jewish faith becomes a topic of conversation in the life of the statesman. Among these other incidents are the following:

1. Alexander Hamilton's friendship with Rabbi Seixas.
2. His many responses to anti-Semitism in his life.
3. The *New York Daily Advertiser* and the Jews (1788).
4. George Washington's treatment of the Jews.
5. Hamilton was accused of being Jewish.

One aspect of Alexander Hamilton's relationship to Judaism has to do with Rabbi Gershom Seixas (1746–1816), the first native-born Jewish clergyman in the United States. Rabbi Seixas was an ardent patriot and spokesman against religious intolerance in regard to his faith. Rabbi Seixas is important for our purposes of this study because Alexander Hamilton was instrumental in getting the rabbi appointed in 1787 as a regent of Columbia College that was still at the time under the auspices of the Episcopal Church.[149]

In the same year, Mr. Hamilton helped Rabbi Seixas be appointed as one of the first regents of the State University of New York, which was the beginning of New York's SUNY system. Rabbi Seixas remained dedicated to Columbia for the rest of his life and was elected as a regent to the SUNY system. He was appointed by the legislature that included Robert Livingston, John Jay and Alexander Hamilton.[150]

In 1796, Rabbi Seixas was also appointed a trustee of the New York Humane Society and was also, through the auspices of Alexander Hamilton, invited to participate in the inauguration of President George Washington as the official spiritual representative of the Jewish citizenry. The rabbi marched in procession along with other clergy that preceded the ceremony at New York's Federal Hall.[151]

The rabbi and his wife also socialized with Alexander and Eliza Hamilton. There is a folder of letters between the two in the Seixas family papers owned by his congregation in New York City called "Congregation Shearith," where the rabbi held the position of *Hazzan*, or "Chief Rabbi."[152]

When Alexander Hamilton served in the New York State Legislature, the great American statesman issued a scathing denunciation of anti-Semitism in his closing remarks before the highest court in the state of New York.[153] It was a legal performance that some of his admirers considered to be one of the most powerful and forceful of his illustrious legal career. While practicing law in New York, Mr. Hamilton represented a number of prominent Jewish businessmen and merchants, many of whom the statesman suspected that his clients often were sued just for being Jewish.[154]

In fact, information at the New York State Archives and the various court cases where Mr. Hamilton represented Jewish clients that even the editors of Alexander Hamilton's four-volume legal papers were not seen until some recent research. Interestingly enough, many of these clients were connected in one way or another to the most prominent members of Rabbi Seisas' Shearith Israel congregation, which, at the time, was the only synagogue in New York City.

Alexander Hamilton gave a three-hour speech—some say the most emotionally invested speech of his career—before the New York State Assembly while defending a French Jew who had been falsely accused of fraud. In the prosecutor's remarks at the trial, he employed anti-Semitic stereotypes.[155]

One of the conclusions we can make about these facts is that Alexander Hamilton was an early champion of religious liberty and toleration in his political career and legal practice. He also found Jewish merchants to be key partners in his plan to invigorate the American financial system and to make the US a major center of global finance and economic stability.

In a lot of ways, Alexander Hamilton and others like him had to respond to the widespread anti-Semitism that existed across Europe in his lifetime and in the American colonies, as well. Globally, Frederick II of Prussia limited the number of Jews in his kingdom in places like Breslau.[156] The Archduchess of Austria, Maria Theresa, ordered all Jews out of Bavaria.[157] The Russian Orthodox Church discriminated against the Jews when Poland was partitioned.[158] In France, philosopher and writer Voltaire, in works like *Candide,* his *Philosophical Dictionary*, and his *lettres philosophiques*, were saturated with negative comments about the Jews.[159]

Things were not much better in the British colonies. In September 1654, twenty-three Jewish refuges arrived in the Dutch colony of New Amsterdam and on Manhattan island seeking asylum from Europe. They were met on the dock by Peter Stuyvesant, the director general of the colony and the Rev. Johannes Megapolensis, an official of the Dutch Reform Church, and a man who did not want Jews to settle in the colony.[160]

Peter Stuyvesant severely limited the Jews' right to live, worship, own land, and trade in the colony while he was in power. In those years of the seventeenth century, many of the colonies limited settlers to Protestants. Jews and Catholics had their ability to worship heavily regulated. They were also usually charged "special taxes" that Protestant worshippers did not have to pay.[161]

Mr. Stuyvesant described the Jews in New York in his time to be "deceitful," "very repugnant," as well as being "hateful enemies" and "blasphemers of the name of Christ."[162] Before the time of Stuyvesant, the inhabitants of the Dutch settlement had declared that "the law of love, peace, and liberty were to be extended to Jews, Turks, and Egyptians."[163]

By the time of Alexander Hamilton in the second half of the eighteenth century, there was still much anti-Semitism to be found in New York, but the rules were greatly relaxed in regard to the Jews. Many of the clients Mr. Hamilton served in the New York Courts were sued as much for the fact that they were Jews as the causes of action in their legal cases.

On July 17, 1788, the city of New York was planning a "procession" or celebration of the city. However, the procession was postponed at the insistence of Alexander Hamilton and others, because the ceremony was scheduled during a Jewish holiday. *The Daily Advertiser* in New York reported that the ceremony would be postponed until July 23. Peter Collin, the writer of the article, wrote at the time:

> It is said that the Procession is postponed until
> the 23rd in order to give the Jews an opportunity
> to join the Festivals, the 22nd still being one of
> their holidays.[164]

What is significant about this event, at least for our purposes, is that it was the great American statesman, the object of this study, who was responsible for getting the date of the procession or festivals changed. And clearly, one impetus on his part was his respect, friendship and admiration of the Jews.

Another event that went into the making of Alexander Hamilton's perspectives on the Jews was the influence of the views of another of his mentors, George Washington, on the Jews and Judaism. One way to see those views of the first president is in a famous letter Washington sent to the Hebrew congregation in New Port, Rhode Island, on August 21, 1790.

Mr. Washington had recently returned from a trip to Newport, and, in the letter, he is returning a missive sent by the Jewish congregation. He begins by thanking the Rhode Island Jews, and in the second paragraph, he tells them:

> All possess alike liberty of conscience and immunities of citizenship. It is now no more that toleration is spoken of, as if it were by the indulgence of one class of people, that another enjoyed the exercise of their inherent natural rights. For happily the government of the United States, which gives to bigotry no sanction, to persecution no assistance requires only that they who live under its protection should demean themselves as good citizens...

In the final paragraph to the Newport Hebrew congregation, President Washington returned to some familiar themes when he wrote:

> May the Children of the Stock of Abraham, who dwell in the land, continue to merit and enjoy the good will of the other inhabitants; while everyone shall sit in safety under his own vine and fig tree and there should be none to make him afraid...

Alexander Hamilton was perfectly aware of both this letter to the Hebrew congregation in Newport and the president's desire that the Jews exercise their religious freedoms like all other citizens, as well as being tolerated by them. And this view of Mr. Washington was perfectly consistent with his one-time aide-de-camp.

In his Farewell Address to the American people on September 19, 1796—much of which was written by Alexander Hamilton—was delivered by the first president after his second term in office and before retiring to his Mount Vernon estate. The speech, which was published as a letter, called for unity, checks and balances, the separation of powers, and an emphasis on religion, morality and education.

In the letter, Mr. Washington, or Mr. Hamilton, again uses the "vine and fig tree" image and speaks of the religions of Abraham that should be protected and tolerated in the new nation.[165] And those religions, of course, include Judaism, as well as Islam, or what the Islamic faith calls "the Peoples of the Book." This expression in classical Arabic is *Ahl al-Kitab*, and refers to Jews, Christian denominations, and, of course, to the Muslim faith.

In more recent history, some Christian denominations, such as the Baptists, Methodists, Seventh-Day Adventists, the Puritans, and the Shakers, among others, have embraced the term "People of the Book" in reference to themselves.[166] Some forms of modern Judaism also employ the term *am Ha-Sefer*, or "People of the Book" in classical Hebrew, to refer to both the Jewish people as well as to the Torah.[167]

This brings us to one final topic in this first section of Chapter Four, in which we will explore the views and findings of some new research about the great American statesman Alexander Hamilton that he was, in fact, Jewish.

The research to which we refer was conducted by Dr. Andrew Porwancher of the University of Oklahoma, who has been researching the life and times of Alexander Hamilton since 2011. In his research, Porwancher came across materials suggesting that Alexander Hamilton may have been Jewish. Since 2011, Dr. Porwancher has traveled to Denmark, England and the Caribbean and has read through thousands of historical documents bringing the scholar to the opinion that great American statesman Alexander Hamilton was, in fact, Jewish.

Andrew Porwancher's findings are to be published by Harvard University Press in a book entitled *A Jewish Founding Father: Alexander Hamilton's Hidden Life*.[168] The gist of Professor Porwancher's argument consists of the following facts:

1. Rachel, Hamilton's mother, married a Jewish man, Johann Michael Lavien.
2. Rachel came from a French Huguenot family of French Protestants who held Reformed or Calvinist beliefs in the sixteenth to eighteenth centuries.
3. Under Danish Jewish law, she would have been required at the time to convert to Judaism.
4. Danish law at the time forbade the inter-marriage of Christians and Jews.

5. Rachel sent her son Alexander to the Jewish school on Nevis because first, his parents were Jewish, and secondly, because he was illegitimate, he could not have attended the Anglican school on the island.

6. There is no record that either Alexander or his brother were baptized.

7. Porwancher found parish records from Nevis indicating that, at the time of Alexander Hamilton's birth, a full 25 percent of the population of the island was Jewish.

8. Rachel was not buried in the local church's cemetery but rather at home on her family property.

9. If Rachel did convert to Judaism, as Porwancher suspects, it would mean that Alexander Hamilton had a Jewish mother, the main Biblical and Talmudic requirement for being a Jew.

10. Dr. Porwancher theorizes that Hamilton's ties to Judaism were severed at the age of thirteen when his mother died. The scholar said in a recent interview, "He wasn't going to tie himself to a second-class religious status, so he became a Christian."

In the same interview, the scholar at the University of Oklahoma Law School said this,

> The best argument is the one that accounts for the most pieces of the evidence. The argument that Alexander Hamilton was Christian accounts for none of these facts. The argument that he was Jewish explains them all.[169]

Needless to say, conventional Hamilton scholars and other academics have been resistant to Dr. Porwancher's thesis. They argue that Rachel's husband Johann is not described as Jewish in any of the Danish records. If Rachel converted, there is no direct evidence for that fact. It may explain why Hamilton appears to have an unusual fondness for Judaism, but at this point, the jury is still out on the matter.

One final fact concerning Alexander Hamilton and Judaism relates to a discovery made by historian Malcolm Stern and his wife in 1957. The couple had taken a cruise that stopped in Nevis, and while the pair was there, they located an old Jewish cemetery on the island that was then being used as a field for grazing goats. Stern and his wife were tipped off by local people on the island who told them that Jews had once used the field as a burial site.[170]

In his investigations, Mr. Stern soon discovered sixteen Hebrew epitaphs, accompanied by box-like burial structures. Stern later wrote extensively about Nevis's lost Jewish community. The Jewish cemetery is approximately 200 feet by 75 feet. Locals call it the "Jews' Cemetery."[171] The site contains sixteen raised graves, with accompanying epitaphs that range in death dates from 1684 until 1768. They vary from complete legibility to absolute obliteration.[172]

If Rachel Fawcett Lavine had indeed converted to Judaism, then that raises the question of why, when she died on February 19, 1768, she was not buried in the cemetery discovered by Malcom Stern. Instead, Alexander Hamilton's mother Rachel is interred in the Lytton family cemetery at the Grange Estate, near Christiansted on the island of St. Croix.[173]

At any rate, what to make of the thesis put forward by Andrew Porwancher is not entirely clear. Perhaps in the future, scholars will find additional evidence of the original religious identity of great American statesman Alexander Hamilton.

This brings us to the second section of Chapter Four on Alexander Hamilton and comparative religion, in which we will explore what Mr. Hamilton believed, said and wrote about Roman Catholicism. It is to the Catholics and Alexander Hamilton, then, to which we turn next.

Alexander Hamilton and Roman Catholicism

Over the course of the life of the great American statesman, Alexander Hamilton had many occasions where his beliefs, written words and speeches reflect his views of Roman Catholicism. Among the sources of these beliefs, words, and writings were the following sources:

1. Hamilton's mother's French Huguenot views of Catholicism.

2. Hamilton's father's Presbyterian perspective on the Catholics.
3. The point of view of the Rev. Hugh Knox on Catholicism.
4. The stance of the thirteen colonies and the Catholics.
5. Catholics in the New York State of Hamilton's time.
6. Hamilton's friendships with the two Catholic signers of the Declaration of Independence and the US Constitution.
7. The Quebec Act (1774).
8. Hamilton Defense of Rights of Catholics (late 1780s).

Each of these eight items will give us an avenue into the views of Alexander Hamilton on Catholicism. We should begin by pointing out that both Mr. Hamilton's French Huguenot mother and his Presbyterian father most likely had anti-Catholic biases, as did most non-Catholic English speakers in the New World. This was also most likely true of the theological views of the Presbyterian theological mentor of Alexander Hamilton, the Rev. Hugh Knox.

The first three items on our list in this section were undoubtedly related to the fourth item on the list. American anti-Catholicism had its roots in Europe in the Protestant Reformation. In fact, British colonists were predominantly Protestants, opposed not only to the Catholic Church but in many cases to the Church of England, as well, which they believed perpetuated Catholic doctrine and religious practices, for they deem them not to be sufficiently Reform.[174]

Catholic historian, John Tracy Ellis, wrote this about the first settlements in the American colonies,

> A universal anti-Catholic bias was brought to Jamestown in 1607 and vigorously cultivated in all thirteen colonies from Massachusetts to Georgia. Indeed, although Massachusetts was first settled by English religious dissenters, Quakers, Jews and Catholics were not permitted to enter the colony. Laws passed there in 1647 and 1700 forbade Catholic priests to reside in

the colony under the "pain of imprisonment and
even execution."[175]

In the Maryland colony, Catholicism was introduced in 1634 in
southern Maryland by Cecil Calvert, the second Baron of Baltimore.
But in 1646, the defeat of the Royalists in the English Civil War led
to more stringent laws against Catholics in the Maryland colony.
Meanwhile, in Connecticut, the colony was established in 1633, but
they later established anti-Catholic legislation, as well.[176]

The Dutch colony of the seventeenth century was established at
New Amsterdam, later to be called New York. The General Assembly
of New York passed its first law outlining Catholic worship in the
colony in August of 1664. The Dutch Reform Church, on the other
hand, became the established church. In fact, at the same time, Jesuits
were banned from the colony. Later in New York, officeholders were
required to sign a declaration against the idea of transubstantiation.[177]

These kinds of anti-Catholic laws existed throughout the colonies,
and many of them were not repealed until after the Revolutionary War
and the establishment of the United States. And what was true of the
British colonies in North America was just as true as those among the
Caribbean islands in the seventeenth and eighteenth centuries.

Then came an important moment in the late 1780s in the state of New
York. The Catholic Church in the state was still outlawed and had been for
nearly 100 years. Catholics had been denied religious liberties and their
political and civil liberties, as well. Catholics in British North America
could not be trusted with essential liberties, and their primary allegiance
was presumed to be the pope, whom many believed at the time was intent
on dissolving secular rulers and assume authority for himself.[178]

Alexander Hamilton vigorously defended the political rights
of Roman Catholics in New York, where they had been denied these
rights for nearly a century. The great American statesman's view came
at a pivotal moment in the founding of the United States. Mr. Hamilton,
however, was not always in favor of the religious rights of Catholics.
After coming to New York in 1774 from the West Indies as a young
man, he plunged into the escalating crises between Britain and its North
American colonies.

This crisis was known as the "Quebec Act," in which Britain recognized the preeminent position of the Catholic Church in Canada and allowed officeholders to takes oaths without renouncing their allegiance to the papacy. Mr. Hamilton wrote in 1775,

> If they had been friends to the Protestant cause,
> they never would have provided such a nursery
> for its greatest enemy.[179]

The official name of the Quebec Act was "An Act for Making More Effectual Provision for the Government of the Province of Quebec in North America." It was an attempt by the British to gain the loyalty of the French Canadian Catholic population of Quebec. The Americans saw the act as part of the British effort to eliminate representative government in the North American colonies.

On June 22, 1775, Alexander Hamilton wrote an essay entitled "Remarks on the Quebec Bill." The great American statesman begins his essay this way:

> Having considered the nature of this bill,
> with regards to Civil Government, I am next
> to examine it with relation to religion and to
> endeavor to show that the Church of Rome has
> now the sanction of a legal establishment in the
> Province of Quebec in order to do this more
> satisfactorily.

Mr. Hamilton goes on in this essay to denounce the signing of the Quebec Bill, suggesting, "This act makes an effectual provision not only for the protection but for the permanent support of Popery." This essay of Mr. Hamilton goes on for another twelve, large paragraphs and in each of them, he makes several central points about why the Quebec Bill was a bad act. At the end of his essay, Alexander Hamilton wrote this as the conclusion:

> Hence, while our ears are stunned with the dismal
> sounds of New Englander's Republicanism,
> bigotry, and intolerance, it behooves us to be upon
> our guard against the deceitful wiles of those,

who would persuade us, that we have nothing
to fear from the operation of the Quebec Act.
But we should consider it as being replete with
danger, to ourselves and as threatening to our
posterity. Let us not, therefore, suffer ourselves
to be terrified at the prospect of an imaginary
and fictitious Syllabus that by this means, be led
blindfold into a real and destructive Charybdis.

The image of Charybdis employed here is a reference in Greek
mythology of a sea monster who lives under a small rock on one side of
a narrow channel. Opposite her was Scylla, a much larger sea monster,
hiding under a much larger rock. In Hamilton's use of the mythological
images, the smaller monster is Canada and the larger one is the United
States.

It is important to point out that Alexander Hamilton had ambiguous,
or even contradictory views, regarding Roman Catholicism. On the one
hand, he supported and defended the rights and toleration of American
Catholics, while on the other hand, he was critically against Canadian
Catholics in relation to the Quebec Act.

Another aspect of his views of Roman Catholics had to do with
the relationship that the great American statesman had with Charles
Carroll (1737–1832) of Carrollton, Maryland, the only Catholic signer
of the Declaration of Independence and the US Constitution. The two
had a cordial and friendly relationship that included a series of letters
in 1800 between these two Founding Fathers.

In one letter from Carroll to Hamilton from August 7, 1800, the
Marylander, knowing Hamilton's views on the French Revolution
and Thomas Jefferson's admiration of it, speaks of the "Arts and lies
& indefatigable industry of the Jacobins in this State." Later, in the
same letter, Carroll specifically mentions Burr and Jefferson and what
the Marylander believed the choice of Jefferson and Burr might be a
"Jacobinical President."

In a letter to Hamilton around the same time, Charles Carroll
accused Thomas Jefferson and his supporters to be "Jacobins of arts
and lies" because he believed the Virginian was attempting to secure

the state of Maryland electoral votes by legislative manipulations, even though a majority of its residents favored the Federalist Party.

The letters that Hamilton wrote back to Carroll express admiration for his Catholic faith, as well as gratitude for the Maryland signer's support against the wiles and manipulations of Jefferson, Burr and the Jacobins. Thus, Alexander Hamilton's ambiguous views of Roman Catholicism may also be seen in the exchange of letters with Carroll.

Alexander Hamilton also had a relationship at the Continental Convention with Pennsylvania delegate Thomas Fitzsimons (1741–1811), the second Catholic signer of the US Constitution. Fitzsimons was born in Ireland and came to America in 1760. At the convention, he spoke infrequently, but when he did, Alexander Hamilton was impressed with him. After the convention, Fitzsimons supported many of Mr. Hamilton's fiscal policies. Mr. Fitzsimons is another Catholic, then, with whom Alexander Hamilton was friendly with and deeply respected. There are extant a few letters between the two.[180]

This brings us to the third and final section of this Chapter Four on Alexander Hamilton and comparative religion of this study of his religion. In the next section, we will explore what Mr. Hamilton believed, said and wrote about the faith of Islam. As we shall see, he had several encounters with the faith of the Prophet Muhammad.

Alexander Hamilton and Islam

In the life of the great American statesman, Alexander Hamilton had occasion to observe and comment on the Islamic faith. Among these occasions and events, there are the following:

1. Comments from other Founding Fathers about Islam and Muslims.
2. A discussion at the Continental Convention about "Who was an American."
3. A discussion of the Ottoman Empire about collecting taxes.
4. The influence that Islam may have had on the formation of the founding documents.
5. The treatment of the North African Barbary pirates.

In this third and final section of Chapter Four, we will discuss each of these five items in the hope of discerning some of what Alexander Hamilton believed, said and wrote about the Islamic faith.

Among the other Founding Fathers who have commented on Al-Qur'an and the Islamic faith, we may include George Washington, John Adams and Thomas Jefferson. And many other figures from the late colonial period in America as well as in England. John Locke, for example, in *A Letter Concerning Toleration*, insisted that all Muslims and anyone else who believed in God should be tolerated in England.[181]

Thomas Jefferson, a great admirer of Locke, campaigned for what he referred to as the religious liberty for the "Mahamadan," the Jews and the pagan.[182] Richard Henry Lee, who first proposed a motion of independence from Britain in Congress on June 7, 1776, also thought that "True freedom should embrace the Mahomitan and the Gentoo [Hindu], as well as the Christian Religion."

In his autobiography, Mr. Jefferson relates that when his bill on religious freedom was first proposed in the Virginia legislature, the legislators rejected by a great margin an effort to limit the bill's scope in that they wanted to exclude "the Jew and the Mohametan."[183] George Washington proposed a relief from this exclusion in the Virginia bill if Muslims were to pay taxes to support Christian worship institutions.[184] In point of fact, Washington most likely already had a number of Muslims working on his Mount Vernon farms, including a man named Sambo Anderson, a West African who was most likely a member of the Muslim faith.[185]

On another occasion, Washington was asked whether he would allow other religions to work at his Mount Vernon estate. His answer was this, "I would welcome Mohametans to Mount Vernon if they were good workmen."[186] The 1780 state constitution of Massachusetts "afforded the most ample liberty of conscience…to Deists, Mahometans, Jews, and Christians."[187] Chief Justice Theophilus Parsons reaffirmed this point in an 1810 Supreme Court decision.[188] This decision was known as *Barnes v. First Parish of Falmouth, Massachusetts*.

Ezra Stiles, the president of Yale College, cited a study showing that "Mohametans morals were far superior to those of the Christians."[189] A Boston newspaper reporter in the 1770s related that

"A Mahometan is excited to practice his good morals in the hopes that after the resurrection he will enjoy the beautiful girls of Paradise to all eternity."[190]

Both John Adams and Thomas Jefferson owned copies of the Muslim Holy Book Al-Qur'an. The latter even attempted to learn classical Arabic, so he could read the holy book in the original language.[191] A petition circulated in Chesterfield, Virginia, and brought to the Virginia Assembly on November 14, 1785. In part, the petition included the following words:

> Let Jews Mehometans and Christians of every
> denomination enjoy religious liberty And thrust
> them not out now by establishing the Christian
> Religion and thereby we become our own
> enemies and weaken the infant state.[192]

It should be clear from this analysis that the topics of the Islamic faith, as well as their Holy Book Al-Qur'an, were central topics among the Founding Fathers, the Supreme Court, academics, newspapermen and the common people in the lifetime of great American statesman Alexander Hamilton.

There were also several other instances when the Muslim faith came up in the context of Mr. Hamilton. One of these was a discussion during the Continental Congress of whether "Mahometans and atheists" could be fully American. Alexander Hamilton was clearly on the side of the affirmative and suggested that the holders of "all religious persuasions or none at all" should be welcomed into the new union.[193]

Another way that Islam and the life of Alexander Hamilton came together was when he borrowed some ideas from the Ottoman Empire about taxation. Scholar Azizah Al-Hibri provides an overview of Hamilton's political thinking and how it was appropriated from the Ottoman Empire. She comments:

> Alexander Hamilton argued for giving the
> federal government the right to impose taxes by
> referring to the example of the Ottoman Empire.
> He noted that the Sovereign of that empire had
> no right to impose a tax.[194]

Professor Al-Hibri continues when she says that Hamilton concluded, "who can doubt that the happiness of the people in both countries would be permitted by competent authorities in the proper hands..." Al-Hibri also said Mr. Hamilton believed that "From our perspective, the Turkish Sultan was, in fact, weak and had limited powers." Hamilton concluded a strong central government would protect people from oppressive local governments.

Finally, Alexander Hamilton had another relation with Islam during what was known as the Barbary Wars, in which Sweden and the United States fought against four North African states known collectively as the "Barbary States." Three of these states were independent. They were Tripoli, Algiers and Tunis of the Ottoman Empire, while the fourth was the Sultanate of Morocco.

The cause of the hostilities with the Barbary States were pirates who began seizing American merchant ships bound for the Mediterranean Sea. The crews of the American ships were held by the Barbary States and subsequently demanded that the US pay tribute to the Barbary rulers. President Thomas Jefferson, however, refused to pay. Sweden, as well, had been at war with Tripoli since 1800.

Earlier, in 1797, the United States had signed a treaty with the Barbary States in which John Adams, the second American president, wrote at the time, "The US government has in itself no character or enmity against the laws, religion or tranquility of Muselman [Muslims].[195]

Now, from 1801 to 1805, the US had to decide how to respond to the Barbary States. Most American leaders at the time weighed in on the debate. In *The Federalist Papers* Essay 24, for instance, Alexander Hamilton argued that "Without a federal navy...of a respected weight... the genius of American merchants and navigators would be stifled and lost."

Alexander Hamilton suggested the Barbary problem could be fixed by establishing a large and powerful navy, which America did not have. Other Founding Fathers—John Adams among them—made the argument that it was better to pay the tribute because it was cheaper than the loss of trade and "a battle against the pirates would be too rugged for our people to bear." Adams put the matter even more starkly when he wrote, "We ought not to fight them at all unless we are determined to fight them forever."[196]

This brings us to the major conclusions we have made in Chapter Four. The subject matter of Chapter Five of this study of great American statesman Alexander Hamilton's religion shall be an examination of his beliefs and writing about ethics and morality.

Conclusions to Chapter Four

In the Introduction to this fourth chapter, we indicated that this chapter would explore what Alexander Hamilton believed, said and wrote about what might be called the phenomenon of comparative religion. More specifically, we have written in the same introduction that the chapter will focus on Hamilton and Judaism, Hamilton and Catholicism, and Hamilton and the Islamic faith. To that end, Chapter Four has consisted of three main sections—Judaism, Catholicism and Islam in relation to the life of Alexander Hamilton.

We began the first section with a short review of a few things we already know about Mr. Hamilton and Judaism: that he went to a Hebrew school as a child; that he learned how to read the Ten Commandments and to recite them in their original language, classical Hebrew; and that there was an extensive Jewish population on the island of Nevis during Mr. Hamilton's childhood.

We continued this section by referring to and then discussing, at some length, five other incidents where Alexander Hamilton had some contact with Jews or the Jewish faith. These were the statesman's friendship with Rabbi Seixas, Hamilton's many responses to anti-Semitism in his life, a *New York Daily Advertiser* about the Jews, George Washington's treatment of the Jews and influence on Hamilton, and the accusation that Alexander Hamilton was Jewish.

In each of these contacts of Alexander Hamilton with Judaism, we have given a lengthy analysis. Regarding Rabbi Seixas, we have shown that Alexander Hamilton was instrumental in getting the rabbi a place on the Board of Regents of Columbia University, as well as Seixas being invited to participate in the inauguration of President George Washington.

We also pointed out that Alexander Hamilton gave a scathing denunciation of anti-Semitism in his closing remarks before the New

York State Supreme Court and the statesman's sneaking suspicion that his clients were sued more because of the Jewishness than the legal merits of their cases.

In the first section of Chapter Four, we also indicated that when the city of New York had planned a celebration that fell on a Jewish holiday, Mr. Hamilton got them to change the date so Jewish citizens and officials could participate in the event.

We also introduced the research of University of Oklahoma scholar Andrew Porwancher and his thesis that Alexander Hamilton was, in fact, a Jew. After giving a catalog of Dr. Porwancher's argument, we concluded that the jury should still be out in regard to evaluating the thesis.

In the second section of Chapter Four, we began by suggesting that eight different pieces of information went into the making of Alexander Hamilton's views on Roman Catholicism. From these eight pieces of information, the major conclusion we made about them is that Mr. Hamilton had an ambiguous or ambivalent view of the Catholic Church. On the one hand, he had many Catholic friends and stood up for Catholic religious liberty when the proper time came. On the other hand, however, he was staunchly against the Quebec Act.

We also indicated that the most likely reason Mr. Hamilton was against the Quebec Act was because of his anti-Catholic Huguenot and Presbyterian parents. Another reason was the strong anti-Catholic sentiments in many legislatures of at least ten of the thirteen colonies, including the colony-state of New York, who had this kind of legislation on the books for nearly a century.

In the third and final section of Chapter Four, we introduced, analyzed and discussed a number of occasions in the life of Alexander Hamilton when the great American statesman had some contact with the faith of Islam. We began the section by enumerating five principal ways in which we find Muslims, the Al-Qur'an, or the Islamic faith in contact in some way with Alexander Hamilton.

More specifically, these events were the comments of other Founding Fathers about Islam, including a discussion at the Continental Congress about what counted as an "American," A discussion of the Ottoman Empire and how they collected taxes, the influence that Islam may have had on the economic policies of Alexander Hamilton, and the great American statesman's views on the Barbary Wars at the beginning of the nineteenth century.

We pointed out that in addition to Alexander Hamilton, his mentor George Washington, John Adams, Thomas Jefferson, Richard Henry Lee, Yale president Ezra Stiles, and many other figures in the late colonial period said many positive things about Muslims, Al-Qur'an, and the Islamic faith.

Also discussed in the third section of Chapter Four was that at the Continental Congress, during a discussion of whether "Mohametans and atheists were Americans," Alexander Hamilton argues forcefully in the affirmative of answering that query. In the same way that Hamilton responded forcefully to anti-Semitic and anti-Semitic expressions in the early American nation, he did precisely the same thing about Muslims and their Holy Book Al-Qur'an as well.

In this same section, we also examined how Alexander Hamilton made use of the way that the Turkish Ottoman Empire collected its taxes, which affected what later would become the Internal Revenue Service instituted when Alexander Hamilton was Secretary of the Treasury.

Using the scholarly work of Azizah Al-Hibri, we again maintained, as she does, that some of Hamilton's ideas about taxation originally had Islamic origins. Professor Al-Hibri also suggests that the idea of a strong central government, endorsed by Alexander Hamilton, was also an Islamic idea from the Ottoman Empire.

Finally, during the crisis known as the Barbary Wars, when North African pirates had confiscated American merchant ships, detained their crews and demanded the payment of tribute for their release, we indicated that there were many comments in the Jefferson Administration about how to respond to the pirates. Jefferson refused to pay the bribes. John Adams was in favor of meeting the demands of the Barbary pirates, but Mr. Hamilton's response regarding the Barbary pirates was completely different.

Alexander Hamilton pointed out that the problem of the Barbary pirates indicated the fact that the US was in great need of a larger and more powerful navy. Mr. Hamilton wrote at the time, "Without a federal navy...of a respected weight...the genius of American merchants and navigators would be stifled and lost."[197]

In short, Alexander Hamilton believed the "Barbary Problem" might have been easily fixed simply by building a larger and more powerful navy—something that America did not have at the time. And, clearly, Mr. Hamilton could not have been more correct about the matter. He was not as convinced that the cause of anti-Islamic movements deserved the same amount of political attention as anti-Semitism and anti-Catholicism, but he was very clearly in support of the rights of Muslims to exercise their religious liberties in the same way as every other religious tradition in America.

It is just as clear that when it came to the idea of religious toleration in late eighteenth-century America, the same toleration should be extended to all other religious groups, Mr. Hamilton believed, to members of the Islamic faith, as well.

This brings us to Chapter Five. The subject matter will be an analysis of what the great American statesman believed, said and wrote about the phenomena of ethics and morality. As we will see, Mr. Hamilton had a great deal to say about those issues. Thus, it is to Hamilton and ethics to which we turn next.

Chapter Five
Hamilton on Ethics and Moral Responsibility

In fact, there is a wonderful story that there was a tomcat at
Washington's headquarters at Morristown—and this tomcat
was always meowing and having a good time at night. And
Mrs. Washington nicknamed the tomcat Hamilton.
—**Thomas Fleming,** *Alexander Hamilton*

The story of the life of Alexander Hamilton is a story that the
most gifted novelist could not have invented. Too much of it
would seem implausible in terms of what happened to this
man in the space of forty-nine years. I mean, it is just better
than a novel.
—**Ron Chernow,** *Alexander Hamilton*

My religious and moral principles are strongly opposed to
the practice of duelling, and it would ever give me pain to be
obliged to shed blood of a fellow creature in a private combat
forbidden by the laws.
—**Alexander Hamilton,** *Letters*

Introduction

Of all the extant material on the life and beliefs of Alexander Hamilton,
what he thought, believed, did, and wrote about ethics, or the Moral
Good, as well as the idea of Moral Responsibility, is the most ambiguous
and ambivalent aspect of the great American statesman's life.

In Chapter Five, our major concerns will be the following issues: First, what were the sources of Alexander Hamilton's views on ethics and morality? Secondly, what did the great American statesman Alexander Hamilton say directly about ethics, morality and the notion of Moral Responsibility? Thirdly, what gleanings about ethics can be found from Mr. Hamilton's contributions to *The Federalist Papers*? And finally, what conclusions may be made about Alexander Hamilton's moral character and actions from the 1791–92 affair that the statesman had with Maria Reynolds, the wife of James Reynolds?

Chapter Five will proceed, then, with four sections, one each on the questions raised in the previous paragraph, beginning with the sources of Alexander Hamilton's views on ethics and Moral Responsibility.

The Sources of Alexander Hamilton's Ethics

There can be no doubt that the primary source for determining the views of Alexander Hamilton on ethics and morality was the ethics and philosophy of the person of Jesus Christ of Nazareth. Like many of the other Founding Fathers—George Washington, Benjamin Franklin and Thomas Jefferson, for example—Alexander Hamilton believed that the most important aspect of the life of Jesus Christ was his ethical and moral views.

We made this same claim earlier in this study in the third section of Chapter Two. In the chapter on Hamilton's views of the Bible, we have also shown that many of the New Testament passages that the statesman most valued were related to ethical matters and/or moral virtues. Indeed, in the New Testament section of Chapter Two, we indicated Mr. Hamilton's fondness for certain Moral Virtues that he wished to be exemplified in his life and the lives of his family members, such as Luke 6:20–26, which generally speaks about virtue. Romans 12:7–22 that extolls the importance of love. Ephesians 4:25–32 that gives a general understanding of Jesus' position against lying and falsehoods. And First Peter 2:16–17 that indicates the role of compassion in the early church and, by extension, the life of Alexander Hamilton.

We also indicated that the most fundamental passage of Jesus' for which Alexander Hamilton had the most affection was the Gospel of Mark 12:30–31, that in the King James version tell us this:

> Love the Lord your God with all of your heart
> and with all your soul and with all your mind and
> with all your strength. The second is love your
> neighbor as yourself. There is no commandment
> greater than these.

Two other sources of Alexander Hamilton's views on ethics and Moral Responsibility are classical writers from Greco-Roman times and seventeenth- and eighteenth-century classical, Western philosophy and literature. Regarding Greek and Roman sources, we might mention Aristotle and his views on virtue, as well as Romans Julius Caesar, Cicero and poet Virgil.

In regard to modern philosophy, we should add David Hume, John Locke, Francis Bacon, Machiavelli, Thomas Hobbes, the Baron Montesquieu and Edmund Burke. Among pieces of modern literature that may have influenced the ethics of Alexander Hamilton, we may list Joseph Addison's drama *Cato*, Montaigne's *Essays*, Daniel Defoe's and Alexander Pope's verse, and the dramatic writings of Frenchman Jean-Baptise Poquelin, also called Moliere.[198]

Of these works, the most important of the Greco-Roman sources, at least for the purposes of this chapter, is Aristotle's *Nicomachean Ethics*, in which the Greek philosopher sets out his understanding of Moral Virtue.[199] Mr. Hamilton had a copy of Aristotle's book in his personal library, which was marked-up with many notations to suggest that the volume was thoroughly read.[200]

In this work, Aristotle sets out the view that later in history would be called "Virtue Ethics." In it, the Greek philosopher suggests that a moral man is one who has over time acquired a collection of moral behaviors that eventually become permanent parts of the individual's personality. Mr. Hamilton very much liked this idea of the Greek philosopher and admired Aristotle's ethics more than any of the other Founding Fathers, with the exception of Benjamin Franklin, who employed Virtue Ethics as the heart of his understanding of the Moral Good.[201]

In the same work, Aristotle suggested that a Moral Virtue is a "mean" between two vices, one that is a lack of virtue and the other an over-abundance of it. Thus, for the Greek philosopher, Courage is a mean between Rashness and Cowardice; Truthfulness is a mean between Boastfulness and Modesty. Justice is a Virtue between Injustice and Over-justice, that is, giving one more than he or she is due.[202]

Many of the personal books of Alexander Hamilton are now to be found at the Columbia University Library. The great American statesman's copy of Aristotle's *Ethics* is still there, as well as another facsimile copy that is available to readers at the statesman's alma mater in New York City. Many of Mr. Hamilton's other personal books were given to what was called the Irving Library Association in the 1870s by one of Mr. Hamilton's descendants in Irving, Texas.[203]

When Alexander Hamilton was a student at the Elizabethtown Academy in New Jersey, and afterward when he applied to the College of New Jersey that later became Princeton University, we get an indication of some of what the statesman must have studied in his preparatory school, as they were then called. The applicants of the College of New Jersey had to know "Virgil, Cicero's orations, and Latin grammar," while at the same time being "conversant with the Greek of the four evangelists," and those texts into "Latin or English."[204]

In one of Mr. Hamilton's notebooks, he jotted down passages of Homer's *Iliad* in Greek.[205] The classical Roman figure of Emperor Julius Caesar also came up several times in the life of Alexander Hamilton. When he visited Jefferson at his lodgings in 1791, he inquired about the three portraits hanging in the Virginian's study. Jefferson said, "They are the Trinity of my great men, Sir Francis Bacon, Sir Isaac Newton, and John Locke." Mr. Hamilton supposedly responded, "The greatest man who ever lived was Julius Caesar."[206] Ron Chernow reports that after that, "Whenever Hamilton wanted to revile Jefferson as a populist demagogue, he invariably likened him to Julius Caesar."[207]

On one occasion, on May 21, 1798, the use of the image of Julius Caesar even went the other way when New York Republican attorney William Ketelas chastised Mr. Hamilton because he thought he was ingratitude for the nation who took him in as a young man, and then Mr. Ketelas likened him to Caesar.

Mr. Ketelas said about Mr. Hamilton:

> But like Caesar, you are ambitious and for that
> ambition to enslave his country Brutus sley

him. And are ambitious men less dangerous to
American than to Roman liberty?[208]

If Alexander Hamilton read Cicero carefully while at King's, he
found in his work, *De Officiis*, or "On Obligations," a work divided
into three books, the first of which describes what the Roman thought
of as the four main virtues (Truth, Justice, Fortitude and Decorum), as
well as the moral duties that these virtues require.[209] The second book is
about how one morally improves his life and focuses more on political
advancement and how to attain wealth and power.[210]

The third book of Cicero's *On Obligations* deals mostly with
how to behave when one's Moral Virtues in some way conflict with
expediency. Cicero states that "True Virtue can never be seen as
conflicting with private advantage. Thus, nothing should be accounted
useful or profitable if not strictly virtuous, and there ought to be no
separation of the principles of virtue and expediency."

Ron Chernow correctly speaks of the training that Alexander
Hamilton had at King's College when it came to his study of the Greco-
Roman classics. Chernow writes:

> After Kings, he could rattle off the classical
> allusions and exhibit the erudition that formed
> part of the intellectual equipment of all of the
> founding fathers. Also, he would be able to draw
> freely from a stock of lore about Greek and
> Roman antiquity, providing essential materials
> for the unending debates about the fate of
> Republican government in America.[211]

The same can be said of Mr. Hamilton's readings of classical
modern philosophy, such as Thomas Hobbes, John Locke, David
Hume, Francis Bacon and Edmund Burke. It is likely that Hamilton
was first introduced to the works of David Hume when he was a
student to Scotsman Robert Harpur at King's, as well as other worthies
of the Scottish Enlightenment. Hamilton was clearly impressed with
the Scottish philosopher when he read about the idea of government,
"Every man ought to be supposed a knave and to have no other end but
his private interests."[212]

The Rev. Richard Price wrote a description of the main points of David Hume's *Political Discourses*, which Hamilton read, and Col. Timothy Pickering gave the statesman a brush-up course on money matters when Mr. Hamilton became the secretary of the treasury.[213] Mr. Hamilton also alluded to David Hume's essays in endorsing government guidance in trade, which he denied was self-regulating and self-correcting.[214]

In *The Federalist Papers* Essay 85, Alexander Hamilton reminded his readers that no constitution is a perfect document, and he quoted David Hume that "Only time and experience could guide political enterprises to completion." In Mr. Hamilton's first report to Congress as secretary of the treasury, he quotes David Hume's *Political Discourses* in which the Scot suggested that "public debt can revitalize business activity."[215]

In addition to Alexander Hamilton's admiration of the works of David Hume, he also admired John Locke, Thomas Hobbes, Hugo Grotius, and the political writings of the Baron de Montesquieu, who suggested, among other things, the idea of three separate branches of government.[216]

Hamilton was firmly against the views of Thomas Hobbes and his understanding of human nature that in the state of nature, human beings are "wolfish and brutish." The great American statesman much more preferred Jean-Jacques Rousseau's view of the state of nature that "Man is naturally peaceful and timid."[217] Perhaps this is a nod in the direction of some of the Scottish Enlightenment thinkers.

Alexander Hamilton also admired literary works like Joseph Addison's drama *Cato*. The drama was based on the events of the last days of Cato the Younger (95–46 BCE) and his resistance to the tyranny of Julius Caesar and thus made him an arch-typical example of republicanism, virtue and liberty.[218] Because Addison's play dealt with issues like individual liberties versus government tyranny, republicanism versus monarchy, and logic versus emotions, Addison's play became very popular in America at the time of the Revolution and Independence.

In fact, in May of 1778, Col. William Bradford, while at Valley Forge, when Alexander Hamilton was there as well, wrote a letter to his sister revealing that Addison's *Cato* was performed at Valley Forge before "a numerous and splendid audience."[219] Alexander Hamilton also owned an eight-volume set of the *Spectator*, composed by Joseph Addison and Richard Steele, a collection of essay that the great statesman frequently recommended to young people to improve their writing style, as well as inculcating virtues.[220]

Alexander Hamilton also admired literary works like the essays of Michel Montaigne and the dramas of Moliere for similar purposes. He liked these works for many reasons, such as their writing styles, as well as some republican ideas he found in them.

This brings us to the second section of this fifth chapter on Alexander Hamilton and ethics, in which we speak of places in his works where the great American statesman wrote specifically about ethics, morality, and the phenomenon of Moral Responsibility. It is to explicit mentions of morality, then, to which we turn next.

Alexander Hamilton's Direct Quotations about Ethics and Moral Responsibility

In this second section of Chapter Five, we will identify and discuss a number of places in the speeches, letters and published works where the great American statesman Alexander Hamilton remarked on ethics, morality, virtue and the nature of Moral Responsibility.

In his first address to Congress on June 21, 1788, after becoming treasury secretary, Alexander Hamilton said this about the US Constitution and ethics:

> Allow a government to decline paying its debts and you overthrow all public morality—you unhinge all the principles that preserve the limits of free constitutions. Nothing can more affect national prosperity than a constant and systematic attention to extinguish the present debt and to avoid as much as possibly the incurring of any new debt.

Mr. Hamilton indicated that a nation that does not pay its debts becomes devoid of any public morality that lies behind its existence and any moral principles that inform that country's existence. He also points out that a nation that does not pay its debts will most likely incur more debt.

In another speech, Mr. Hamilton spoke of the moral problem of slavery and its relation to the moral character of the nation that practices it. Mr. Hamilton observed:

> Were not the disadvantages of slavery too obvious to stand in need of it, I might enumerate and describe the tedious train of calamities inseparable from it. I might show that it is fatal to religion and morality; that it tends to debase the mind, and corrupt its noblest springs of actions. I might show that it relaxes the sinews of industry, clips the wings of commerce, and introduces misery and indigence in every shape.[221]

In these comments, as well, Mr. Hamilton speaks of the issue of slavery and the many moral affects and effects that it has on a nation that practices it, which will be discussed later in Chapter Eight of this study. It is enough now, however, to point out, as this quotation does, that Alexander Hamilton was staunchly against the idea of the practice of slavery in the United States, as well as being very critical of those owners of slaves like many of the Virginia Founding Fathers, including Thomas Jefferson.

In another of his letters, Alexander Hamilton makes a very general remark about morality and ethics when he speaks of,

> So numerous indeed and so powerful are the causes which serve to give a false bias to the judgment, that we may, upon many occasions, see wise and good men as well as on the right side of questions of the first magnitude to the Society.[222]

Mr. Hamilton points out here that, at times, it is not easy to pick a "good and wise man" out from a host of others that are not either wise or good. Clearly, Hamilton thought this was true in the general population of a nation and in its political and perhaps moral leaders.

In another public speech, Alexander Hamilton appears to be speaking directly of Aristotle and/or Cicero's accounts of virtue, when the great American statesman observed:

> This circumstance, if duly attended to, would furnish a lesson of moderation to those who are ever so much persuaded of their being to be in the right in any controversy. And a further reason for caution, in this respect, might be drawn from the reflection that we are not always sure that those who advocate the truth are influenced by purer principles than their antagonists.[223]

Mr. Hamilton refers here to the reliance of Aristotle and Cicero on the idea of the Mean or "Moderation" in ethical matters, as well as the idea that a certain kind of person is of the view that he is always right in any controversy, without being influenced by what he refers to as "purer principles."[224] In the same text, Alexander Hamilton continued by observing more about the subject of ethics when he wrote:

> Ambition, avarice, personal animosity, party opposition, and many other motives not more laudable than these, are apt to operate as well upon those who support as those who oppose the right side of a question.[225]

In this general observation about ethics and morality, Mr. Hamilton again points out that ambition, avarice and these other attributes are as often seen among good men as they are among those who are less than good men. This is a theme that Alexander Hamilton repeated many times over the course of his life, in government, as well as among his family and his friends.

In one of the epigrams for this chapter, we employed another comment of Alexander Hamilton on the phenomenon of dueling. This comment was solicited from a colleague when he asked the great American statesman, in light of his son Philip's murder, what Mr. Hamilton now thought about dueling. The statesman answered the question by saying:

> My religious and moral principles are strongly
> opposed to the practice of Dueling and it would
> ever give me pain to be obliged to shed blood of
> a fellow creature in a private combat forbidden
> by the laws.[226]

The *New York Evening Post*, a newspaper started by Alexander Hamilton, featured an editorial after the death of Philip Hamilton in a duel, lamenting that the practice of dueling should be outlawed. It is likely that the editorial was written by Mr. Hamilton himself, though it was unsigned. The article said:

> Reflections on this horrid custom must occur
> to every man of humanity, but the voice of
> the individual or the press must be ineffectual
> without additional strong and supportive
> legislation interference.[227]

Alexander Hamilton also appeared to have been writing about believing and dying for a moral cause when he wrote to his friend, Edward Stevens, on November 21, 1769, whom the statesman called "Ned." He told his friend,

> To confess my weakness, Ned, my ambition is so
> prevalent that I disdain the groveling conditions
> of a clerk to which my fortune condemns me.
> I would willingly risk my life, though not my
> character, to exalt my station...Oh, how I wish
> there was a war!

Later, of course, Mr. Hamilton would receive his wish when he served bravely from 1775 to 1782.

Mr. Hamilton expresses his belief that there are some higher moral causes worth dying for, that one does not usually find these traits among one working as a "groveling clerk," and the soon-to-be American statesman understood the importance of what only can be called the "higher moral character." But what strikes us most about this passage is that it was written when Alexander Hamilton was only fourteen years old.

Finally, Dr. Kate Elizabeth Brown, author of the recent book *Alexander Hamilton and the Development of American Law*, gave a January 2019 talk in which she suggested that the 1790 "Remitting Act" that permitted the executive branch to waive penalties under the revenue laws if there were mitigating circumstances. In her remarks at the lecture, she suggested that there were many "important principles illustrated" in her view.

The first of these, Dr. Brown illustrated, "the importance of intent." If there were no criminal intent, a perpetrator would be treated more leniently. Secondly, is the question of judicial discretion, whereby a statute is not implemented automatically (as by a computer), but the "circumstances are taken into account." "Such a principle," Brown related, "lay behind the establishment of courts of equity, which were able to mitigate the letter of the law judgments which were seen as perpetrating an injustice, or violation of a moral law."[228]

At first blush, these observations by Professor Brown would seem to have little do with Alexander Hamilton's direct references to ethics, morality and, more specifically, to the idea of Moral Responsibility. But if we consider the passages in Aristotle's *Nicomachean Ethics*, where the Greek philosopher speaks about the notion of full Moral Responsibility, the relevance of Dr. Brown's 2019 lecture becomes clear for our purposes.

In Aristotle's *Ethics* sections 1110 to 1114, a book that Alexander Hamilton owned, the Greek philosopher sets out four conditions for full Moral Responsibility. These are:

1. Intentions
2. Knowledge of Right and Wrong
3. Knowledge of the Circumstances
4. The Ability to do otherwise

What Aristotle means by I. above is that moral actions must be "deliberate, they cannot be accidental." By II., that any moral action must be done within the context of already knowing what is generally considered morally right and morally wrong. Moral decisions, Aristotle tells us, are not made in a vacuum, so one must understand the circumstances under which the action and decision take place (item III). And finally, in any moral choice, the agent of choice must have the ability to not perform any given action, or what the Greek philosopher called the "ability to do otherwise."

If Dr. Brown is correct about why the "Remitting Act" was important for American law, then her two points about it—the importance of intent and taking circumstance into account, are nothing more than conditions I. and III. of Aristotle's account of full Moral Responsibility. Thus, another item in Alexander Hamilton's account of ethics and morality is that if Dr. Brown is correct, the great American statesman relied very heavily on Aristotle's notion of full Moral Responsibility.

This brings us to the third section of Alexander Hamilton's perspectives on ethics, morality and the notion of Moral Responsibility, in which we will identify and then discuss many pieces of moral advice that the great American statesman gave to people over the course of his life.

Alexander Hamilton on Moral Advice

Another aspect of Alexander Hamilton's perspective on ethics can be seen in several pieces of moral advice that the great American statesman gave over the years. There are many of these, but we will confine our discussion to ten of them in this third section of Chapter Five. We will list these ten pieces of moral advice here and then speak about them one at a time. They are:

1. Genius comes from hard work.
2. Do not procrastinate.
3. Do not fight for a cause you do not believe in.
4. Do not take on debt you cannot repay.
5. Always look sharp.
6. Do not forget to spend time with your family.
7. Do not let the haters get to you.
8. Embrace adversity.
9. Honor your commitments. Keep your promises.
10. Forgive your enemies.

In regard to number one on our list of moral advice, as we have indicated earlier in this study, Alexander Hamilton observed to a friend, "All the genius that I have lies in this when I have a subject in hand, I study it profoundly. Day and night, it is before me. I explore it in all its bearings. My mind becomes pervaded with it. Then the effort I have made is what people are pleased to call genius, but it is the fruit of labor and thought."[229]

Alexander Hamilton had an extraordinary work ethic throughout his life. What some saw as his genius, the great American statesman believed it was nothing more than working harder than everybody else. Mr. Hamilton wrote fifty-one essays of *The Federalist Papers* in a surprisingly short period of time, and he did it while keeping his day job, working full-time as an attorney.[230]

Many times in his life, Alexander Hamilton warned people not to procrastinate. He made this point in one letter from 1795 when he simply wrote, "I hate procrastination."[231] When Mr. Hamilton was treasury secretary, he was required to make periodic reports to Congress about the "books" of the country. Most of those scheduled reports were delivered two weeks early.[232]

In Hamilton's piece of moral advice number three above, he makes this point after talking a case of a man he suspected was guilty of what he was being accused. He later wrote about it, "I will never again take up a cause in which I was convinced I ought not to prevail."[233]

Many times while treasury secretary and also later in his life, Alexander Hamilton wrote things like, "The creation of debt should always be accompanied by the means of extinguishment." He said this in 1790 during a campaign to have the federal government assume the debts of states from the war. In other words, for Hamilton, debt can be good and fine, as long as you have a way to pay it back.

One aspect of the personal life of Alexander Hamilton is that the great American statesman "always dressed the part," as we would put it in contemporary American parlance. "A smart dress is essential," he wrote in a 1790 letter. He was speaking in the context of the attire of soldiers in the Continental and American armies.[234] By everyone's standards, Alexander Hamilton was always a dapper dresser, and this frequently made him attractive to people, particularly to women.

Alexander Hamilton was famously divisive in his adult life. While he was a beloved adviser to George Washington, he was loathed by many others who surrounded the general/president, particularly with other Founding Fathers like Jefferson, Madison, Adams and, of course, Vice-President Aaron Burr.

While Alexander Hamilton was busy in his full-time law practice and his help in the birth of a fledgling nation, the great American statesman still found time for his family. In 1801, Mr. Hamilton wrote a letter to Eliza that said, "Experience more and more convinces me that true happiness is only to be found in the bosom of the family." A report from the Hamilton family doctor tells us that when one of his children became ill, he rushed home to nurse the child back to health, at times even insisting that he administer the medicines himself.[235]

Regarding number seven on our list—don't let the haters get to you—Alexander Hamilton was indeed a hated man for much of his public life. Some of that had to do with his, at times, testy personality or perhaps the fact that he began life on the "wrong side of the tracks." But Mr. Hamilton never treated his role in public life as a popularity contest. In 1795, the great American statesman wrote a letter to George Washington that included the passage, "I have learned to regard public opinion as having little value."[236]

On many occasions, Alexander Hamilton experienced great tragedy and turmoil in his life, as we have seen many times in this study. In a letter to a friend in 1780, he spoke of the value of adversity, suggesting it may be a way of "testing" one's character or even "making that character morally better in some way."[237] Elsewhere, we have suggested that such theological responses to adversity are sometimes known as the "Test View" or the "Moral Qualities" perspective. It appears that Alexander Hamilton was a firm believer in these philosophical notions.[238]

Alexander Hamilton was a man who considered his word his bond, both in politics and in his personal life. On December 5, 1791, the great American statesman wrote a letter to his then nine-year-old son, Philip. He told his son, "A promise must never be broken, and I will never make you one, which I will not fulfill as I am able."

Finally, Alexander Hamilton was a firm believer that one must forgive his enemies. Following his fatal duel with Vice-President Burr,

Mr. Hamilton lay on his deathbed in intense pain for a day and a half. Before he finally passed away at 2:00 pm in the afternoon of July 12, 1804. One of his physicians, a Dr. Wilser, reported that in one of his final lucid moments, Mr. Hamilton reported, "I have no ill will toward Col. Burr. I met him with fixed resolution to do him no harm. I forgive all that happened.[239]

Both Dr. Mason and the Rev. Moore reported similar comments made by the great American statesman on his deathbed, to which both ministers attended. There can be little doubt that Alexander Hamilton held fast to the dictum of Jesus of Nazareth that one should "Love his enemies as himself."[240]

This brings us to what can be gleaned from his contributions to the *Federalist Papers* in regard to Alexander Hamilton's perspectives on the Moral Good and Moral Responsibility, the topic of the next section of Chapter Five.

Hamilton, Ethics and *The Federalist Papers*

Another way to ascertain the many views of great American statesman Alexander Hamilton's views on ethics and Moral Responsibility is what he had to say about these matters in his fifty-one essays of *The Federalist Papers*. Among the essays of the *Papers* that speak specifically about ethics are numbers 10, 31 to 34, 54, 68, and 84. Most scholars now conclude that Essays 10 and 54 were written by James Madison, with 31 to 34, 68, and 84 by Alexander Hamilton.[241]

In an essay called "The Moral Foundations of Republican Government," Edwin Meese provides a collection of moral ideas that Mr. Meese believed can be gleaned from these particular essays of the *Papers*.[242] Among these moral ideas were the following:

1. The idea of Natural Law
2. The idea of Natural Rights
3. The idea of the Consent of the Governed
4. A definition of Politics
5. The Implications of Good Government
6. The Nature of Republican Government
7. Moral and Religious Motives in Government

8. The Role of Commerce in Government
9. The Role of Moral Sentiments in Government
10. The importance of Federalism in Government

Needless to say, we will concentrate our attention here on those assumed to be the products of Alexander Hamilton, that is 31 to 34, 68, and 84. Essay 68 begins this way,

> The process of election affords a moral certainty
> that the office of the President will never fall
> to the lot of any man who is not in an eminent
> degree endowed with the requisite qualifications.

In contemporary American politics, of course, those on the left believe that Donald Trump did not meet the "qualifications" that Mr. Hamilton had in mind, while those on the right argue that President Biden is "locked up in the White House" because his mental acuity has now faded to the point of also being unqualified.[243] Essays 31 to 34 of the *Papers* are principally about the "general power of taxation." But along the way, Mr. Hamilton makes several moral claims about both state and federal taxes.

Essay 84 of the *Papers*, written by Hamilton in July and August of 1788, raises the question of whether the Bill of Rights should be included as part of the US Constitution. Mr. Hamilton thought yes, Mr. Madison believed no.

Of the ideas listed by Mr. Meese, he finds numbers one, two and three are most clearly in the very first of the *Papers*, another essay written by Mr. Hamilton. The idea of the "Science of politics," as Mr. Meese points out, "like most of the other sciences," as Mr. Hamilton points out, "has received greater improvement. The efficiency of various principles is now well understood, which were not known at all, or imperfectly known to the Ancients." The comment of Mr. Hamilton is in *Papers* Essay 34, Mr. Meese suggests, is based on David Hume's desire adopted by Alexander Hamilton that "Politics may be reduced to a science."

In the first of the essays of the *Papers*, as well, Mr. Meese points out that Alexander Hamilton asked, "Whether societies of men are really capable or not of establishing good government from reflection and choice, or whether they are forever destined to depend for their political constitutions on accident and force?" In Essay 33 of the *Papers*, Mr. Hamilton takes up the question of number eight in Mr. Meese's list.

In that regard, in Essay 32, Mr. Hamilton tells us that "Commerce has long been thought to be the primary cause of corruption of the manners and the morals of free people," and "private vice, the prevailing belief held, could never produce true virtue." In the same essay, however, Mr. Hamilton argued against both of these ideas.

Alexander Hamilton also discussed at some length in the *Papers* the necessity of the separation of powers and the continuing importance of Federalism, or item number ten on the list of Mr. Meese. In conclusion, both Alexander Hamilton and Edwin Meese believed that many moral observations of the great American statesman may be found in his contributions to *The Federalist Papers*.

This brings us to the fifth and final section of Chapter Five, in which we will discuss the great American statesman Alexander Hamilton's affair with Maria Reynolds, the wife of James Reynolds, and the moral character and consequences of that affair.

Hamilton, Ethics and Maria Reynolds

One final element in the life of statesman Alexander Hamilton related to ethical matters is the year-long affair he engaged in between the summers of 1791 and 1792 with Maria Reynolds, the wife of James Reynolds. In this final section of Chapter Five, we will proceed in the following fashion. First, we will give an account, as best we can, of the facts of the case, including, as we shall see, some unanswered questions about the incident. Second, using Aristotle's account of full Moral Responsibility introduced earlier in this chapter, we will raise some questions about who is morally responsible for what in the story of James and Maria Reynolds and Alexander Hamilton. And finally, we will offer some conclusions about what sense to make of the story.

In the summer of 1791, twenty-three-year-old Maria Reynolds came to the door of the thirty-four-year-old Alexander Hamilton in Philadelphia to request some monetary assistance from the statesman. She claimed that her husband, James Reynolds, was abusive to her and their daughter by abandoning the two of them. Maria Reynolds was now staying at a boarding house in the city after the abandonment.[244] Mr. Hamilton told Mrs. Reynolds that he was willing to help her, but he had no cash with him at the time.

Mr. Hamilton jotted down the address of the boarding house and promised to bring money the following evening. When he arrived, Maria Reynolds took Mr. Hamilton up to her room. Alexander Hamilton later recounted in a text that has come to be called the "Reynolds Pamphlet," "I took the bill out of my pocket and gave it to her. Some conversation ensued in which it was quickly apparent that other than pecuniary consolation would be acceptable."[245]

Thus, the two began an illicit affair that would last, with varying frequency, until June 1792. Over the course of those months—most likely in December of 1791—James Reynolds had become well aware of the tryst between Hamilton and his wife. As a response, Mr. Reynolds began to blackmail Mr. Hamilton, threatening to tell the statesman's wife if he did not agree to pay money to Mr. Reynolds.[246] The common practice of the day was for the "wronged" husband to seek retribution in a pistol duel, but Mr. Reynolds insisted instead for monetary compensation.

In the same month, on December 15, Mr. Hamilton received two letters from Mr. and Mrs. Reynolds, one from him and the other from his wife. The one from Maria arrived first in the post telling Hamilton that her husband is aware of the affair and James' attempt to blackmail the statesman. Over the next several months, Alexander Hamilton paid James Reynolds a sum of $1,300 in exchange for secrecy.[247] In today's money, this would be worth somewhere between $25,000 and $35,000.

However, Mr. Reynolds began to tell others that Hamilton was providing him with insider trading information about government securities.[248] When a group of congressmen began investigating these accusations in 1797, Alexander Hamilton was forced to reveal the truth about the tryst with Maria by sharing his love letters to her with his accusers, as well as those missives back from Maria to Alexander. Soon after, Mr. Hamilton published his famous *Reynolds Pamphlet*, a nearly 100-page document that gave an account of the affair from beginning to end.

After the pamphlet was released, Maria Reynolds was publicly scorned, and she decided to move with her second husband to Britain. His name was Jacob Clingman, a man who had allegedly been involved in the Reynolds affair. Mr. Clingman also assisted Mr. Reynolds in swindling army vets out of money the government owed them. In fact, James Reynolds was later arrested for this crime and subsequently served time in prison.[249]

Later, Maria returned to Philadelphia and changed her name to Maria Clement. In Philadelphia, she became a housekeeper for a physician named Dr. Matthew, and in 1806, she married the doctor, though there is no record of a divorce from Mr. Clingman. In 1808, the Reynolds' daughter, Susan, moved in with her mother. Susan was married several times and had two daughters, one of which was named Josepha Philips, who was raised by her grandmother.[250]

Later on, Alexander Hamilton suggested that his "real crime" was what he had done to his dear wife, Eliza. We will say more about Eliza's reaction to the word of her husband's affair with Mrs. Reynolds later in this section of this chapter. It is enough now, however, to indicate that she forgave him for his indiscretion.

In terms of the facts of the affair, one overarching question is who knew what and when? For example, were Maria and her husband in the game of blackmail together? When did James Reynolds first learn, or even suspect, the tryst was going on? Did Eliza have any doubts about the fidelity of her husband?

If any of the answers to these questions were in the affirmative, or if James Reynolds sent his wife to the Hamilton house in Philadelphia, the moral status of the situation would be different for the Reynolds pair from the beginning.

Regarding Aristotle and the nature of Mr. Hamilton's Moral Responsibility in the affair, he intended to betray his wife. He certainly knew it was morally wrong. He understood the circumstances under which it was conducted, and later on in the pamphlet, he believes that he was blackmailed by both the Reynolds—husband and wife. And, Mr. Hamilton certainly had the "ability to do otherwise." Thus, we may conclude that Alexander Hamilton was fully, morally responsible for the affair, something that was decidedly outside his normal moral character for the rest of his moral life.[251]

The only other character that appears to be fully morally responsible for his actions is James Reynolds. His intentions were self-serving. He acted out of spite. He profited from the affair and fully understood the circumstances he had put Mr. Hamilton in. And he certainly could have kept from doing what he did. Thus, James Reynolds appears to have been morally wrong in his actions as well, at least in regard to the affair of Mr. Hamilton with his wife, Maria.

Alexander Hamilton had no reason to expect forgiveness from his wife, Eliza. Yet, somehow, she forgives him. After the death of their son, Philip, also in a duel, the family had to deal with yet another tragedy in the life of the Hamilton family. In taking his children to church and returning to God at the end of his life, Mr. Hamilton asks for forgiveness, and, ironically, he gets it.

In the musical *Hamilton*, amid the revelation of the affair with Mrs. Reynolds, Eliza takes her husband's hand and draws near to him and then says, "There are moments that the words do not reach/There is a grace too powerful to name."[252] Alexander Hamilton was the recipient of the Divine grace, even at the expense and at the behest of his faithful and loving wife.

This brings us to the major conclusions of Chapter Five. The subject matter in Chapter Six of this study of Alexander Hamilton's religion shall be the phenomena of religious freedom and religious toleration in the life of great American statesman Alexander Hamilton.

Conclusions to Chapter Five

In the Introduction to Chapter Five, we began by indicating that the chapter would have four parts and sections. There we suggested we would explore, first, the sources of Alexander Hamilton's ethics, followed by his direct pronouncements about morality and Moral Responsibility; the third section on what Mr. Hamilton said about ethics in *The Federalist Papers*, and the final section on the moral character and moral evaluation of Mr. Hamilton's affair with Mrs. Maria Reynolds.

In the initial section of Chapter Five, we indicated that the principal sources of Alexander Hamilton's views on ethics were the teachings of Jesus, Greco-Roman sources, including ideas from Cicero, Vigil, Julius Caesar and Aristotle's *Nicomachean Ethics*. In addition, we also suggested that the Greek philosopher's Virtue Ethic was one that Mr. Hamilton found very attractive.

We also indicated in the "sources" section of Chapter Five, that several modern European philosophers and literary artists were also employed by Alexander Hamilton in constructing his theory of ethics. Among these philosophers were Thomas Hobbes, John Locke, Edmund Burke, the Baron Montesquieu, and, most importantly, Scottish philosopher David Hume.

Among the literary figures that Alexander Hamilton found helpful in cobbling together his views on ethics, as we have shown, were Michel Montaigne's *Essays*, the dramas of Moliere, and Joseph Addison's drama *Cato*.

In the second section of Chapter Five on Alexander Hamilton's views on ethics, we introduced and discussed thirteen separate passages of the great American statesman where he specifically talked or wrote about morality and the phenomenon of Moral Responsibility. Indeed, at the end of our analysis of this material, we introduced the work of contemporary scholar Dr. Kate Elizabeth Brown, who, among other things, has shown how reliant Alexander Hamilton was on Aristotle's account of Moral Responsibility.

In the third section of Chapter Five, we analyzed and discussed ten pieces of moral advice that Alexander Hamilton frequently gave to young people, including his own children, as we have shown. These ten pieces of advice were about genius, procrastination, debt, looking smart, spending time with family, embracing adversity, keeping your promises, and forgiving one's enemies, which, in Mr. Hamilton's case, included his forgiveness to Vice-President Aaron Burr on his deathbed. We indicated that each of these ten pieces of advice often had profound moral attributes, as well as moral implications to be found in them.

Hamilton, ethics and *The Federalist Papers* was the subject matter of the fourth section of Chapter Five. In that section, we employed an essay by former US attorney general of the United States, Edwin Meese III, who found a list of ten separate political and moral categories in *The Federalist Papers*.

In this analysis of the fourth section of Chapter Five, we have shown that the items on Mr. Meese's list are addressed quire explicitly in several of the essays of *The Federalist Papers* written by the great American statesman Alexander Hamilton. Among those essays, as we have shown, were *The Federalist Papers* numbers 31 to 35, 54, 68, and 84.

In the final section of Chapter Five on Alexander Hamilton's ethics, we discussed the moral nature and character of the affair that Alexander Hamilton conducted with Mrs. Maria Reynolds from the summer of 1791 to June of 1792. In that analysis, we made the following moral conclusions: First, the great American statesman was fully morally culpable in his actions in the tryst. Secondly, regarding the affair, is that Maria Reynolds' husband, James, was also fully morally responsible for untoward behavior in the episode. Thirdly, we concluded that Alexander Hamilton's behavior in the affair with Maria Reynolds was decidedly out of character when it came to his normal moral behavior throughout the rest of his moral life. Fourthly, we have shown that Eliza Hamilton forgave her husband, but she clearly need not have done so. What her motivations were are not entirely clear. But she outlived her husband for half a century, and in that time, she spoke no ill of her brilliant and clever husband.

This section also shows that the *Reynolds Pamphlet* stated that the entire affair might have been a "set-up" constructed by the Reynolds couple and Maria's second husband, Jacob Clingman. And given the reports of the criminal moral characters of both men, it seems likely that Mr. Hamilton was correct about that matter.

At the very end of Chapter Five, we suggested that the forgiving action of Eliza Hamilton toward her husband's affair with Mrs. Reynolds can only be explained by what both Eliza and Alexander could only explain as an act of Divine Grace.

This brings us to Chapter Six. The major focus of this chapter, as we shall see, will be the phenomena of religious freedom or liberty, the term Hamilton usually preferred, and religious toleration in the thoughts, speeches, and writings of the great American statesman Alexander Hamilton.

Chapter Six
Hamilton on Religious Liberty and Toleration

Napoleon, Charles James Fox, and Hamilton, the greatest men of
his age and that if he were forced to decide among the three, I
would give without hesitation the first place to Hamilton.
—Charles Maurice Talleyrand

Washington chose him to be part of what Washington called
his family. He gathers around him young men of promise and
talent. And Hamilton gets picked. What could be more wonderful than to be brought into George Washington's family?
—Carol Berkin, *The Tartan Apple: The Scots of New York*

I am conscious of no ill-will toward Colonel Burr, distinct from
political opposition, which, as I trust, has proceeded from
pure and upright motives.
—Alexander Hamilton, prayer before his duel with Mr. Burr

Introduction

The purpose of this Chapter Six is to explore what the great American
statesman Alexander Hamilton thought, said and wrote about the
phenomena of religious freedom, or the expression that Mr. Hamilton
preferred of "Religious Liberty," as well as the idea of religious
toleration in Mr. Hamilton's time and thought.

To those ends, we will divide Chapter Six into four separate
sections. In the first of these, we will identify and discuss many general
observations that Alexander Hamilton made about religious liberty. In

the second section, we shall identify and discuss the places in the essays of *The Federalist Papers* written by Mr. Hamilton, in which religious liberty is discussed by him.

In the third section, we shall explore what the sources may have been for what Alexander Hamilton believed, said, and wrote about the phenomenon of religious toleration. And, in the fourth and final section of Chapter Six, we will discuss more about what great American statesman Alexander Hamilton explicitly believed, said and wrote about the idea of religious toleration.

Hamilton's General Comments About Religious Liberty

Among the places in the works of Alexander Hamilton where he spoke in general terms about religious liberty were his *The Farmer Refuted;* the statesmen's comments at the Constitutional Convention in Philadelphia in June of 1787; in his essay, "A Full Vindication of the Measures of Congress," from December 15, 1774; as well as in a number of his other public speeches and published works.

In one place in *The Farmer Refuted,* from February 23, 1775, Alexander Hamilton turned his attention to what he called "Sacred Rights of Mankind." The statesman related:

> The Sacred Rights of Mankind Are not to be
> Rummaged for among old parchments of musty
> records. They are written, as with a sunbeam, in
> the whole volume of human nature by the hand
> of the Divinity itself. And they can never be
> erased or obscured by mortal power.

Here Mr. Hamilton wrote of how God wrote natural rights into human nature, "like a sunbeam by the hand of Divinity itself," and that these natural rights, including religious freedom, were to be a permanent mark on human nature.

So, presumably then, among these "Sacred Rights" that Mr. Hamilton had in mind were those connected to Religious Liberty and described in the US Constitution. In another place in the same work, Hamilton told us, "There is a certain enthusiasm of liberty that makes human nature rise above itself in acts of bravery and heroism."

Undoubtedly, Mr. Hamilton was referring to the bravery and heroism that he would later see, as well as exhibit himself, on the battlefield.

At the Constitutional Convention on June 16, 1787, Delegate Robert Yates reported Alexander Hamilton had said, "We are now forming a republican government. Real liberty is never found in despotism or the extremes of democracy but in moderate governments." Here Mr. Hamilton expresses his lifelong view that religion in any "extreme form" is likely to be harmful to society and religious liberty, as well.

In another place in *The Farmer Refuted*, Alexander Hamilton observed more about the nature of religious liberty when he wrote, "Civil liberty is only a natural liberty, modified and secured by the sanction of civil society." In yet another section of the same work, Alexander Hamilton again wrote about the most pristine form of civil liberty. He wrote:

> I consider civil liberty in general unadulterated
> sense, as the greatest of terrestrial Blessings.
> I am convinced that the whole human race is
> initiated to it; and that it can not be wrestled
> from no part of them, without the blackest and
> most aggravated guilt.

In his essay entitled "A Full Vindication of the Measures of Congress," published on December 15, 1774, Alexander Hamilton said more about the relationship between civil and religious liberties. He observed, "Remember, civil and religious liberty always go together; if the foundation of one is sapped, the other will soon fall, of course." Thus, the great American statesman appears to have believed in a symbiotic relationship between civil liberty and religious liberty.

In another portion of the same work, Mr. Hamilton spoke of the foundations of the law and civil and religious liberty. He observed,

> I would die to preserve the law upon a solid
> foundation, but take away liberty, and that
> foundation is destroyed.

From these general observations of Alexander Hamilton about religious liberty, we may make the following conclusions:

1. The great American statesman believed that religious freedoms were "Sacred Rights" given to "all of Mankind."
2. These rights come from God.
3. That despotism is the worst place to find the expression of these religious liberties.
4. A government with moderation is the best place to find religious freedoms.
5. Hamilton believed these religious liberties could not be taken from human beings.
6. The great American statesman was convinced that there is a symbiotic relationship between civil rights and religious rights.
7. At times, human nature is perfectly capable of great acts of heroism and bravery.
8. Mr. Hamilton was sure that he and others should be willing to die for a just cause but never at the expense of his, or their, religious liberties.

Often in the published speeches and works of Alexander Hamilton, his comments about religious liberties are to be found in the context of other political issues that the statesman was engaged in. Often these pronouncements came in very short and pithy statements such as,

> To be more safe, they [Americans] at length become willing to run the risk of being less free.[253]

Or consider this comment from his *Collected Works*, edited by his son John C. Hamilton,

> However weak our country may be, I hope we shall never sacrifice our liberties.

Or,

> A large and well-organized republic can scarcely lose its liberty from any other cause than that of anarchy, to which a contempt of the laws in the high road.

Or,

> The vigour of government is essential to the
> security of liberty.[254]

Alexander Hamilton gave us another pithy statement about
religious liberty when he observed:

> The standing army can never be formidable
> [threatening] to the liberties of the people, while
> there is a large body of citizens, little if at all
> inferior to them in the use of arms.[255]

At other times, Alexander Hamilton's observations about liberty
in a political context are more lengthy, such as,

> Safety from external danger is the most powerful
> director of national conduct. Even the ardent
> love of liberty will, after a time, give way to its
> dictates.[256]

Consider this comment of Mr. Hamilton's about authority, force,
and liberty:

> The instrument by which it [government] must
> act are either the authority of the Laws or
> Force. If the first be destroyed, the last must be
> substituted; and when this becomes the ordinary
> instrument of government there is an end to
> liberty.[257]

On another occasion, Mr. Hamilton again turned his attention to
the relation of government to liberty when he observed:

> We may safely be received as an axiom in our
> political system, that the state governments will
> in all possible contingencies afford complete
> security against invasions of the public liberty
> by the national authority.[258]

Mr. Hamilton made it clear what values and moral virtues he saw
as the backbone of religious liberty when he wrote,

> A struggle for liberty is in itself respectable and
> glorious... When conducted with magnanimity,
> justice, humanity, it ought to command the
> admiration of every friend to human nature. But
> if sullied by crimes and extravagancies, it loses
> its respectability.[259]

At many points in Mr. Hamilton's works, he spoke eloquently about the human capacity that God had written in human nature so that certain men might display human acts of incredible heroism and bravery, such as Mr. Hamilton's behavior in his seven years as an army officer.

From these general observations on religious liberty, we may make the following four conclusions.

1. The vigor of government must depend on human liberty.
2. Liberty is either the product of chance or force.
3. Forced liberty never works.
4. Religious liberty and civil liberties always come together.

Mr. Hamilton also made a very general observation about e relation of liberty to power in his 1788 essay "Energy in the Executive is a Leading Character in the Definition of a Good Government." In that work, the great American statesman observed:

> In a government framed for a durable liberty, no
> less regard must be paid to giving the magistrate
> a proper degree of authority, to make an execute
> the laws with rigour, than to guarding against
> encroachments upon the rights of the community.
> As too much power leads to despotism, too little
> leads to anarchy, and both eventually to the ruin
> of the people.[260]

Mr. Hamilton believed there must be a delicate balance when it came to questions of religious and civil liberties. Too much emphasis either way in these matters could easily lead to despotism or anarchy.

In addition to these general observations that Alexander Hamilton made about religious liberties, as well as liberties in general, he also frequently commented on these same concerns in the essays of *The Federalist Papers*, of which he was the author. In the next section of Chapter Six, we will identify and discuss several of these observations.

Hamilton, Religious Liberty and *The Federalist Papers*

In general, questions of religious freedom and religious strife are not major themes of *The Federalist Papers*. Not a single essay of the eighty-five takes up the question of religious liberty. Nevertheless, nine different essays of the *Papers* spoke about the issues at hand. These included Essays 1, 2, 10, 23, 47, 51, 52, 55, and the next to last essay of the *Papers*, number 85.

We must remember, however, that during this period of American history, from the Revolution through the ratification and amendment of the Constitution, from 1775 until 1791, the protection of religious liberty, as well as the proper relation of religion to politics, were of very great concern to the founders.

Still, the question must be posed, why is the single most important contemporaneous commentary on the US Constitution say so little about the idea of religious liberty? Also, when the subject is raised in the *Papers*, it is always just in passing. Nevertheless, we can point to the following observations about the issue at hand.

In the very first of *The Federalist Papers*, Alexander Hamilton made many comments on liberties in general and religious liberty in particular. Consider,

> I would die to preserve the law upon a solid foundation but take way liberty, and the foundation is destroyed.

In *Papers* Essay 8, Alexander Hamilton again talks of safety, danger and freedom when he wrote:

> Safety from external danger is the most powerful director of national conduct. To be more safe,

nations at length become willing to run the risk
of being less free.

Again, in the same essay, Mr. Hamilton spoke of the origin of
religious liberty and its relation to civil liberty when he wrote,

> Natural liberty is a gift of the beneficent Creator
> to the whole human race, and that civil liberty
> is founded in that and cannot be wrestled from
> any people, wihout the most manifest violation
> of justice.[261]

In the first essay of *The Federalist Papers*, as well, Alexander
Hamilton told us more about the nature of religious liberty as well as
how it is related to civil liberty, when he observed,

> For in politics, as in religion, is it equally
> absurd to aim at making proselytes by fire and
> sword. Heresies in either can rarely be cured by
> persecution.

This is another theme that we see throughout the life of Alexander
Hamilton; that the worst forms of religion and religious worship in
any state are almost always in those states where people are coerced to
believe and act in certain ways. Mr. Hamilton was always against the
imposition of views by "fire and sword."

In Essay 57 of the *Papers*, Alexander Hamilton observed,

> The genius of the whole system, the nature of
> just and constitutional laws, and above all the
> vigilant and manly spirit which actuates the
> people of America, a spirit which nourishes
> freedom, and in return is nourished by it. If this
> spirit shall ever be so far debased as to tolerate
> a law not obligatory on the Legislature, as well
> as on the people, the people will be prepared to
> tolerate anything but liberty.

In Essay 70 of *The Federalist Papers*, Alexander Hamilton also
observed,

> When sometimes there is an interruption of
> the ordinary course of justice, to the security
> of liberty there is against the enterprises
> and assaults of ambition, of faction and of
> anarchy.

In *Papers* Essay 78, in a discussion of the judiciary, the great American statesman again turned his attention to the idea of oppression and liberty. He observed:

> It equally proves that though individual
> oppression may now and then proceed from
> the courts of justice, the general liberty of the
> people can never be endangered from that
> quarter. I mean so long as the judiciary remains
> truly distinct from both the legislature and the
> executive branches.

In Essay 26, entitled "The Idea of Restraining the Legislative Authority in Regard to the Common Defense Considered," Alexander Hamilton wrote:

> The citizens of America have too much
> discernment to be argued into anarchy. And I am
> much mistaken if experience has not wrought a
> deeper and solemn conviction in the public mind,
> that greater energy of government is essential to
> the welfare and prosperity of the community.

In this essay, Mr. Hamilton speaks of the respect that he had for the judgment of the average American when it came to the welfare and prosperity of the community. He firmly believed that citizens were largely capable of making their own decisions for themselves, their families, and the community, as well.

On November 20, 1787, in the context of writing *Papers* Essay 8, entitled, "The Consequences of Hostilities Between the States," the great American statesman again turned his attention to some common themes when he told us this:

> The violent destruction of life and property
> incident to war, the continual effort and alarm
> attendant on a state of continual danger will
> compel nations the most attached to liberty, to
> resort to repose and security, to institutions,
> which have a tendency to destroy their civil and
> political rights. To be more free, they at length
> become willing to run the risk of being less free.

In Essay 75, Alexander Hamilton spoke of the idea of virtue and the make-up of the American nation. He observed:

> The history of human conduct does not warrant
> that exalted opinion of human virtue which would
> make it wise in a nation to commit interests of so
> delicate and momentous a kind as those which
> concern its intercourse with the rest of the world
> to the sole disposal of a magistrate created and
> circumstanced as would be a President of the
> United States.

Alexander Hamilton in Essay 63, written in 1788, speaks of the notion of Moral Responsibility and its relation to freedom. He observed:

> Moral Responsibility in order to be reasonable,
> must be limited to its objects within the power of
> the responsible party. And in order to be effectual
> must relate to operations of that power, of which
> a ready and proper judgment can be formed by
> the constituents.

Mr. Hamilton makes the following points in this passage.

1. Moral Responsibility has to occur within the context of reason.
2. The responsibility of an individual may be very different than that of a group.
3. Proper judgment of Moral Responsibility in any given

case must be interpreted by a "judgment formed by the constituents."

What that meant in practical terms is that there may also be a deep distinction between the concept of general responsibility and that of Moral Responsibility.[262]

Finally, in Essay 84 of *The Federalist Papers*—which may have been written by Mr. Madison or by Mr. Hamilton—in the context of whether the United States needed a separate Bill of Rights, the author said, "the Constitution is itself in every rational sense, and in every useful purpose, a bill of rights," would thus safeguard all liberties including religious freedom.

The Federalist Papers emphasized that the essential goal in designing and constructing a constitution for a free people is not the use of fine words about rights that amount only to a "parchment barrier" against tyranny (Essay 47), but instead it was "The design of an internal structure [number 23] that tilts all the outcomes of the political process in the direction of natural freedoms."

From these fourteen passages on religious freedom from Alexander Hamilton in his contributions to *The Federalist Papers*, we may make the following conclusions.

1. That Americans are sometimes willing to give up or limit freedom for the sake of safety.
2. Religious liberty comes from God.
3. Personal ambition is sometimes an obstacle to the expression of religious liberty.
4. Citizens are often the best judges for evaluating the exercise of religious liberty and religious toleration in regard to others.
5. The idea of Moral Responsibility is a subtle notion that is often not so easy to determine.

This brings us to the third section of Chapter Six, in which we will explore the views of great American statesman Alexander Hamilton on the phenomenon of religious toleration regarding the United States in the second half of the eighteenth century.

Hamilton on Religious Toleration

When we use the term "Religious Tolerance" or "Religious Toleration" in the study, we mean that citizens are required to allow other citizens to think, believe or worship any way they see fit. In a nation with a state religion, religious toleration at the government level means that the state allows other faith to be there. In past centuries, many countries permitted other religions to exist but only in a private way. This was, however, a rare phenomenon. Other nations allowed different faiths to exist but practiced religious discrimination in other ways. This was often the case in the original thirteen American colonies, where Catholics, for example, were often discriminated against.

When Alexander Hamilton's French Huguenot maternal grandfather arrived in the New World in 1658, he selected a British-controlled island of Nevis in the British West Indies to settle. Mr. Hamilton's grandfather, Dr. John Faucett, as well as other Protestant French subjects, were themselves fleeing religious discrimination following the revocation of the Edict of Nantes by King Louis XIV of France in 1685.[263] The Edict of Nantes was first promulgated at Nantes in Brittany on April 13, 1598, by King Henry IV that granted a large measure of religious freedoms to his Protestant, or Huguenot subjects.[264]

Nevertheless, it is rare in the speeches and published written works of Alexander Hamilton that a passage that specifically speaks about the idea of religious toleration can be found. What is much clearer on the matter are the sources that went into making the perspectives on Religious Toleration in the life of Mr. Hamilton. As we shall see later in this third section of Chapter Six, when the great American statesman does speak of Religious Toleration, it was often in speeches the statesman had written for George Washington, both as a general and as a president.

In addition to the founding documents of the United States that speak of both religious freedom and religious toleration, it is very clear that George Washington, both as a general and as a president, should be seen as a key source for discerning Mr. Hamilton's views on the matter of religious toleration.

One interesting fact about the discussion of eighteenth-century interests in religious toleration is that the English language did not even have a word for the phenomenon in discussion until the 1780s.[265] The French term *Tolerantisme* can first be seen in the 1760s. The French *Dictionaire de France* from 1762 gives us this definition of the equivalent French term for "toleration." It said, "The characteristics or system of those who believe that one should tolerate in a state all sorts of religions."

Twenty years later, at the end of 1780s on August 26, 1789, Article 10 of the *Declaration of the Rights of Man and Citizen* proclaimed that:

> No one should be disturbed for his opinions, even
> in religion, provided that their manifestation does
> not trouble public order as established by law.

Meanwhile, in America, toleration of varying points of view, especially in regard to religion, had become a hallmark of American republicanism. On August 18, 1790, George Washington wrote to the Hebrew Congregation of Newport, Rhode Island, including the words,

> Tolerance in return requires that they who under
> the protection of the government should demean
> themselves as good citizens in giving it on all
> occasions their effectual support.

In the letter, Mr. Washington was attempting to soothe the sensibilities of the Jews in New England and their concern for the lack of religious toleration. Many historians have pointed out that our first president did not write these words. They were written by his former aide-de-camp, Alexander Hamilton, the great American statesman who is the object of this study.

George Washington's "Farewell Address to the Nation," delivered and published on September 19, 1796, was his final words to his fellow American citizens before retiring to his Mount Vernon estate. The address is important for our purposes for two reasons. First, like the letter to the synagogue in Newport, Rhode Island, the "Farewell

Address" also came from the pen of Alexander Hamilton. Second, in several places in the address, President Washington turned his attention to issues of religion and ethics. About two-thirds along in the address, he related that these words originated from the hand of Alexander Hamilton, his speechwriter:

> Of all the dispositions and habits, which lead to political prosperity, religion and morality are indispensable supports. In vain would that man claim the tribute of patriotism, who should labor to subvert these great pillars of human happiness, these firmest props of the duties of men and citizens.

A few sentences later, Hamilton, by way of Washington, turned his attention to the relation of religion to morality. Washington said:

> And let us with caution indulge the supposition that morality can be maintained without religion. Whatever may be conceded to the influence of refined education on minds of peculiar structure, reason and experience both forbid us to expect that national morality can prevail in exclusion of religious principle.

If these were indeed the original words of Alexander Hamilton, then he assents here to the moral theory known as Divine Command Theory, which essentially says that the Moral Good is nothing more than what God commands, such as the Ten Commandments and the Golden Rule, for examples.

A few paragraphs later, the first president, or Mr. Hamilton through George Washington, came very close to an observation about religious tolerance by saying:

> Observe good faith and justice towards all nations; cultivate peace and harmony towards all. Religion and morality enjoin this conduct; and can it be that good policy does not equally enjoin it?

And what Washington said of nations could also have been said about the American nation's citizens, "Good faith and justice toward all faiths and denominations. Let them cultivate peace and harmony for the whole."

Ron Chernow, in his *Alexander Hamilton*, points out that years later, Eliza Hamilton said of the Farewell Address of Washington, "The whole or nearly all of the Address was read to me by him as he wrote it and a greater part, if not all, was written by him in my presence."[266] Mr. Chernow also relates a memory of Eliza that she and her husband were "strolling down Broadway when they were accosted by an old soldier on the street who was selling the Farewell Address. Alexander Hamilton bought a copy, and his wife reported that he then said, "That man does not know he has asked me to purchase my own work."

Some of the state constitutions also may have been sources of Alexander Hamilton's views on religious toleration. The Virginia Constitution from June 12, 1776; the Pennsylvania Constitution from September 28, 1776; the Delaware Constitution of September 10, 1776; and the Massachusetts Constitution of 1779 all had provisions for the phenomenon of religious toleration built into their state documents.

In addition to President Washington, a few seventeenth-century sources also went into the making of Alexander Hamilton's views on religious toleration. Two of those sources could be found in Alexander Hamilton's personal library. The first is John Locke's *An Essay on Toleration*, which included several ideas that Mr. Hamilton found attractive. In addition to advocating for religious toleration in the essay, Mr. Locke also argued for drawing a clear line or boundary between civil power and religion.

In other words, Mr. Locke would seem to have argued for what we would call the separation of church and state. Locke's argument was so clear that it deserves repeating here. The English philosopher wrote:

> The Civil Power can either change everything in
> religion, according to the prince's pleasure, or
> it can change nothing. If it be once permitted to
> introduce anything into religion, by the means
> of laws and penalties, there can be no bounds

> put to it… Whereas, if each of them [the church
> and the state] would contain itself within its
> own bounds—the one attending to the worldly
> welfare of the Commonwealth, the other to the
> Salvation of Souls—it is impossible that any
> Discord should ever happen between them.

These words in Alexander Hamilton's copy of John Locke's *An Essay on Toleration* are marked up with a black pen. It is clear that the great American statesman apparently was in full agreement with the ideas of religious toleration and the separation of church and state.

Apparently, Mr. Hamilton was impressed with another portion of John Locke's essay, which was also heavily marked up in his personal copy. The text of that passage is this:

> Men being by nature all free, equal, and
> independent, no one can be put out of this
> estate and subjected to the political power of
> another without his consent, which is done by
> agreeing with other men, to join and unite into
> a community for their comfortable, safe, and
> peaceable living… in the secure enjoyment of
> their properties.

The other volume is French philosopher Pierre Bayle's 1686 work *Philosophical Commentary on these Words of Jesus Christ*. This was one of the first tracts in French to use toleration of religious differences in a positive way.

Another volume to be found in Alexander Hamilton's library, in addition to his *Candide*, was Voltaire's *Treatise on Toleration on the Occasion of the Death of Jean Calas*, published in Paris in 1763. In this work, Voltaire targets both religious intolerance, as well as what we might call religious fanaticism.

Jean Calas, a French Protestant merchant, was accused of murdering a man who was supposedly trying to get Calas to convert to Catholicism. Mr. Calas was executed for the murder on March 10, 1762, after he confessed after being tortured for many hours. In Voltaire's account of the case, he makes this statement:

> Sir, there are forty million inhabitants in Europe
> who are not members of the Church of Rome,
> should you go up to every one of them and say,
> "Sir, since you are infallibly damned, I shall
> neither eat, nor converse, nor have any other
> connection with you?"

In Alexander Hamilton's copy of Voltaire's book, held at the Columbia University Library, this argument is underlined and otherwise marked up in such a fashion that it appears to be one with which the great American statesman agreed.

As indicated earlier in this section on religious toleration, we are now pretty sure that Alexander Hamilton wrote George Washington's letter to the Jewish community in Newport, Rhode Island. In that same letter, Mr. Hamilton wrote:

> We all possess alike a liberty of conscience, for
> happily the Government of the United States,
> which gives to bigotry no sanction, to persecution
> no tolerance. It requires only that those who live
> under its protection should demean themselves
> as good citizens, in giving it on all occasions
> their effectual support.

The expression, "To persecution no tolerance," if Alexander Hamilton was indeed the author, then it stands as the most archetypal comment that the great American statesman Alexander Hamilton made on the issue of religious toleration in America.

Finally, in the summer of 1787, delegates from the former thirteen colonies were slowly working their way to Philadelphia, where the Constitutional Convention would convene to draft the founding document that still governs us today. George Washington was the overwhelming choice to preside over the assembly. As the chairman, he was among the first to arrive in Philadelphia.

Despite the fact that Roman Catholics and other minority faiths were despised and discriminated against, and many lurid tales of debauchery in convents, the fears of Roman Catholic conspiracies and papist plots were still an everyday part of the folk religion for many Americans.

And what did George Washington do? On Sunday, May 14, 1787, after his arrival in Philadelphia, he and several other delegates went to mass at a local Roman Catholic Church. The Anglican George Washington went to mass, without fanfare, without any press release, without any photo-ops. The gesture, nevertheless, sent a powerful, symbolic message of religious tolerance. And one might guess that one of those fellow delegates who attended mass with George Washington was none other than a brilliant delegate from the New York delegation by the name of Alexander Hamilton.

Interestingly enough, on subsequent Sundays in Philadelphia during the Constitutional Convention, Mr. Washington attended the services of other denominations as well, including a Friends Meeting Service and a Presbyterian church, still further evidence of the views of George Washington, as well as those around him at the Constitutional Convention, toward the phenomenon of religious toleration; and again, this most likely included the great American statesman Alexander Hamilton, as well.

This expression on the part of George Washington must have been in the mind of Alexander Hamilton—if he did accompany his general to these houses of worship—another plank that went into the making of the structure of the great American statesman regarding the issues of religious liberty and religious toleration. *If the general can be this way, then I must be this way, as well.*

In the Presbyterian church attended by General Washington and some other delegates that may have included Alexander Hamilton, the Rev. William Rogers said a special prayer for the Constitutional Convention on July 4, 1787, at the Reformed Calvinist Church of Philadelphia. The Rev. Rogers observed that morning,

> We fervently recommend to Thy fatherly notice...our federal convention...Favor them from day to day with Thy immediate presence; be Thou their wisdom and their strength. Enable them to deviser such a measure as may prove happily instrumental for healing all divisions and promoting the god of Thy good whole... that

the United States of America may furnish the world with one example of a free and permanent government.

This brings us to the major conclusions we have made in this Chapter Six. The central feature of Chapter Seven, as we shall see, is the phenomenon of prayer in the life and times of great American statesman Alexander Hamilton. It is to prayer, then, to which we turn next.

Conclusions to Chapter Six

We began this sixth chapter on religious freedom and religious toleration in the life and works of Alexander Hamilton by suggesting that the chapter would have three main sections. The first of these was to be very general comments that the great American statesman had made or written about religious liberty.

To that end, in the first section of Chapter Six, we provided sixteen separate examples of Mr. Hamilton's where he spoke, in very general terms, about religious liberty. Among the Hamilton texts we have gleaned for these observations, we relied on: *The Farmer Refuted*; "A Full Vindication of the Measures of Congress," and a number of other tracts in his *Complete Works of Alexander Hamilton*.[267]

In the second section of Chapter Six, we turned our attention to many of the places of the essays that Alexander Hamilton wrote for *The Federalist Papers*, in which the great American statesman made observations about religious liberty. In that section, we employed comments of Mr. Hamilton from Essays 1, 8, 26, 57, 65, 70, 75, 78 and 84.

Altogether, in the second section of Chapter Six, we provided thirteen different comments made by Mr. Hamilton in *The Federalist Papers*, and, for the most part, his observations about civil and religious liberties are consistent with the general remarks we introduced in the first section of Chapter Six.

In the third section of Chapter Six, we turned our attention to the phenomenon of religious toleration in the life and works of Alexander Hamilton. We began that section by reviewing what we see as the many sources of religious toleration in the thought of Mr. Hamilton.

We mentioned several European sources from the seventeenth and eighteenth centuries, including Pierre Bayle, Voltaire's *Treatise on Toleration*, John Locke's 1689 *An Essay on Toleration*, comments that Mr. Hamilton made at the 1787 Constitutional Convention on religious toleration, the state constitutions of Pennsylvania, Massachusetts, Virginia, Delaware, and others, as well as George Washington's influence on Mr. Hamilton, both as a general and a president.

In the final portion of Chapter Six, we also indicated that the principal place that Mr. Hamilton's views on religious toleration can be seen is in many of the speeches he wrote for George Washington. Chief among these include Washington's letter to the Hebrew Congregation of Newport, Rhode Island, in 1791, and Washington's Farewell Address to the nation on September 19, 1796.

From these two documents—a letter and an address—we may glean the general views about religious toleration that American statesman Alexander Hamilton made or wrote from his army days until the death of Mr. Washington.

The major elements of those views of Mr. Hamilton on religious toleration are clear. First, he was a stringent supporter of the founding documents of the United States that contained observations about religious freedoms in general, and religious toleration in particular, such as the First Amendment and Article Six of the US Constitution that disallowed any "religious test" in America.

Secondly, Mr. Hamilton fully supported the idea of religious toleration to be extended to religious sects and other religions that were not his own, particularly to Judaism and to Roman Catholics and Muslims, as we have seen in Chapter Four of this study on Alexander Hamilton's religion.

In the third and final section of Chapter Six, we have also shown that during the summer of 1787, when the Constitutional Congress was meeting in Philadelphia, General Washington attended churches of Roman Catholics, Presbyterians and the Quakers to show his support of the idea of religious toleration in America. General Washington did this despite the fact that two of these denominations—the Catholics and the Society of Friends—were both targets of religious discrimination for much of the eighteenth century.

We also indicated that when Mr. Hamilton attended mass at a Philadelphia Catholic church, as well as services at a Presbyterian church and the Friends Meeting House in the city, he was accompanied by several of his fellow delegates from the Constitutional Convention of which Mr. Washington was the chair. One only wonders if, among the New York delegates, there was not a former military officer under the command of General Washington who also accompanied the soon-to-be-president to the houses of worship with his mentor.

We also pointed out in the final section of Chapter Six that there was no word for "toleration" in American English until the very early part of the nineteenth century and that before that time, some Enlightenment thinkers in America, perhaps including Alexander Hamilton, on the French *Tolerantisme*, to express the idea in American English.

It was not until Article 1, Section 1, of the State of Florida's 1838 Constitution that the idea of religious toleration was built into the state's pact. It was also in the state of Florida that on May 7, 1947, that the Miami Beach City Council unanimously approved a one-page ordinance drafted by the Anti-Defamation League that outlawed signs displaying the coded words "restricted," "gentiles" and "gentles only," or other discriminatory words phrases in any "hotel or apartment house or other establishment which caters to the public in the City of Miami Beach."

This Florida case, which was called *Shelly v. Kraemer*, was brought before the US Supreme Court, and the court held that discriminatory deed restrictions were unenforceable in the state courts. At any rate, this was the first time in an American court where the idea of religious toleration was the subject of a legal decision. In this case, it was discrimination against Jews in Miami Beach, Florida.[268]

Given what we have said of great American statesman Alexander Hamilton on religious toleration, it is likely that we may guess what Mr. Hamilton would have said about the *Shelly v. Kraemer* case. He simply would have been appalled by it and that it would go against his life-long view that religious toleration should always be extended to worshippers of other religions, or even other sects, than one's own.

This brings us to Chapter Seven. The chief topic of this chapter on this study of Alexander Hamilton's religion is what the great American statesman thought, said, and wrote about the phenomenon of prayer.

Chapter Seven
Hamilton on Prayer

Let it be ordered therefore that the members of the House do attend ...with the Speaker, and the Mace, to the church in this City, for the purpose of the aforesaid; and that the Reverend Mr. Price be appointed to read prayers, and the Reverend Gwatkin, to preach a sermon.
—Thomas Jefferson, "Proclamation of a Day of Fasting and Prayer" (1774)

I now make it my earnest prayer that God would have you, and the State over which you preside, in his holy protection, that he would incline the hearts of citizens to cultivate a spirit of subordination and obedience to Government.
—George Washington, "Address to State Governors" (1783)

The consolation of Religion, my beloved, can alone support you; and these you have a right to enjoy. Fly to the bosom of your God and be comforted. With my last idea, I shall perish with the sweet hope of meeting you in a better world. Adieu best of wives and best of Women. Embrace all my darling children for me. Ever yours, Alexander.
—Alexander Hamilton letter to his wife, Eliza, on July 4, 1804

Introduction

The main goal of this chapter is to explore what the great American statesman Alexander Hamilton believed, said and wrote in his published writings about the phenomenon of prayer. To achieve that central goal of Chapter Seven, we will divide it into three separate parts. The first of these will be what many of the other American Founding Fathers believed, said and wrote about prayer.

In the second section of this chapter, we will describe and discuss what keys we may find concerning Alexander Hamilton's early life when it came to the issue of prayer. We speak here of the time in Alexander Hamilton's life from his birth on the island of Nevis, through his early education at Hebrew School and with the Rev. Hugh Knox, to his preparatory school in New Jersey, and up to his time at King's College in New York City.

In the third and final section of Chapter Seven, we will examine the roles that prayer played at the end of Alexander Hamilton's life on July 12, 1804. In this section, we will examine the uses of prayer in Mr. Hamilton's family life, as well as activities related to the end of his life. That is, the role of prayer on his deathbed as well as his death, his will and his final letter to his wife, Eliza.

Prayer and the other Founding Fathers

Founders such as Thomas Jefferson, James Madison and Benjamin Franklin resisted any sectarian or exclusively Christian basis for the new nation. They believed in genuine religious liberty for all people. Yet, across the theological spectrum of Americans, from deists to evangelicals of the First Great Awakening, the Founding Fathers agreed on the importance of religion in the life of the new republic. As George Washington put the matter in his 1796 Farewell Address, an address written by Alexander Hamilton, "Faith and Morality are indispensable supports of the new Government."

Be that as you may, there were, nevertheless, two events among the Founding Fathers of America that brought the discussion of the idea of prayer into early American focus among these men. The first event took place in the Virginia House of Burgesses on May 24, 1774, when

Thomas Jefferson called for a "Day of Fasting and Prayer" in response to the effort of the British government to close the Boston Harbor after the infamous Boston Tea Party in late 1773.

The British Crown issued the Boston Port Act on March 7, 1774, designed to destroy the economy of Boston, as well as the Massachusetts Bay Colony.[269] A young Thomas Jefferson, farther south in the colony of Virginia, believed that this dictatorial act required a political response of some kind.

The response devised by Mr. Jefferson was to draft a resolution in the Virginia House of Burgesses calling for a "Day of Fasting and Prayer." The day in question was to be held on June 1, 1774, the very day the British blockade of the Boston Harbor was scheduled to begin. Mr. Jefferson's resolution was proposed on May 24, 1774, and unanimously adopted that same day in a vote.

Immediately, several supporters stepped up to support Mr. Jefferson's resolution. Among those original supporters were Patrick Henry, Richard Henry Lee—one of the signers of the Declaration of Independence—and George Mason, the Father of the American Bill of Rights. In Mr. Jefferson's resolution, he enjoined:

> Let it be ordered therefore that the members of
> the House do attend ...with the Speaker, and the
> Mace, to the church in this City, for the purpose
> of the aforesaid; and that the Reverend Mr. Price
> be appointed to read prayers, and the Reverend
> Gwatkin, to preach a sermon.

The Rev. Mr. Price mentioned by Mr. Jefferson was Dr. Richard Price (1723–1791) of the Anglican Church and the Rev. Mr. Gwatkin was Thomas Gwatkin (1741–1900). Note that Mr. Jefferson's Resolution was "Ordered" and not simply recommended or urged. And it was actually the Virginia Legislators themselves, to the man, who went to the Anglican Church to participate in the "Day of Prayer and Fasting." Even George Washington participated in this day of prayer. He wrote in his diary that day, "Went to Church and fasted all day."

Now Mr. Jefferson's proposed Day of Prayer and Fasting was not accepted by everyone. In that, the proposal had fierce and angry opposition aimed at the supporters of the resolution. British Royal Governor John Murray, the 4th Earl of Dunmore, was so incensed by the Day of Prayer and Fasting that two days later, the earl disbanded the Virginia House of Burgesses in Williamsburg, leaving the colony with no representative government.

What did Jefferson and his colleague do? They did not quit. Instead, they marched down the street to the Raleigh Tavern, where they made a momentous decision to convene a Continental Congress. It met for the first time three months later, and two years after that produced the Declaration of Independence, which brought the United States of America into being.[270]

The Raleigh Tavern in Williamsburg, Virginia, was one of the largest taverns in the colonies. It gained some fame as a watering hole for legislators. After the House of Burgesses was dissolved in the city, which was then the capital of Virginia, the House delegates met in the tavern on the Duke of Gloucester Street. The tavern was named after Sir Walter Raleigh, an important figure in the settlement of Virginia. A lead bust of Mr. Raleigh sat above the front entrance to the tavern. The acts of Mr. Jefferson and his House colleagues were one of the earliest impetuses for the American Rebellion from Britain, as well as the subsequent formation of the United States.

Thomas Jefferson's views on prayer are quite ambiguous. He dismissed certain Biblical miracles as myths and implied doubts about the efficacy of prayer while recognizing an obligation of human beings to worship God and even prayed publicly, at least in very broad terms.

The other event that crystalized the Founding Fathers on the phenomenon of prayer took place at the Constitutional Convention on May 28, 1787. On June 28, 1787, delegate Benjamin Franklin, the oldest of the delegates, proposed a prayer be said to open the sessions. As part of his prayer proposal, Mr. Franklin said:

> I therefore beg leave that henceforth prayers imploring the assistance of Heaven, and its blessings in our deliberations, be held in this Assembly every morning before we proceed to

business, and that one or more of the clergy of
this city be requested to officiate in that service.

When Mr. Franklin's motion was put to a vote a day or so later, it
was easily defeated, with only a handful of delegates voting in favor of
the proposal. Mr. Franklin was miffed by the whole experience and said
so in his diary. During the discussion portion of the proposal, several
delegates to the convention spoke against the idea. One might have
thought it would be the so-called "free thinkers" among them, atheists
or deists. But in fact, some of the best arguments against Mr. Franklin's
proposal were voiced by some of the leading Founding Fathers present,
including Alexander Hamilton, who was reported to have declared
during the discussion session:

> For my own part, I sincerely esteem it a system
> without which the finger of God never could
> have been suggested and agreed upon by such a
> diversity of interests.

James Madison spoke next. He related:

> It is impossible for the man of pious reflection not
> to perceive in it a finger of that Almighty hand
> which has been so frequently and signally extended
> to our relief in the critical stages of the revolution.

Both the comments by Mr. Hamilton and Mr. Madison seemed
more to be about the actions of God in helping to establish the
new nation rather than to be about Mr. Franklin's proposal. George
Washington, the chair of the proceedings in Philadelphia, spoke next
to the assembled. He, too, said nothing about the proposal on prayer.
Instead, the general said this:

> As to my sentiments with respect to the merits
> of the new Constitution, I will disclose them
> without reserve. It appears to me then little
> short of a miracle that the delegates from so
> many different states...should unite in forming
> a system on national government.

Rather than voting yea or nay on Mr. Franklin's proposal, General Washington pointed instead to the need for a centralized Federal government. Delegate Benjamin Rush (1745–1813), a physician and philosopher, was next in line to speak. He related,

> I do not believe that the Constitution was the offspring of inspiration, but I am as perfectly satisfied that the Union of the States in its form and adoption is as much the work of a Divine Providence as any of the miracles recorded in the Old and New Testament were the effects of a Divine Power.

Like Hamilton, Madison and Washington, during the discussion of beginning the meetings of the Constitutional Convention with a prayer, Dr. Rush also said nothing of the idea of prayer in his remarks.

It appears that what was really going on in the discussion is that most of the delegates wanted to keep theological language out of the founding documents of the United States, which is also most likely why God is not really mentioned in the Constitution. From these two events, Thomas Jefferson's proposal calling for a day of prayer and fasting and Benjamin Franklin's proposal to begin each session of the Constitutional Convention with a prayer, put the issue of prayer directly in the center of religious discussions of the Founding Fathers.

These two events occasioned much debate about the exercise of religion in the new nation. One side believed that the US began as a Christian nation, while another faction thought there were no Christian influences in the country's Constitution.

Some of the Founders were deists, some Bible-believing Christians, and some held other beliefs. Many were skeptical of certain aspects of the Christian faith, such as the divinity of Jesus of Nazareth, as we have shown earlier in Chapter Two of this study.

At any rate, at least seven major Founding Fathers, in one way or another, said or wrote something about the phenomenon of prayer. Among those are the following figures:

1. George Washington
2. John Adams

3. Thomas Jefferson
4. John Carroll
5. Benjamin Franklin
6. James Madison
7. Alexander Hamilton

We already examined some of the views of these early American Founding Fathers one at a time in discerning their perspectives on prayer, while keeping in mind that we already have mentioned some of the views on the matter by Washington, Jefferson, Franklin, Madison and Hamilton.

The first public record of George Washington's views on prayer comes in the context of the 1777–1778 winter at Valley Forge. There we find the following prayer by the soon-to-be first president of the United States:

> I was riding with Mr. Potts near Valley Forge, where the army lay during the war of the Revolution, when Mr. Potts said, "Do you see the woods and that plain? ...There laid the army of Washington."[271]

Mr. Potts himself gives his narrative of the tale:

> I saw the great George Washington on his knees, alone, with his sword on one side and his cocked hat on the other. He was at prayer to the God of the Armies, beseeching to interpose with his Divine aid, as it was ye Cause & Crisis of the Country of humanity and of the world. Such a prayer I never heard from the lips of man. I left him alone praying. I went home and told my wife. We never thought a man could be a soldier and a Christian, but if there is one in the world, it is General Washington. We thought it was the cause of God & America that would prevail.[272]

The "Mr. Potts" to whom Mr. Washington referred was Isaac Potts (1750–1803), the founder of Potts Grove and Pottstown, Pennsylvania, as well as Mount Joy Forge. Mr. Potts' house served as George Washington's Headquarters in the winter of 1777–1778.

On George Washington's first day in office as President of the United States, in his very first address on April 30, 1789, he said:

> I now make it my earnest prayer that God would
> have you and the State over which you preside,
> in his holy protection, that he would incline
> the hearts of citizens to cultivate a spirit of
> subordination and obedience to Government.

In this address, George Washington is speaking to an assembly of state governors, and he encouraged these men that, by the power of God, they should show love and obedience and "entertain a brotherly affection" for each other. Thus, the first act of George Washington as president was a prayer.

On October 3, 1789, George Washington began a long-standing precedent of declaring the first national Day of Thanksgiving and Prayer, as set forth in the new Constitution. In that pronouncement, Mr. Washington observed,

> It is the duty of all nations to acknowledge the
> providence of the Almighty God, to obey His
> will, to be grateful for His benefits, and humbly
> to implore His protection and favor.

Over the course of his two terms in office, George Washington proclaimed a number of other days of prayer and fasting, including one on February 19, 1790, and another on January 1, 1795. The first of these called for "A Day of Public Thanksgiving and Prayer," and the second, the one from 1795, Mr. Washington proclaimed a "Day of Public Thanksgiving and Prayer," and on that day to meet together, and to render their sincere and hearty thanks to the Great Ruler of Nations.

Congress requested President Washington to proclaim a day of thanksgiving and prayer at the end of the first session of the meeting of Congress in 1789. By the time John Adams did the same thing, the political temperatures had heated up quite a bit and the Republicans— Thomas Jefferson's party—opposed Mr. Adams' suggestion.

Nevertheless, our second president, John Adams, also declared a Day of Fasting and Prayer on March 23, 1798. His proclamation, however, had a very different moral flavor to those of George Washington. Mr. Adams entitled his declaration, "Proclamation 8: Recommending a National Day of Humiliation, Fasting, and Prayer," in which he asked the American citizens to "abstain from their customary worldly occupation and to offer their devout addresses to the Father of Mercies."

At the close of Mr. Adams' 1798 proclamation, he related this:

> And finally, I recommend that on the said day the duties of humiliation and prayer be accompanied by fervent thanksgiving to the Bestower of Every Good Gift, not only for His having hitherto protected and preserved the people of these United States in the independent enjoyment of their religious and civil freedom, but also for having them prospered in a wonderful progress of population, and for conferring on them many and great favors conducive to the happiness and the prosperity of a nation.

John Adams also frequently showed his assenting to the efficacy of prayer, for example, in many of his letters, including some of these to his wife, Abigail. On September 16, 1774, Mr. Adams wrote to tell her about the sermon he had just heard in Philadelphia from the Rev. Mr. Duche, an Anglican preacher in the city. President Adams related to his wife:

> After this, Mr. Duche unexpected to every Body struck out into an extemporaneous prayer, which filled the Bosom of everyone present. I must confess I never heard a better Prayer or one, so well pronounced. Episcopalian as he is, Dr. Cooper himself never prayed with such fervor, such Ardor, such Earnestness, and Pathos, and in language so elegant and sublime.

This reference to "Mr. Rev. Duche," by President Adams is the Rev. Jacob Duche (1737–1798), was the Rector of Christ Church in Philadelphia and the first chaplain on the Continental Congress. He first came to the attention of the First Continental Congress in September of 1774 when he was summoned to Carpenters Hall to lead the opening prayer. His text was from Psalm 35, and his comments, apparently, greatly moved all who were present.

In another letter to Abigail Adams on November 2, 1800, her husband related that he had just arrived at the President's House in Washington, DC. At the close of this missive, Mr. Adams included this prayer, "I pray to Heaven to bestow the best of Blessings on this House and all that shall hereafter inhabit it. May none but honest and wise Men ever rule under this roof."

One of the interesting features of President Adams' 1798 proclamation called on citizens to ask God,

> Through the Redeemer of the World, freely
> to remit all our offenses, and to incline us, by
> His Holy Spirit, to that sincere repentance and
> reformation which may afford us reasons to hope
> for prosperity in the years to come in this nation.

This blatant reference to Jesus Christ as "Redeemer," as well as the hope for the "remission of sins," and the reference to the "Holy Spirit," would be more than enough to keep such a prayer from a public venue in the United States after Supreme Court decisions in 1962 and 1963.[273]

Our second president, John Adams, also made a number of declarations and pronouncements, one of which he made at the president's residence in 1997,

> I pray to Heaven to bestow the best of blessings
> of this house and all that shall hereafter inhabit
> it. May none but wise men ever rule under its
> roof.[274]

Already in this chapter, we have spoken of our third president Thomas Jefferson and his November 1779 response as a call for a "Day of Thanksgiving and Prayer" to the blockade of the port of Boston in the Massachusetts colony. Like the presidents before him, Mr. Jefferson also advocated a "National Prayer Day of Peace," the text of which told us this:

> Almighty God, Who has given us this good land for our heritage; we humbly beseech Thee that we may always prove ourselves a people mindful of Thy favor and glad to do Thy will. Bless our land with honorable ministry, sound learning and pure manners.[275]

In his first inaugural address on March 4, 1801, Mr. Jefferson began with this prayer:

> We humbly beseech Thee that we may always prove ourselves a people mindful of Thy favor and glad to do Thy will...Save us from violence, discord, and confusion, from pride and arrogance and from every evil way.

Even on the final day of his life, on July 4, 1826, after he had declined to attend a celebration to honor the fiftieth anniversary of the Declaration of Independence, Mr. Jefferson, nevertheless, expressed, "His most fervent hope that the Declaration be to the world what I believe it to be, to some parts sooner and to others later, but finally, to all."

Another of the Founding Fathers, American Archbishop John Carroll (1735–1815), in November of 1791, was asked by George Washington and Congress to give a "Prayer for America." In the text of that prayer, Bishop Carroll asked of the Divine:

> Let the light of your Divine wisdom direct the deliberations of Congress, and to shine forth in all their proceedings and laws framed for our rule and government, so that they may tend toward the preservation of peace, the promotion of national happiness, the increase of industry, sobriety and useful knowledge; and may perpetuate to us the blessing of equal liberty.

Already in this chapter, we discussed the suggestion of Benjamin Franklin in the Constitutional Congress in Philadelphia that each day's proceedings should begin with a prayer. On another day of the convention, after Mr. Franklin's proposal on prayer had been defeated, he observed:

> In the beginning of the contest with Britain, when we were sensible of danger, we had daily prayers in this room for Divine protection. Our prayers, Sir, were heard and they were graciously answered...Do we imagine that we no longer need assistance?

This comment by Benjamin Franklin is part of an overall view among the American Founding Fathers that America was to be understood as a "New Israel," a "New Chosen People," if you will, and this new nation was afforded many special kinds of Grace not given to other nations.

Benjamin Franklin and other Founding Fathers openly acknowledged that the frequent prayers throughout the Revolution had been answered. God was responsible for the United States to become an independent nation rather than remain subjugated as a British colony. Franklin, as well as other Founding Fathers, firmly believed that it was answered prayers that changed the course of the new nation.

On many occasions in Mr. Franklin's life in Philadelphia, he spoke of his relationship with English preacher George Whitefield and the idea of prayer. Mr. Franklin often related, "He [the Rev. Whitefield] sometimes used to pray for the conversion of my soul, but he never had the satisfaction of believing that his prayers were heard."[276]

Our fourth president, James Madison, issued two prayer proclamations during his presidency, one on July 23, 1813, and the other during the War of 1812. In the former, Mr. Madison intoned:

> If the public homage of a people can ever be worthy of a favorable regard of the Holy and Omniscient Being to Whom it is addressed, it must be that in which those who join in it are guided only by their free choice, by the impulse of their hearts and

dictates of their consciences; and such spectacle must be interesting to all Christian nations as proving their religion, that gift of Heaven for the good of man, freed from all coercive edicts.

President Madison also issued a prayer proclamation during the War of 1812 at the request of Congress, but he later expressed regret for having done so. In an undated essay that scholars call the "Detached Memorandum," believed to have been written in 1817, Madison spoke of the issue at some length. In the memorandum in question, the fourth president observed:

> Religious proclamations by the Executive recommending thanksgivings & fasts are shoots from the same root with the legislative acts reviewed. Although recommended only, they imply a religious agency, making no part of the trust delegated to political rulers.[277]

Of all the Founding Fathers we have discussed so far, the views of James Madison on both public prayer proclamations and his personal views on the matter are far more subtle and extensive than those of the other politicians we have discussed. Mr. Monroe realized that the nature and function of public proclamations for prayer and fasting are sometimes complicated matters.

From these materials from other Founding Fathers on the idea of prayer, we may make three conclusions.

1. All of the first four presidents of the United States issued proclamations calling for prayer and thanksgiving.
2. There is evidence in each of their personal lives that they had a place for prayer in their lives.
3. James Madison regretted the fact that he had issued days of prayer and fasting.

On December 11, 1776, the then Secretary of Congress made a proclamation that,

> All the States appoint a Day of solemn Fasting,
> Prayer, and Humiliation to implore of Almighty
> God the forgiveness of the many Sins prevailing
> among the Ranks, and to beg the Countenance
> and Assistance of his Providence in the
> Prosecution of this just and necessary War.

A few months later, on October 1, 1777, the Continental Congress
appointed a day of prayer and summoned Americans to,

> A penitent confession of their manifold sins...
> and humble and earnest supplication that it
> might please God, through the merits of Jesus
> Christ, mercifully to forgive and blot their
> transgressions out of remembrance.

If these congressmen mean God's "remembrance," they must
have forgotten about the view in traditional Christianity that God is
said to be Omniscient. Or All-Knowing, and the act of "forgetting" is
not one that God's nature would allow.

This brings us to the second section of Chapter Seven, in which
we will discuss the phenomenon of prayer in the early life of great
American statesman Alexander Hamilton, from his birth in Nevis on
January 11, 1757, to his time at King's College in New York City in
October of 1772 to 1775, when he joined the army.

Prayer in Hamilton's Early Life

Most of what can be said about the idea of prayer in the early life of
Alexander Hamilton are nothing but surmises. It is likely, for example,
that when the great American statesman studied at the Hebrew School in
which he learned to read the Ten Commandments in classical Hebrew,
that he also learned some Hebrew prayers, but there is no independent
evidence for this possibility.

Similarly, the religious instruction that the young Alexander
Hamilton received from the Rev. Hugh Knox probably also included
some Calvinist and Presbyterian prayers in the lessons, though we
cannot be sure of this. Mr. Hamilton may also have learned some

Christian prayers in the readings that he did in the Rev. Knox's personal library in his home.

We can be sure that the curriculum at the Elizabethtown Academy he attended in 1771 involved daily prayers before and after school, as well as before and after meals at the school.[278]

We also know that one of Mr. Hamilton's college roommates at King's College, a fellow student named Robert Troup, testified to his piety, telling us,

> He was attentive to public worship and in the habit of praying on his knees night and morning." Mr. Troup added, "I have often been powerfully affected by the fervor and eloquence of his prayers.[279]

Mr. Troup also related about Mr. Hamilton in his college days,

> He had read many of the polemical writers on religious subjects and he was a zealous believer in the fundamental doctrines of Christianity.

In the same interview, Mr. Troup observed about his former college roommate:

> I confess that the arguments with which he was accustomed to justify his beliefs have tended in no small degree to confirm to my own faith in revealed Religion.

Robert Troup (1757–1832) was also a soldier in the Continental Army during the Revolutionary War and later was a United States District Court Judge. Before the war, Mr. Troup was attending King's College. In the *Hamilton Papers*, organized by his son, John C. Hamilton, there are several letters between Troup and Alexander Hamilton, including one from June 15, 1791, and another from Hamilton to Troup on July 25, 1795.

Another influence on the life of Alexander Hamilton in the King's College period was Irish-born Hercules Mulligan (1740–1825). Mulligan attended the college, married Elizabeth Sanders, the niece of

Admiral Sanders of the Royal Navy, but nevertheless was a staunch patriot in the American cause.

The Mulligan family had come from Ireland when Hercules was six years old. They were a fine example of an immigrant family living the eighteenth-century American dream. Hercules' father was a successful accountant before his son made his name as a tailor to the New York elite. Mr. Mulligan is important for our purposes because he allowed Mr. Hamilton to live at the Mulligan household, while the great American statesman was a student at King's. Mulligan was seventeen years older than Mr. Hamilton, so the Irishman was a kind of mentor. The two of them reportedly had many late-night political discussions. In fact, some credit Mr. Mulligan as the catalyst for turning Alexander Hamilton away from the Tory Party to the Federalist Party.[280]

Together, Hamilton and Mulligan joined the Sons of Liberty, a secret society of patriots that was formed to protect the rights of colonists. After his graduation from King's College, Mr. Mulligan became a tailor to many of the rich and famous in New York, including many British officers. By tailoring to the British officers, Mr. Mulligan was able to garner secret information from them that included two different plots to kidnap and kill General Washington.[281]

Twice Mr. Mulligan's garnered information saved the general's life. On one occasion, a British officer came to Mulligan's shop late at night in dire need of a coat. When Mr. Mulligan asked what the big hurry was, the officer reported that his mission was to capture George Washington later in the day. The tailor sent his slave Cato to see Mr. Hamilton immediately after the British officer left the shop, and Mr. Hamilton made it so the general would change locations thwarting the plot.[282]

The second incident when Hercules Mulligan saved the life of George Washington happened in 1781 when Mulligan's brother's import-export firm received a large rush order from the British. It also revealed that the British had plans to capture General Washington in Connecticut. Hercules Mulligan, who had been interrogated twice by the British and narrowly had escaped prison after the betrayal of Benedict Arnold, once again sent his slave Cato with a warning of the kidnapping plan, saving the general's life for the second time.[283]

After the war, a grateful General Washington visited the tailor's shop wanting to thank him and order some clothes. Outside his shop, Mulligan put up a sign that read: "Clothier to George Washington." Later, Mr. Mulligan continued to fight for democratic ideals when he became one of the co-founders of the New York Manumission Society, an anti-slavery organization of which Mr. Hamilton later became a member.[284]

To publicly demonstrate Hercules Mulligan's loyalty to the cause of American freedom, Washington declared the tailor "a true friend of liberty" when he stopped one time in his shop at what was then 23 Queen Street, but today is 218 Pearl Street in Manhattan, Washington is said to have shared "a bit of breakfast" with a man who had saved his life—twice![285]

There is an extant letter to Hercules Mulligan from George Washington's secretary Tobias Lear dated February 6, 1792, in which "The President is desirous of getting black moleskin of which you made him a pair of breeches when he was in New York." Mr. Lear goes on in the letter telling Mr. Mulligan that he needs the moleskin for three more pairs of breeches and he inquires about the "price."

Hercules Mulligan continued to work in his tailor shop and retired when he was eighty years old. He died at age eighty-four. He is most likely interred in the cemetery of Trinity Church in New York City, in the Sanders family tomb, just a few feet from his beloved friend, Alexander Hamilton.

In this period at King's, Alexander Hamilton was only seventeen years old, while Mr. Mulligan was thirty-four in 1774. Two years later, at the age of nineteen, Alexander Hamilton was appointed captain of a New York artillery company, and a year after that—at age twenty—Alexander Hamilton was appointed aide-de-camp to General George Washington with a rank of lieutenant colonel. By age twenty-three, the great American statesman had met and quickly married Elizabeth Schuyler on December 14, 1780, in Albany, New York.

This brings us to the third and final section of Chapter Seven, in which we will identify and discuss the places in Alexander Hamilton's later life where the phenomenon of prayer played some role.

Hamilton and Prayer in Later Life

By "Later Life" in the heading of this section, we mean the period in Alexander Hamilton's life from his marriage in December of 1780 until his death on July 12, 1804. During this time, there were several events and occasions in the Hamilton family life where prayer became important. Many of these events are taken from John Church Hamilton's reflections on his family life, including the practice that the elder sons in the family would take turns before breakfast in which they did a Gospel reading, and then the family prayed together, as we have indicated earlier in this study.

We also indicated earlier that, after the death of Philip Hamilton in a duel, Mr. Hamilton returned to regular church attendance about which he related,

> I take my children to Church on Sunday/a sign
> of the cross at the door/And I pray/ That never
> used to happen before.[286]

John Church Hamilton also told us that his father regularly led the household in prayer and that the "encouragement of prayer" was one of the goals of Hamilton's "Christian Constitutional Society that the statesman established in a letter to his friend, James Bayard in 1802, as we have seen earlier in this study.[287] Mr. Hamilton's son, John Church, also related that after church on Sundays, and sometimes even before church, Alexander Hamilton read to his family in the garden of their house, the Grange, and led them in prayer on those occasions.

Both Dr. Mason and Bishop Moore reported that on his deathbed Alexander Hamilton prayed with both ministers. John Church also reported that the night before his father's death he went into the room and the son tells us, "And in the morning he awakened me and taking my hands in his palms, all four hands extended, he ask me to repeat the Lord's Prayer about which I complied."[288]

There is some difference of opinion concerning Alexander Hamilton's final words. One tradition has it that Mr. Hamilton said,

> I have tender reliance of the mercy of the
> Almighty; through the merits of the Lord Jesus

Christ. I am a sinner. I look to Him for Mercy.
Pray for me.[289]

Another tradition, however, said that Hamilton took his final breath shortly after two o'clock, and before that said, "It is finished."

These two differing accounts come from the two ministers who attended to the great American statesman on his deathbed. They could, of course, both be true. The first view may be the final word on Alexander Hamilton's Christian faith, while the latter view may be a sign that his life is over, and he is ready for a new life.

On July 4, 1804, a week before the duel with Vice-President Aaron Burr, Alexander Hamilton prepared a letter—a kind of prayerful hymn really—in the event that he did not survive the encounter with Mr. Burr. The great American statesman began the letter by saying this,

> The letter, my very dear Eliza, will not be delivered to you, unless I have first terminated my earthly existence to begin, I humbly hope from redeeming grace and Divine mercy, a happy immortality.[290]

After a second paragraph in which Mr. Hamilton speaks about the possibility of "avoiding the interview," the duel, and the heartache it now caused for Eliza and their children. In the third paragraph, however, Mr. Hamilton returned to the theme of Religion and Immortality. The great American statesman wrote to his wife:

> The consolations of Religion, my beloved, can alone support you; and these you have a right to enjoy. Fly to the bosom of your God and be comforted. With my last idea I shall perish the sweet hope of meeting you in a better world. Adieu best of wives and best of Women. Embrace all my darling children for me. Ever yours.

Alexander Hamilton's final letter to his beloved wife, Eliza, was his final hymn and prayer to the deep belief and trust in God that the great American statesman would see his wife again in a "Better world." We can only add, "Amen to that!"

This brings us to the major conclusions we have made in this chapter on Alexander Hamilton and prayer regarding Alexander Hamilton's religion.

The central concern of Chapter Eight to follow is what the great American statesman experienced, believed, said, did, and wrote about the phenomenon of slavery.

Conclusions to Chapter Seven

The main goal of Chapter Seven has been to explore what the great American statesman Alexander Hamilton believed, said and wrote in his public works about the phenomenon of prayer. We then divided the chapter into three separate parts. In the first of these, we examined what many other Founding Fathers, besides Mr. Hamilton, have relayed about these public and personal lives about prayer.

In the first section of Chapter Seven, we made three conclusions. First, that all of the first four US presidents issued declarations of days of prayer and thanksgiving. Second, we have shown that there is evidence in each of the private lives of these first four presidents that they prayed and that they found some uses of prayers in their lives.

Finally, in the first section of Chapter Seven, we have also shown that President James Madison had some misgivings about his prayer proclamations after he was president and expressed those misgivings in a document known as his "Detached Memorandum."

In the second section of Chapter Seven, we explored the phenomenon of prayer as it appeared in Alexander Hamilton's early life, from his birth to the statesman joining the Army in 1775 at the age of eighteen.

In that section, we pointed to several possible influences that may, or may not, have influenced the stateman's attitudes and thoughts about prayer. Among these sources were his attendance at a Hebrew school while still on Nevis; the theological influences from the Rev. Hugh Knox, as well as his personal library; comments about Mr. Hamilton and prayer from his college roommate, Robert Troup. And finally, the possible influence on prayer from Mr. Hercules Mulligan, a Manhattan tailor with whom he boarded when the statesman was a student at King's College in the city.

In the third and final section of Chapter Seven on Alexander Hamilton and prayer, we analyzed and discussed the roles that prayer played in the life of the great American statesman from leaving the army in 1782 until his death on July 12, 1804. We related that the observations we have made about the roles of prayer in Mr. Hamilton's family life came mostly from the statesman's son and biographer John Church Hamilton.

Indeed, from the younger Mr. Hamilton, we garnered the facts that the elder Hamilton sons took turns before breakfast leading the family with a Gospel reading followed by a prayer; that after the death of Philip Hamilton, the statesman eldest son, he returned to attend church in his twilight years, a time when he mentioned prayer; and that Alexander Hamilton led the family in prayer in the garden of their Grange home.

We have also shown in the third section of Chapter Seven that both Dr. Mason and Bishop Moore, the two ministers who were present at Alexander Hamilton's deathbed, report that the great American statesman prayed in his final hours, though the two members of the clergy disagreed about what his last words were.

We also have shown that the final word of Alexander Hamilton regarding the phenomenon of prayer is to glean that view from the prayerful hymn he wrote to his wife Eliza in the event that he did not survive the duel with Vice-President Aaron Burr. In that hymn, Mr. Hamilton spoke of "redeeming grace and Divine mercy" that may lead to a "happy immortality." And that he desired his wife to return to the "bosom of her God" in the "hope of meeting you in a better world."

Thus, Alexander Hamilton appears to have remained prayerful until the very end of his life. There is no record, however, about when Mrs. Hamilton opened the final letter from her husband, nor what her reactions and responses were when she did so.

This brings us to Chapter Eight. The main focus of this chapter will be what the great American statesman Alexander Hamilton experienced, believed, said and did, as well as wrote about the phenomenon of slavery from his time as a child on the island of Nevis, where slavery was practiced from very early on, until his death on July 12, 1804.

Chapter Eight
Hamilton on Slavery

He [Hamilton] advocated one of the most daring invasions of property rights that was ever made—the Abolition of Negro Slaves.
—**John C. Miller, *Alexander Hamilton: Portrait in Paradox***

In his lack of deep concern about either slavery or its concomitant racism (prevalent in the North and the South), Hamilton joined the overwhelming majority of his countrymen, political foes and allies alike.
—**Harry Jaffa, *Crisis of the House Divided***

It may perhaps be replied to this, that whether the states are united or disunited, there will still be intimate commerce between them which would answer to the same ends, which, in the course of these papers, have been intimately detailed. A unity of commercial as well as political interests can only result in a unity of Government.
—**Alexander Hamilton, *The Federalist Papers***

Introduction

The chief focus in Chapter Eight of this study on great American statesman Alexander Hamilton's religion is what sense we can make of what he thought, believed and wrote about the idea of slavery. We will accomplish this goal by dividing it into four separate parts. In the first of these, we will sketch out the traditional scholarly view on Alexander Hamilton and slavery.

In the second section of Chapter Two, we will make some general observations about what we know about the practice of slavery in the eighteenth-century Caribbean. Or, in other words, what experiences the young Alexander Hamilton most likely had concerning the phenomenon of slavery.

In the third section of this chapter, we will explore a new theory about Alexander Hamilton's views on slavery that has arisen in the last several years, which is drastically different from the traditional understanding of the great American statesman on the issue of slavery. This new theory essentially argues that Alexander Hamilton was, in fact, a slave owner, as well as a slave dealer, and we will evaluate this claim at the end of the third section of Chapter Eight, as well.

In the fourth and final section of Chapter Eight, we will analyze and discuss what the great American statesman Alexander Hamilton wrote about the phenomenon of slavery in the portions of *The Federalist Papers* written by Mr. Hamilton, specifically in Essays 6, 7, 8, 11 and 12.

Traditional Scholarly View of Alexander Hamilton on Slavery

By the traditional scholarly view of Alexander Hamilton on the issue of slavery, we mean a view generally held by most historians and other writers since Mr. Hamilton's death that his views on slavery were generally benign compared to many of the other Founding Fathers in his age, many of whom were owners of slaves.

This traditional perspective on Hamilton and slavery can be seen, for example, in the works of John C. Miller,[291] Forest McDonald,[292] Ron Chernow[293] and the scholarly work of Richard Brookhiser[294] on the issue at hand. Additional contemporary perspectives on Mr. Hamilton and slavery also have been provided by Thomas G. West,[295] Jacob Ernest Cooke,[296] Harry V. Jaffa[297] and Michael D. Chan.[298]

John C. Miller gives us a representative example of this traditional view when he wrote, "He [Hamilton] advocated one of the most daring invasions of property rights that was ever made—the Abolition of Negro Slaves."[299] Forest McDonald wrote, "Hamilton was an Abolitionist, and on that subject, he never wavered."[300]

Ron Chernow suggested that "Hamilton's childhood surrounded by the slave system of the West Indies would shape Alexander's attitudes about race and slavery for the rest of his life."[301] Chernow goes on to say that this may be because "He was an outcast from the very beginning." In a different part of the same book, Mr. Chernow wrote, "Few, if any, other founding fathers opposed slavery more consistently or toiled harder to eradicate it than Hamilton."[302]

Richard Brookhiser also assents to what we have been calling the "traditional scholarly view of the great American statesman and slavery, when he wrote, "No existing documents from his early life support the claim that he was against slavery."[303]

Broadus Mitchell's *Alexander Hamilton: Youth to Maturity*[304] published in 1957, Henry Cabot Lodge's *Alexander Hamilton*[305] published in 1886, and James Oliver's *Alexander Hamilton*[306] published in 1961, all held the benign view on the great American statesman and slavery.

Mitchell, Lodge and Oliver all cite the same evidence from which they arrived at their conclusions, including the fact that Mr. Hamilton was one of the founding members of the New York Manumission Society, along with Robert Troup and the society's first president, John Jay.[307]

One of the most interesting aspects of the New York Manumission Society is how and why the organization began. It was not, interestingly enough, due to the fact that African American people have the same rights guaranteed by the Founding documents of this country. Rather, the society began in 1785 when there was a widespread practice in New York City in the early 1780s when black New Yorkers were being kidnapped—both slave and free—and then sold as slaves elsewhere.[308]

Later, in 1799, the society lobbied to pass a law that granted gradual manumission to New York's slaves. The organization also provided legal assistance to both free and enslaved African Americans who were being abused.

The society also founded the New York African Free School in 1787, two years after the founding of its own organization. Members raised money for the salaries of teachers, for supplies, and eventually for the construction of a new building to accommodate the growing number of children at the school. The board members were also responsible for checking in on the school periodically and reporting on the progress that they found there, especially among the students.[309]

All of the founding members of the society agreed that they had to sign a pledge in regard to the idea of manumission. The pledge from 1785 said this:

> The Benevolent Creator and Father of Men having given to them all, an equal Right to Life, Liberty, and Property; no Sovereign Power on Earth can justly deprive them of either; but in Conformity to impartial Government and laws to which they have expressly or tacitly consented.[310]

Alexander Hamilton made an early resolution in the society that anyone who wanted to be a member had to manumit their slaves. Although his proposal was defeated, the traditional view still points to the proposal as further evidence of Mr. Hamilton's benign opinions on slavery.

These same scholars mentioned above, such as Mitchell, Lodge and Oliver, also point to Alexander Hamilton's support of a plan by John Laurens of South Carolina to enlist blacks into the army as proof of the statesman's egalitarian views on slavery. Mr. Hamilton supported the idea of Mr. Laurens as a way to give slaves their freedom if they joined the Continental Army because the statesman believed it was in the best interest of the United States.[311]

Alexander Hamilton argues that the only way to keep black soldiers loyal was to give them their "freedom with their muskets," and their service had ended.[312] Mr. Hamilton wanted to win the war against Britain, and giving black soldiers their freedom seemed the best option at the time. In Ron Chernow's treatment of the Laurens-Hamilton collaboration, he observed, "Laurens and Hamilton were both unwavering abolitionists who saw emancipation of slaves as an inseparable part of the struggle for freedom."[313]

A recent *New York Daily News* article also took up a belief in the traditional view we have been developing in this section of Chapter Eight. The op-ed piece by Philo Hamilton called "Alexander Hamilton's Slavery Smear" was published on January 16, 2021. The writer called Mr. Hamilton a "staunch abolitionist."[314] The *Huffington Post*, as well, from the July 7, 2020, edition, celebrates the great statesman's "strong opposition to slavery" as a primary reason to keep Mr. Hamilton on the ten-dollar bill.[315]

In his 1997 *Vindicating the Founders*, Thomas G. West also assented to the traditional view of Alexander Hamilton on slavery, as did Jacob Ernest Cooke's *Alexander Hamilton*, published by the University of Chicago Press in 1959. However, Cooke does say that "Neither Hamilton nor Jay championed the cause of abolition."

Harry Jaffa, in his study *Crisis of the House Divided*, also published in 1959 by the University of Chicago Press, for the most part, took the traditional view on Hamilton and slavery, but he also wrote in the same work observations such as the following:

> In his lack of deep concern about either Slavery or its concomitant racism (prevalent in the North) as well as the South, Hamilton joined the overwhelming majority of his countrymen, political foes and allies alike.[316]

In his recent essay, "Alexander Hamilton on Slavery" by Michael D. Chan, after evaluating the evidence for the traditional view of Alexander Hamilton on slavery, Mr. Chan finally concluded:

> We must, therefore, establish Hamilton as a bona fide opponent of slavery, who left no ambiguity as to how he interpreted America's fundamental principles.[317]

Thus, the traditional scholarly view in regard to great American statesman Alexander Hamilton and the phenomenon of slavery is that the New York politician was a "staunch abolitionist" filled with egalitarian ideas of black Americans in the late eighteenth century. Later, in section three of this Chapter Eight, we will evaluate those claims. However, it is enough now, early on in Chapter Eight, to at least introduce the traditional view.

This brings us to the second section of Chapter Eight, in which we will give a general summary of the practice of slavery on the Caribbean islands in the seventeenth and eighteenth centuries in the hopes of determining what attitudes and views of slavery may have been engendered in Alexander Hamilton's early life on the idea of slavery on the islands of Nevis, St. Kitts and St. Croix, where he spent his childhood.

Slavery in the Caribbean: Seventeenth and Eighteenth Centuries

Spain was the first country to colonize the Caribbean during the fifteenth century. The Spanish came to the New World in search of gold and silver, but they found very little. Christopher Columbus came to the Caribbean in 1492 believing that he had sailed to the "Indies," as Asia was known in his time. At the time, Europeans did not know that he had discovered a completely different part of the world, but it was still only natural to call the inhabitants he found in the New World "Indians."[318]

The Dutch also came early to the Caribbean. By 1654, they had established sugar plantations on some of the islands. This made sugar a more valuable commodity in the New World. The Dutch also aided both the English and the French by bringing slaves to settlements in the Caribbean. By 1654, the Dutch had 600 men in the Caribbean along with 300 slaves.[319]

By 1650, there were 15,000 white Frenchmen in the Caribbean, and the British, by that time, had already brought 52,000 African slaves to Barbados, Nevis and St. Kitts. In the eighteenth century, the French has established sugar plantations on Jamaica and Santo Domingo, as well as Martinique.[320]

European slavery in the British and French Caribbean began on the islands of St. Kitts and Barbados in 1623 and 1627, respectively, and a short time later in Jamaica in 1655. By the middle of the seventeenth century, slaves were brought from Africa to the Caribbean by European merchants.

Between 1662 and 1807, the British shipped 3.1 million African captives across the Atlantic Ocean by way of the Middle Passage in the British transatlantic slave trade. Africans were forcibly brought to British-owned colonies in the Caribbean and sold as slaves, chiefly to work on plantations.

The first Africans to arrive on St. Kitts and the island of Nevis came in the late seventeenth century due to this same slave trade. These two islands had a climate that was well-suited for sugar plantations. These early slaves on the two British islands, then, came there to help in the cultivation of sugar.

The first census on the island of Nevis was conducted in 1671, which recorded that the island had 1,739 African slaves.[321] Six years later, that number had increased to 3,849.[322] The Royal African Company had its West Indian Headquarters in Charlestown from 1674 until 1678, and more than six thousand slaves were sold at auction there is those years.[323]

In the earliest years when slaves came to St. Kitts and Nevis, the captives were forced to clear the forests so that the sugar cultivation could begin. The difficulty of this work, plus poor diet, made the mortality rates of workers engaged in clearing the islands very high. By the end of the eighteenth century, about two-thirds of the slave populations on the two islands were Caribbean-born. By 1800, the number of slaves imported to both islands had dwindled to fewer than one hundred.[324]

There is very little recorded information about the family structure among slaves on St. Kitts and Nevis, but slave marriages appear to have been encouraged by their owners, and at times these marriages were recorded by their white owners. Children were put to work in the fields by the age of five or six, usually doing light work such as feeding the animals and weeding. A group of five or six children was known as a "Hog Meat Gang." A slave woman supervised each gang.[325]

These slave children were fed at night, eating meals prepared by their mothers that mostly consisted of imported grains. At Christmas time and on other holidays as well, the slave population was given slightly more freedom and often given extra rations of beef and pork.[326] The white populations of the two islands organized guards to monitor the activities of slaves during their free time.

In general, slave quarters on both islands were downwind of their masters' houses. The general white population was also wary of slave revolts. In fact, in 1639, the French had to dispatch ships to put down an uprising of slaves on the island of St. Kitts. Sixty slaves took a defensive position on Mount Misery, only assessed by a narrow path. It took five hundred French soldiers to put down the rebellion. Some of the slaves were burnt alive, re-captured or hanged. Their bodies were cut into pieces and put on display for other slaves to see.

There was another significant slave rebellion in the 1830s, when thirty slaves on St. Kitts, led by a man named Markus, also called the "King of the Woods," raided the homes of plantation owners, spreading mayhem and terror on the island. Markus' men were called "Maroons." In 1834, he organized a work stoppage, and many captives walked off of these places where they labored.[327]

After the many tragedies and turmoils experienced by Alexander Hamilton early in his life, he most likely experienced his first direct contact with the institution of slavery. His mother, Rachel, left her orphaned son the remainder of her property, including a slave boy named Ajax.[328] However, neither Hamilton nor his brother James Jr. received any of their inheritance because, under the eyes of the law, both boys were illegitimate and could not own property.

Thus, Alexander Hamilton did not become a slave owner on the island of St. Croix as his mother had intended. He did, however, appear to be fully cognizant of the trials and tribulations of plantation life since the island's economy was fully dependent on the institution of captivity.

Mr. Hamilton spent his teenage years working as a clerk with the St. Croix trading firm Beekman & Cruger, which imported everything needed for plantation life, including enslaved people from West Africa. Hamilton must have watched hundreds of captives come ashore after making the Middle Passage voyage. It is also likely that he took part in the inspection and the pricing of captives traded by this firm. A 1772 letter in Alexander Hamilton's youthful handwriting sought the acquisition of "two or three poor boys" for plantation work, and he asked that they be "bound in the most reasonable manner you can."[329]

Scholar Ankeet Ball, in his essay "Ambition and Bondage: An Inquiry on Alexander Hamilton and Slavery," tells us about Hamilton's early life:

> Hamilton witnessed firsthand the intense struggles that plantation slaves faced, and he

began to loathe the institution of Slavery through this direct exposure.[330]

Mr. Ball does point out in his essay, however, that the Nicholas Cruger family, the young lad Alexander Hamilton's employer, sometimes engaged in slave trading on the island. He related,

> Hamilton, through his employment, must have witnessed the cramped conditions of the slave ships where hundreds of Africans were chained in "fetid holds."

Mr. Ball adds:

> The conditions on these ships were said to be so vile that people on shore on St. Croix could smell the foul effluvia from miles away.

At the end of Mr. Ball's essay, he suggests that,

> [Hamilton's] later feelings on slavery found grounds in economic jealousy along with than ideological and philosophical opposition.

Mr. Ball adds,

> Despite his fundamental disapproval of the institution, Hamilton recognized, nevertheless, that most of the powerful elite on the island were slaveholders or slave traders.

In his essay, Mr. Ball makes the following conclusions about Alexander Hamilton and the issue of slavery.

1. As a child, he began to find the practice of slavery to be repugnant.
2. That his long-held aversion to slavery was life-long.
3. That the bottom-line regarding Alexander Hamilton and slavery is that he was never a slave owner and was decidedly against the idea of the practice, in America or anywhere else for that matter.

Thus, we should add Ankeet Ball to our list of scholars who hold the traditional view of Alexander Hamilton on slavery. But, unfortunately, the many observations he makes about the young Alexander Hamilton and the notion of slavery, are completely without evidence. Mr. Ball may be correct about his surmises, but there is no evidence to show that he is.

This brings us to the third section of Chapter Eight, in which we will identify and discuss a new theory that has recently been put forward that great American statesman Alexander Hamilton was, in fact, a slave owner. For the most part, two scholars have promulgated this theory, Ms. Jessie Serfilippi, who works at the Schuyler Mansion State Historic Site in Albany, New York; and Harvard Professor Annette Gordon-Reed, who also holds the same view. We also will evaluate this new theory at the close of section three to follow.

New Theory on Hamilton and Slavery

A new research paper published in November of 2020 takes a swipe at the long-held, traditional view of Alexander Hamilton and slavery that we have described and discussed in the first section of Chapter Eight. The paper is entitled "As Odious and Immoral a Thing: Alexander Hamilton's Hidden History," and its author is Jessie Serfilippi. Her research was originally published o the New York State Park System website.[331]

Ms. Serfilippi examined letters, account books, and many other Hamilton-Schulyer family documents. Her conclusion is put quite forcefully when she wrote, "Not only did Alexander Hamilton enslave people, but his involvement in the institution of slavery was essential to his identity, both personally and professionally."

At the beginning of her article, Ms. Serfilippi points out that "Hamilton is almost universally depicted as an Abolitionist in popular modern works from Ron Chernow's 2004 biography *Alexander Hamilton* to Lin-Manuel Miranda's Tony-Award winning show, "Hamilton: An American Musical."

After poring over the ledgers and letters of Hamilton and his wife Eliza Schuyler Hamilton, Serfilippi wrote, "It is vital that the myth of Hamilton as the Abolitionist Founding Father must come to an end."

At the heart of Ms. Serfilippi's arguments are a series of transactions that Mr. Hamilton was involved in after doing business for his wife's family after their marriage in December of 1780. On November 11, 1784, for example, one of Eliza's sisters asked for the return of a slave from another party. For Ms. Serfilippi, this is evidence that Alexander Hamilton at times was in the slave business.

Mr. Hamilton's cash books report the payment of $250.00 to Philip Schuyler in 1796 for "A Negro servant purchased by him for me." Another entry records receiving $100.00 for "lending a Negro boy to another person." Ms. Serfilippi also points out that in an inventory of his property made out by Mr. Hamilton to settle his affairs after his death, it included "servants valued at four hundred pounds."

These and other account books, journals and letters of Alexander Hamilton, as well as those of his wife, Eliza, lead Ms. Serfilippi to conclude, "not only did Hamilton enslave people, but his involvement in the institution of slavery was essential to his identity…" Over and against Ms. Serfilippi's article are a number of facts and questions that must be raised about her approach. Why, for example, does the 1800 census show that the household of Alexander Hamilton owned no slaves? The 1800 census records do show that the Hamiltons had four free black persons living in their household, but these were most likely domestic servants.

Ms. Serfilippi also points to some transactions Alexander Hamilton undertook for his brother-in-law, John B. Church, while the latter was in Europe and returned to the United States in May of 1797. After returning, Mr. Church purchased a black woman and her son with Mr. Hamilton acting as Church's agent. The great American statesman records Mr. Church's payment in his cash book.

In a 1784 entry from Alexander Hamilton's cash books, there is a mention of the sale of a woman known as "Peggy." Ms. Serfilippi took the entry as another example that the great American statesman was given the cash payment because he owned Peggy and conveyed her in a sale. But it could just as easily have been that someone in the Schuyler family had owned Peggy, and the money was being collected for that person with Hamilton as his or her agent.

In the Schulyer mansion essay of Ms. Serfilippi, she records the purchase for Mr. Church mentioned above as two separate transactions, even though the amount given for both is exactly the same figure. Does it not make more sense to say it was only one purchase event for both the mother and son and together they were worth one hundred pounds?

The smoking gun in the Serfilippi essay is that Hamilton wrote down the values of various items in his estate, including his servants, who were worth a collected four hundred pounds. Calling someone a "servant" is clearly not the same as calling that person or persons a slave or slaves. Most likely, these four individuals were domestic house servants who helped Mrs. Hamilton keep what was a very large house and estate.

At the same time, Ms. Serfilippi seems to ignore other exculpatory evidence such as Hamilton's support of John Laurens attempt to raise companies of black soldiers, or Mr. Hamilton's participation, and his presidency in 1790 of the New York Manumission Society, which also led to an act for the "Gradual Abolition of Slavery." In New York, Alexander Hamilton was also instrumental in establishing the African Free School for the education of the children of slaves.

The Hamilton's slave owner thesis also has been taken up by Harvard Professor Annette Gordon-Reed. In an interview with the *Harvard Gazette* from October 7, 2016, she responded to one question from the interviewer by saying this about Alexander Hamilton, "He was not an Abolitionist. He bought and sold slaves for his in-laws and opposing slavery was never at the forefront of his agenda."

A little further on in the same interview, Professor Gordon-Reed adds, "He [Hamilton] was not a champion of the little guy...he was an elitist, he was in favor of having a president for life." One might respond by saying that buying and selling slaves for his in-laws is not the same as saying that Alexander Hamilton was a slave owner. And it is not entirely clear why being president for life is necessarily a bad thing. With some of our greatest presidents in the history of America, it might have been a good idea.

In 1781, the Hamilton family hired a woman to help clean a house where they were soon to move. After the move, the statesman wrote to Governor Clinton of New York stating that he "had to pay for the value of the woman Mrs. H had of Mrs. Clinton." Ms. Serafilippi concludes that this was Hamilton paying for the purchase of a slave.

But Mr. Hamilton used the past tense "had," which may indicate the woman had returned home. Clearly, however, the woman in question had been hired and not purchased.

Finally, Ms. Serfilippi and Dr. Gordon-Reed say nothing about what *The Federalist Papers* have to say about the issue of *Slavery*, a major unargued collection of texts in the Alexander Hamilton body of work. In point of fact, there are at least four of Mr. Hamilton's contributions in the *Papers*, the subject matter of the next section of Chapter Eight.

Hamilton, Slavery and *The Federalist Papers*

One final aspect of great American statesman Alexander Hamilton's perspectives on slavery is what the New York politician and former treasury secretary said about slavery in *The Federalist Papers*. Among the essays written by Mr. Hamilton in the *Papers*, five of them are more relevant for our purposes in this final section of Chapter Eight. These are Essays 6, 7, 8, 11 and 12.

The first three of these essays—numbers 6, 7, and 8—take up many of the same themes, one of those being slavery. Alexander Hamilton's greatest fear for America was the possibility of a violent death of the Union. There was no doubt in his mind that it was the *sine qua non* for the country's security and liberties, and he warned that without the Union, America would split into mutually hostile Northern and Southern confederacies. Therefore, Hamilton and the other Founders had to be cautious in their push to end slavery, particularly during the national government's infancy.

Alexander Hamilton worried about triggering a rupture that could prostrate the national government and thereby preclude any federal efforts to extinguish slavery. At the same time, the Constitution's concessions to slavery were not intended to be permanent, as evidenced by the expiration date in 1808 of the restrictions on banning the exportation of slaves. Indeed, there are more than adequate grounds to assert that Mr. Hamilton's interpretation of the Constitution, perhaps more than any other Founder's, supplied the federal government with the requisite powers to confine and eventually distinguish slavery.

Alexander Hamilton worried that the Union would crumble over the issue of slavery. He voiced that concern in each of Essays 6, 7 and 8 of *The Federalist Papers*. Little did Mr. Hamilton know he was presaging what would occur in America from 1861 until 1865.

By the time that Alexander Hamilton got to the writing of Essays 11 and 12 of *The Federalist Papers*, he still had the same number one worry—the desire for unity. This can be seen in the opening paragraph number 11:

> The importance of the Union, in a commercial light, is one of those points, about which there is least room to entertain a difference of opinion, and which has in fact commanded the most general assent of men, who have any acquittance with the subject. This applies, as well, with our intercourse with foreign countries, as with each other.

Several paragraphs later, still in Essay 11, Mr. Hamilton returns to the issue of unity when he wrote:

> It may perhaps be replied to this, that whether the states are united or disunited, there would still be intimate commerce between them which would answer the same ends, which, in the course of these papers have been amply detailed. A unity of commercial, as well as political interests, can only result in a unity of government.

Throughout the entire text of *The Federalist Papers* number 11, the shadow of slavery and its possible effects in terms of national unity in relation to the slavery issue is tantamount.

These same themes can be seen again in the opening paragraph of Essay 12. There, Mr. Hamilton tells us:

> The effects of the Union upon the commercial prosperity of the States have been sufficiently delineated. Its tendency to promote the interests of revenue will be the subject of our present inquiry.

Mr. Hamilton goes on, again, to mention the specter of slavery as the principal worry about the cause of "Disunity, if it were to occur." *The Federalist Papers* Essay 12 was published on November 27, 1787, under the pseudonym Publius. Its formal title is "The Utility of the Union in Respect to Revenue." Mr. Hamilton also speaks in this essay of national and state borders and how taxes should be levied in relation to slave states versus non-slave states. The great American statesman concludes Essay 12 by speaking of the essential nature of the funding of the national government, and any failure to do it properly would make the entire effort of the Revolution be in vain.

Although Mr. Hamilton had these concerns about slavery breaking up the American Union, James Madison wrote considerably more about slavery in his essays of *The Federalist Papers*. For example, in Essay 42, Mr. Madison suggested that slavery would only last another twenty years. He repeats the same claim about the duration of slavery in America in Essay 38, as well.

Mr. Madison also turned his attention to slavery in Essays 49 and 54, where he discusses the famous three-fifths compromise for counting slaves in regard to proportioning votes in the House of Representatives. Madison also claims in Essay 54 that "slaves are property, as well as people."

This brings us to the major conclusions of Chapter Eight. The topic for Chapter Nine to follow is the great American statesman Alexander Hamilton and nationalism.

Conclusions to Chapter Eight

In the introduction to Chapter Eight, we indicated that the chapter on Alexander Hamilton and slavery was to have four sections. In the first of these, we described and discussed what can be called the "traditional scholarly view on Hamilton and slavery." As we have shown in the first section of this chapter, this perspective is that, in general, Alexander Hamilton had a much more benign view of slavery for most of his life.

We presented this traditional scholarly view by relying on the work of writers such as John C. Miller, Forest McDonald, Ron Chernow, Richard Brookhiser, Broadus Mitchell, Henry Cabot Lodge, James Oliver, as well as many other writers and scholars, to describe the traditional view.

We dedicated the second section of Chapter Eight to an analysis of what we know of the practice of slavery in the Caribbean islands of Nevis, St. Kitts and St. Croix, where Alexander Hamilton spent his early childhood years. In that section, we made some very general observations about the selling and keeping of slaves on the three islands. We also evaluated a long-held belief by those who hold the traditional view of Hamilton and slavery that, as a small child, he learned to hate the institution of slavery. As indicated, however, there is absolutely no available evidence that this point of view is true.

However, we pointed out in section two that slave revolts or slave insurrections frequently occurred in the Caribbean, and Alexander Hamilton may have heard tales about some of these rebellions, a very large one, for example, took place on the island of Nevis a generation before his birth in 1755 or 1757.

In the third section of Chapter Eight, we took up a description of, and then an evaluation of, a new theory on Alexander Hamilton that is at odds with the traditional perspective from section one of the chapter. This new theory we had in mind was developed by Jessie Serfilippi called "As Odious and Immoral a Thing: Alexander Hamilton's Hidden History." Indeed, we have shown that Ms. Serfilippi has claimed in her essay that Alexander Hamilton was both a slave owner, as well as a slave dealer.

After sketching out the evidence she puts forward in her essay, we then pointed out that Harvard scholar Annette Gordon-Reed is also in full agreement with the two major conclusions in Serfilippi's essay, as evidence by an interview with Professor Gordon-Reed in the *Harvard Gazette* from October 7, 2016. In fact, in that interview, Dr. Gordon-Reed said of Alexander Hamilton, "He was not an Abolitionist. He bought and sold slaves for his in-laws, and opposing slavery was never at the forefront of his agenda."

At the close of section three of Chapter Eight, we supplied a tentative response to the Serfilippi/Gordon-Reed point of view. In that response, we suggested, as others like Ron Chernow also have, that neither female scholar placed their evidence in the context of a larger understanding of Hamilton on slavery that included lots of evidence that still supports the traditional theory of the great American statesman on the phenomenon of slavery.

Among those pieces of additional evidence, we cited that the 1800 US census said nothing of slaves living in the Hamilton household, but it does indicate four black domestic servants living there. Hamilton's work for the New York Manumission Society and his support of John Laurens' plan to raise companies of black soldiers whom, after their service, would be, in Mr. Hamilton's words, "Free with Muskets."

Another criticism we have made of the Serfilippi/Gordon-Reed thesis is that there is nothing in the essay, nor in the *Harvard Gazette* interview, that discusses Alexander Hamilton's comments on slavery or the essays he wrote for *The Federalist Papers*. In fact, we have shown that Mr. Hamilton's over-arching fear about America was that it would falter in keeping its "Unity."

We also have shown that in *The Federalist Papers* 6, 7, 8, 11 and 12, Mr. Hamilton expressed the view that what will keep America from retaining its unity would be the issue of slavery, and his concerns about the fact certainly were some of the earliest presages, which would come to pass later in the century from 1861 until 1865.

Indeed, for Mr. Hamilton, the specter of slavery was forever in the background of the issue of unity. He feared we would become "Two Americas," and in many ways, he was correct about that judgment.

We have also shown in section four of Chapter Eight that James Madison, another author of some of *The Federalist Papers*, also discussed slavery, including Essays 38, 42, 49 and 54, in which Mr. Madison said, "Slaves are property, as well as people."

The bottom-line conclusion made in Chapter Eight is that we see no good reasons for not believing and for promulgating the traditional scholarly view of Alexander Hamilton and slavery described in the first section of Chapter Eight.

Alexander Hamilton held a more progressive view than most of the other Founding Fathers regarding the equality of race. In 1774, he published his first major political essay, "A Full Vindication of the Measures of Congress," in which he drew a direct comparison between American slaves and the colonists being oppressed by the British. In the essay, he asserted that both varieties of "enslavement" were immoral by their very natures.

When defending John Laurens plan of recruiting black companies into the Continental Army, Mr. Hamilton wrote to the Continental Congress:

> I have not the least doubt that the negroes
> will make very excellent soldiers with proper
> management. Their natural faculties are probably
> as good as ours.

However, his lobbying for Mr. Laurens' plan failed to win the support that was needed, and the South Carolinian's plan was soon abandoned. Interestingly enough, George Washington was against the plan from the very beginning.

In that same 1774 essay, "A Full Vindication of the Measures of Congress," Alexander Hamilton clearly stated his bottom-line view on race and slavery. He wrote:

> All men have one common origin, they participate
> in one common nature and consequently have
> one common right.

This does not begin to approach the extreme paradox found in Thomas Jefferson's paradoxical views on these same issues in which he espoused independence of slaves while enslaving hundreds of them.

For Mr. Hamilton, the issue of slavery was a moral dilemma that pitted two moral rights against each other. The slave owner's right to own property versus the slave's right to freedom and autonomy. Clearly, Alexander Hamilton believed that these rights of humanity take precedence over the rights to property when these rights conflict with each other. The great American statesman hoped, however, that a way could be found that would end making such a stark choice an unnecessary one.

Indeed, and finally, much of what Alexander Hamilton had to say about the phenomenon of slavery was often given in the context of ethics and morality. When speaking of the practice of slavery, he often employed the words "odious" and "immoral," such as in the following comment:

In the interpretation of treatises, things odious or immoral are not to be presumed. The abandonment of Negroes who have been induced to quit their masters on the face of official proclamations, promising them liberty, to fall again under the yoke of their masters and into slavery is as odious and immoral a thing as can be conceived. It is odious not only as it imposes an act of perfidy on one of the contracting parties. But as it tends to bring back to servitude men once made free.[332]

In the final analysis, this man who was a fierce defender of private property, a man in whom the idea of a contract was tantamount to a sacred agreement, nevertheless, expressly denied the sacredness of any agreement that took from any human being, no matter what his color, his or her God-given freedom. For Alexander Hamilton, the great American statesman, slavery was "odious" and "immoral."

After the publication of Ms. Serfilippi's essay, the *New York Times* and the *New York Daily News* conducted a battle of sorts in their respective periodicals. The former's headline about Serfilippi's research read, "Alexander Hamilton, Enslaver? New Research Says Yes."[333] The author of this piece was reporter Jennifer Schuessler, and she is, for the most part, supportive of Ms. Serfilippi's thesis that Alexander Hamilton was both a slave owner and a slave dealer for his in-laws, the Schuylers.

A *New York Daily News* article responded to the *New York Times* article, in a piece by Philo Hamilton, published on January 16, 2021, that was headlined: "The Alexander Hamilton Slavery Smear," which both criticized the Schuessler article and put a vote in the camp of what we have been calling the "Traditional Scholarly View" on Alexander Hamilton and slavery. That is, that he was an abolitionist, through and through.

Philo Hamilton said in his piece, "There are a number of other unfair insinuations related to Hamilton's work on behalf of his in-laws and his career as an attorney. Hamilton was engaged as a banker for his in-laws on two different occasions."[334] The *Daily News* writer goes on to suggest that Ms. Serfilippi misinterprets two separate transactions, one in 1784 that involved Peggy Schuyler, and the other in which the statesman purchased a woman and child for his brother-in-law, John Church.

Philo Hamilton ends his article with an assent to the traditional scholarly view when he wrote:

> Hamilton was no friend of slavery. Since Hamilton himself cannot write his way out of his accusation, others who respect his legacy must.

The major focus of Chapter Nine of this study of Alexander Hamilton's religion will be what may be described, as we shall see, as "Alexander Hamilton's Nationalism," or "Alexander Hamilton's Civil Religion." Chapter Nine will be followed by a conclusive chapter in which we will catalog and give a summation of the major conclusions of this study.

Chapter Nine
Hamilton, Nationalism and Civil Religion

Alexander Hamilton's American foreign policy can only be understood in the context of his nationalism.
—**Lawrence S. Kaplan,** *Alexander Hamilton: Ambivalent Anglophile*

Among the four main political principles that distinguish Hamilton and Jefferson from each other were the primacy of the national community versus local communities; the sovereignty of the national people rather than the sovereignty of the states; nationalistic political realism instead of isolationism or world federalism; and a broad understanding of the powers and role of the federal government.
—**David Upham,** *Hamilton's Republic: Readings in the American Democratic Nationalist Tradition*

Let the thirteen states bound together in a strict indissoluble Union, should concur in erecting one great American system, superior to the control of all transatlantic force or influence, and able to dictate the terms of the connection between the old and the new world.
—**Alexander Hamilton,** *The Federalist Papers*

Introduction

In this ninth chapter, the major goal is to discuss the life of great American statesman Alexander Hamilton in terms of two phenomena we will call "Nationalism" and "Civil Religion." The third goal of this chapter will be to discuss these two ideas in terms of the current political situations in the United States, where the Left is deadly afraid of Nationalism, while the Right embraces it. We will also raise and answer the question, "Was Alexander Hamilton a Nationalist?"

The terms "American Nationalism" and "American Imperialism" are discrete phenomena that have not been studied extensively. In his book *Imagined Communities*, Benedict Anderson related that "Nation, nationality, and nationalism—all have proven notoriously difficult to define, let alone to analyze."[335] Nevertheless, Anderson suggested in the same 1983 book that "Nationalism should be studied as cultural artifacts of a particular kind."

Scholar Liah Greenfeld, in her book *Nationalism and the Mind: Essays on Modern Culture*, agrees that Nationalism cannot be defined, and instead, she emphasizes the specific circumstances in England, France, Russia and Germany where Nationalism first appeared in eighteenth- and nineteenth-century Europe.[336]

When we use the word "Nationalism" in this chapter, we will mean the loyalty and devotion to the United States and especially a sense of national consciousness in which the believer in Nationalism place a primary emphasis on the promotion of its culture and interests as opposed to other nations or supranational groups. A concomitant claim of an American Nationalist, as least in terms of how we are using the term, is that the American nationalist believes that the United States is superior to other nations, or even that the United States is the best nation.

In this last sense, sometimes American Nationalism is expressed in the belief that the United States is better than other nations. Those who foster Nationalism in this sense oppose both Globalism and empires of any kind. In 2016, the American people elected Donald Trump, a populist president who, at a Texas rally, declared that he was a Nationalist.[337] We will say more about Mr. Trump and his Nationalism in a later section of this chapter.

We will begin by speaking of the history of the idea of Nationalism in America from the Founding Fathers on. We then will move to the second section, where we will discuss the idea of the American "Civil Religion" and how this idea may have shaped American history.

In the third section of Chapter Nine, we will apply what we have learned about Nationalism and Civil Religion to many ideas and events in contemporary American politics and what are sometimes called the "Culture Wars" in the contemporary United States.

Finally, in section four, we will raise and then answer the question, "Was the great American statesman Alexander Hamilton a Nationalist?" As we shall see, we will give an affirmative response to that question. We move next, then, to the history of American Nationalism.

History of American Nationalism

Many contemporary political scholars hold the view that Nationalism is a uniquely modern idea, but many of its ideas can be traced throughout human history going all the way back to the ancient Hebrews, who conceived themselves as both a Chosen People—that is, as a people superior to all other peoples—as well as a people with a common language, history and culture.[338]

The ancient Greek city-states also believed themselves superior to all other nations around them and also believed in the sense of great loyalty to the political community. These feelings of national and cultural superiority can also be seen in the Roman Empire and in the Christian church when it established itself as the religion of the empire at the end of the fourth century CE.[339]

Strong centralized monarchies grew out of petty feudal states, as regional languages, art and culture began to develop in Europe in the medieval period. The religious wars of the Reformation set nation against nation, although the strongest loyalty still appeared to be toward monarchs. The nationalistic development of the economic doctrine of Mercantilism was one of the by-products of these religious wars.

The rise and growth of the middle class in Europe and their desire for political power and representation became an important theme in European history and helped give rise to the modern theory of "Nationalism." The theorists of the French Revolution held that their people were closely connected with the emergence of modern nationalist nations and governments by establishing the ideas of equality and liberty for everyone.

To the Jacobins, the French nation was inseparable from the French people, and for the first time in history, a people could create a government in accordance with the "general will of the people." Although the aims of the Jacobins were universal, they glorified the nation that would establish their political aims, and nationalism had evinced itself in the doctrine of a kind of Manifest Destiny.

It was only in the nineteenth century, however, that nationalism became a widespread and powerful force. During this period, nationalism expressed itself in many areas to exhibit a drive for national unification and independence. The spirit of nationalism took an especially strong hold in Germany where thinkers such as philosopher Johann Gottfried von Herder and Johann Gottlieb Fichte developed the idea of a *Volk*, or "People."[340]

According to Johann Herder (1744–1803), a great political power was arising in the nineteenth century in Germany that involved "an increasing desire and excitement for romantic "feeling, identity," and liberal demands that were based on a "government by the people rather than the authority of a king, a chancellor, or an empire." Herder pointed out that before that time what he called "romantic identity nationalism" and "liberal civil nationalism" had mostly been middle class movements. Now, in the mid-to-late-eighteenth century, it was a nationwide movement.[341]

The nationalism that inspired the German people, however, gave rise to the antagonism toward Napoleon, and the fragmented German states were now unified. After many years of fighting, Italy was also unified and achieved freedom from foreign domination. Certain areas, such as Trieste in the East, were not included in the new "Italian" nation.

Meanwhile, in America, the British colonies faced a modern identity problem with the decision to view themselves as either Americans or as British subjects. This raised the question of when people living in the British colonies stopped identifying themselves as "British" and began to identify themselves as "Americans."

One way to help us in aiding in arriving at an answer to this question is a study done by researcher Alexander Ziegler entitled "From Colonies to Nation: The Emergence of American Nationalism, 1750–1800," published in 2006. Ziegler's study focused on the content analysis of newspaper articles published in Charleston, South Carolina, from 1750 to 1800. As Ziegler reported, "The goal of this study is to detect trends in the emergence of an American national identity as evidenced by the language used in eighteenth-century Charleston newspapers."[342] In regard to Mr. Ziegler's findings, he tells us this:

> My own case of Charleston newspapers shows that between 1750 and 1800, Colonists went through a gradual process of beginning to think of themselves as Americans, and no longer as Britons.[343]

In his analysis of the South Carolina newspapers from 1750, he could find nearly no articles where colonists thought of themselves as Americans. Most of the news in these articles was European news. By 1755, this trend continued, and the articles tended to be longer and now contained some local subjects. By 1760, however, the news in the newspaper articles is now evenly divided between European events and colonial events.[344]

The Stamp Act passed by the British Parliament on March 22, 1765, was an impetus for the beginning of the emergence of an American identity, and by 1770, there are far more references to American identity than those of 1765. In 1775, Mr. Ziegler argues, we see another large shift toward American identity and American Nationalism. This was also the year that the Revolutionary War began.[345]

Commenting on issues from September 26 and November 14, 1775, Ziegler notes, "references to American identity significantly outnumbered references to British identity." He also tells us that for the first time in the South Carolina newspaper articles, we see the first uses of phrases such as:

1. Representatives of the People.
2. The Good of the People.
3. The Voice of the People.[346]

Ziegler's conclusion about this material is clear, "The tone and content of the 1775 sample of the *Gazette* are markedly different from the previous issues. 1775 appears to be the jumping-off point for an emerging, independent sense of American identity."[347]

Ziegler also cites similar research and findings by Richard Merritt in 1963 and 1966 studies in which he analyzed colonial newspapers from five cities—Boston, Philadelphia, New York, Williamsburg and Charleston.[348] Another researcher Miroslav Hroch, pointed out that nationalist movements "begin with a small group of intellectuals and activists who draw on preexisting conditions to incite a 'national consciousness' among a larger ethnic group."[349]

This brings us to the second section of Chapter Nine, in which we will apply these findings discussed above to the political situation in America from 1755 until 1800.

Nationalism in America: 1755 to 1800

The first thing we can say about this period in American history is that the Founding Fathers, for the most part, were caught up with the Enlightenment ideas of Liberty and Equality. Secondly, it was common among these men to think of the United States as a "New Israel" or "New Chosen People." Thirdly, as Miroslav Hrovch suggested, American nationalism began with a cadre of these "small groups of intellectuals and activists."[350]

This notion of a "New Israel" or a "New Chosen people" can be seen throughout the colonial period in America, beginning with John Winthrop's 1630's dream of "A City on a Hill" in which he called for the Massachusetts Bay Colony to be seen as a "bastion on a hill."[351]

In the Great Awakening year of 1738, Jonathan Edwards said in a sermon that "The beginning of the late work of God in this place was circumstanced that I could not look upon it as a remarkable testimony of God approbation."[352] In 1780, Samuel Cooper preached before the Massachusetts House of Representatives and called the colony "a Hebraic Republic."[353] Three years later, Connecticut pastor and president of Yale College, Ezra Stiles, gave a sermon in the presence of Governor Jonathan Trumbull called, "The United States Elevated to Glory and Honor."[354]

This hundred-page oration began with a text from the Book of Deuteronomy. And in the midst of the sermon, Stiles spoke of "A Discourse Upon the Political Welfare of God's American Israel." It was not unusual, then, to speak of the United States as the "New Israel," the "New Chosen People," up to and beyond the American Revolution.

Miroslav Hroch told us that nationalistic movements tend to begin with a small group of intellectuals and activists. More specifically, that a small group of intellectuals and activists were centered in the party known as the Federalists, the first political party in the United States. This party dominated the national government from 1789 until 1801. The Federalist Party called for a strong national government that promoted economic growth and friendly relations with Great Britain and in opposition to Revolutionary France.

The Federalist Party opposed the Democratic-Republican Party in America during George Washington's first term as president. They were known for their support of a strong national government, as we saw in Chapter Eight in our observations about Alexander Hamilton on "Unity" in his essays of *The Federalist Papers*. The Federalists emphasized commercial and diplomatic harmony with Great Britain following the signing of the 1794 Jay Treaty.[355]

The Federalist party split over negotiations with France during the administration of President John Adams, but it remained a political force until its members were finally absorbed into the Democratic and Whig parties in the 1820s. Despite the party's dissolution, the Federalist Party made a lasting impact by laying the foundations of a national economy, creating a national judicial system and formulating principles of foreign policy for the future.[356]

While Secretary of the Treasury Alexander Hamilton furthered his call for a stronger unity and national government, Thomas Jefferson, the secretary of state under President Washington, was Hamilton's main opponent. In *The Federalist Papers* Essay 17, Mr. Hamilton argued that under the new Constitution, the federal government would be able to act directly upon the citizens of the states to regulate the common concerns of the nation, which he believed was absolutely essential to the preservation of the Union.

The Articles of Confederation, in Hamilton's view, were far too weak to serve the nation well. A stronger, more centralized system was necessary. While arguing for the necessity of a strong Union and a stronger national government, Alexander Hamilton attempted to assuage the fears of many citizens that the proposed new government would destroy state sovereignty and subordinate the legitimate interests of the states.

Alexander Hamilton was also very clear about the necessity of a strong national government in the areas of finance and national security. Alexander Hamilton, while secretary of the treasury, created a national bank in 1791.[357] This bank was not a private entity but a government agency that had the power to print money and to make loans. It acted like most of the central banks in Europe. And in many ways, the creation of the national bank was one of the main points of contention between Mr. Hamilton and Mr. Jefferson.[358]

Hamilton was now responsible for settling the issue of debt incurred during the Revolutionary War. A major part of this task was to ascertain what each state's debts were, how these debts were serviced, how much of the debts had been paid off, as well as who owned the debts.

Thomas Jefferson's state of Virginia, however, had paid off almost all of its debt and was not too interested in having the federal government assume what the state had left. Other states, like Massachusetts, for example, had repaid very little of its debt. Hamilton's idea of a central bank changed the nature of wealth by making paper money a viable form of wealth, whereas before then, land and property had largely been the main form of wealth.[359]

As treasury secretary, Alexander Hamilton envisioned the United States as a national administrative republic engaged in wide-ranging commerce. The national bank would issue banknotes, stimulate commercial growth, provide a safe haven for federal revenue and finance short-term loans.

Mr. Hamilton wanted to foster a mercantile economy where the central government would organize the economic activity in America. To a great extent, the commercial states of the North—New England and New York—supported the secretary's economic plan. Mr. Jefferson and his followers, however, were strongly against Mr. Hamilton's economic vision. For one thing, Jefferson believed that agrarian interests, living off the land and its products, were the major contributors to wealth in America.[360] Thomas Jefferson also opposed the national bank because it was partially to be funded by tariffs. Mr. Hamilton wanted to put tariffs on imports that would compete with manufacturing in the US.

Mr. Hamilton was able to win over George Washington in the debate over the national bank, and the bank was originally given a twenty-year charter by Congress. Slowly, Washington moved in the direction of the Federalist view. Hamilton's vision of a strong national government as the organizer of economic life became a hallmark of political and economic life in the late eighteenth century.

Although both Hamilton and Jefferson played key roles in the Revolution and the founding of the United States, from the very beginning, it was clear that both men harbored a distrust about the other. Jefferson was sure that America's success would lie in its agrarian tradition, while Mr. Hamilton's economic vision hinged on the promotion of manufacturing and commerce. Mr. Hamilton distrusted the popular will and believed that the federal government should wield considerable power. Mr. Jefferson, on the other hand, placed his trust in the people as the true governors.[361]

One thing that Mr. Hamilton and Mr. Jefferson did agree on, however, is the ideas found in the following statement of Alexander Hamilton:

> The safety of the republic depends essentially on the energy of a common national sentiment; on a uniformity of principles and habits; on the exemption of the citizens from foreign bias and prejudice; and on that love of country which will almost invariably be found to be closely connected with birth, education, and family.[362]

Both Jefferson and Hamilton believed the idea of "uniform principles and habits" was at the heart of what it meant to be an American, then and now. Many of those uniform principles and habits are in the Founding documents of the United States, such as the US Constitution. Among those principles, of course, are the many rights guaranteed by the Constitution, including the many rights outlined in the First Amendment of that document.

In addition to those "uniform principles and habits" about which both Jefferson and Hamilton agreed, there were also some other "habits" that all Americans began to share from that time in the late eighteenth century to American society today. In his 1967 essay entitled "Civil Religion in America," American sociologist Robert Bellah expressed what he believed that "uniform principles and habits" are. In section three of Chapter Nine, we will examine Dr. Bellah's thesis.[363]

Hamilton, Civil Religion and Nationalism

According to Robert Bellah, writing in the mid-twentieth century, suggested that Americans embrace what he called "a common Civil Religion with certain fundamental beliefs, values, holidays, and rituals in parallel to, or independent of, their chosen religion." After its publication, Bellah's article became a major focus of sociology of religion conferences and numerous articles and books written on the subject. The debate on American Civil Religion reached its peak with the American Bicentennial celebration in 1976.

Among many of the scholars who commented or wrote about Dr. Bellah's thesis was sociologist Anthony Squiers, who wrote in support of Dr. Bellah's theory, suggesting among other things that the Declaration of Independence, the US Constitution and the Bill of Rights are the "cornerstones of a type of civil religion," in that these texts possess a kind of sacredness in an American political context.

In fact, in his book *The Politics of the Sacred in America*, Dr. Squiers goes so far as identifying fourteen principles of the American Civil Religion. These are the following:

1. Filial piety.
2. Reverence to certain sacred texts and symbols such as the Constitution, the Declaration of Independence and the flag.
3. The sanctity of American institutions.
4. The belief in God.
5. That rights are Divinely given.
6. The notion that freedom comes from God through government.
7. That government authority comes from God.
8. That God can be known through the American experience.

9. That God is the Supreme Judge.

10. That God is Sovereign.

11. That America's prosperity results from God's providence.

12. That America is a "City on a Hill" or a bastion of hope and righteousness.

13. The principle of sacrificial death and rebirth.

14. America serves a higher purpose than self-interests.[364]

The idea that America was a new Israel or New Promised Land, of course, may be seen as an implication from combining Dr. Squiers' beliefs numbers six, twelve, and fourteen, that the United States is to have a "Higher Purpose" than other nations.

It should be clear that both Thomas Jefferson and Alexander Hamilton assented to all fourteen of these propositions. What it meant to be an American for both of these Founding Fathers was bound up in these propositions, for each of them can be found in the Declaration, the Constitution and the Bill of Rights.

After serving as a crucial adjutant to George Washington during the Revolution, Alexander Hamilton, as a leader of the Federalists, took a leading role in the formation of American Nationalism. He was able to dump the "Articles of Confederation" to create a durable national government. Mr. Hamilton became a prime actor behind the Constitutional Convention and wrote roughly two-thirds of *The Federalist Papers*.

In his conclusion to Essay 11 of *The Federalist Papers,* Alexander Hamilton wrote:

> Let the thirteen states bound together in a strict and indissoluble Union, concur in erecting one great American System, superior to the control of all transatlantic force or influence and able to dictate the terms of the connection between the old and the new world.

Mr. Hamilton points to at least two other aspects that will go into the making of what can be called American Nationalism. First, that

America, with its peculiar version of Nationalism, may be in conflict with other nations. And secondly, America is superior to those other nations. When the United States was in conflict with the Soviet Union during the Cold War, American schoolchildren were taught that the Soviets were "Godless," and secondarily, they were dangerous. The two empires of the Cold War competed against each other, and the citizens of both sides were instructed as children about how their system was the superior one.[365]

In addition, then, to the fourteen propositions suggested by Dr. Squiers in the American Civil Religion, we now may add two more:

15. American will compete with other nations and conflict with them.
16. The American system is superior to other systems.[366]

It should be clear that both Mr. Jefferson and Mr. Hamilton would have assented to proposition numbers 15 and 16, as well. Since the end of World War II, however, when another of those "World Systems," the Nazis, were soundly defeated, the so-called "Best Generation" had once again demonstrated the superiority of the American brand of Nationalism.

In the generation after the best generation, baby boomers were taught another collection of elements that went into the making of the American brand of Nationalism. Among these new supplemental beliefs that all American schoolchildren learned were the following:

1. That school should begin with the Pledge of Allegiance.
2. That the America flag should be venerated and not be allowed to touch the ground.
3. That citizens should stand for the National Anthem with their right hands on their hearts.
4. That America is One Nation Under God.
5. That the United States is the best nation on Earth.
6. That America is a New Israel or a New Chosen People.[367]

Not only were these six new supplemental beliefs true, no one among the baby-boomer generation ever thought about questioning them. This certainly changed, however, in subsequent generations, which is the focus of the next section of Chapter Nine when we will speak of the phenomenon of America's Nationalism in contemporary America.

American Nationalism in Contemporary America

"From this day forward, a new vision will govern our land. From this day forward, it is going to be only America First, America First." President Donald J. Trump uttered these words during his inaugural address on January 20, 2017. It was a clear distillation of what was to come and his Nationalist politics, a politic that claimed to prioritize American interests above the interests of anyone else. On the surface, this does not appear to be particularly controversial. The problem seems to be, however, with what Mr. Trump meant by "America."

For many Americans, Trump's "America First" is defined by race and rooted in disdain for foreigners. In that regard, many of Trump's critics on the Left called him a racist, a white supremacist and a homophobe. In policies like the Muslim ban and the border wall, Trump's critics were certain that the forty-fifth president of the United States was out of step with the values held by Americans after his baby-boom generation.

One way to see these values of the two American generations after Mr. Trump's is to look at an experiment I conducted in the final five years of my teaching undergraduates in America from 2011 until 2016. In that period, I gave my students a one-question survey. That one question was this: *In your mind, which is more important to American life, diversity or freedom?*

In those five years, I surveyed 1,632 undergraduates in American colleges and universities. Of those students, two out of three, or 66 percent, answered "diversity." Of the 1,632, only 549 answered the survey by saying "freedom" is more fundamental than "diversity," or even "identity," for that matter.

Now I must say, I was shocked by the responses of the undergraduates, particularly if we understand that freedom, number

6 on Dr. Squiers list of components of the nature of American Civil Religion, but diversity is nowhere to be found in any of the American values we have discussed in this chapter.

I suspect that the findings of my study have to do with a new set of supplemental core American beliefs that are held by the Left in contemporary America. Among those new core beliefs are the following:

1. Race is more fundamental than any other category when determining identity.
2. White Americans are "systematically" and "inherently" racists.
3. The character of America is rotten at its core.
4. The greatest danger to America is white supremacy.
5. The "America" of "Make America Great Again" was never so great.[368]

Thus, one way to understand the current debate about Nationalism in America is to suggest that it is a debate of the six supplemental American beliefs learned by baby boomers like Mr. Trump mentioned earlier in this section and these five current beliefs largely held by Americans after the baby boomer generation.

Black athletes who refuse to stand for the national anthem breaks rule number three mentioned earlier. The Pledge of Allegiance should not be said daily before school in America because it says, "One nation under God." That the United States is not the best nation on earth—and never has been—breaks rule number five on our list of baby boomer principles.

As Nationalism gained strength in the United States in recent years, some writers have gone so far as saying that "Nationalism is un-American." Bret Stephens of the *New York Times*, Kim Holmes of the Heritage Foundation, and Elan Journo of the Ayn Rand Institute, for example, have all made this claim.[369]

Going all the way back to the 1780s, however, there is a long tradition of Nationalism in America, beginning with the Federalist Party. At that time, because of the failure of the Articles of Confederation, the American nationalists were headed by George Washington, John Adams, John Jay, Robert Morris, James Wilson, Oliver Ellsworth, Rufus King, John Marshall, Noah Webster, and most important for our purposes, Alexander Hamilton.

Today's worries about American Nationalism appear to be more about "White Nationalists" than Nationalism. There are many differences between the two. One is a 200-year movement started by Washington, Hamilton and others. The other is a congregation of angry and patriotic white people who are worried that their Constitutional rights are slowly eroding. The first movement has little or nothing in common with the second.

One final task remains in Chapter Nine—whether Alexander Hamilton was a Nationalist, the subject matter of the final section of this chapter. This will be followed by Chapter Ten, a summary of the major conclusions we have made in this study of Alexander Hamilton's religion.

Was Alexander Hamilton a Nationalist?

In a recent book by Lawrence S. Kaplan called *Alexander Hamilton: Ambivalent Anglophile*, Kaplan suggests that Mr. Hamilton's contributions to American foreign policy can only be understood in the context of his Nationalism. In fact, Kaplan presents Hamilton as a precocious nationalist. Mr. Kaplan gives this judgment as an explanation of the life of Mr. Hamilton from his speeches and publications during the imperial crisis of the 1770s, to his understanding of the shortcomings of the Confederation during the 1780s, as well to his reports on credit, banking and manufacturing in the early 1790s, behind all these activities, according to Mr. Kaplan was Mr. Hamilton's Nationalism.[370]

Mr. Kaplan also points out that the great American statesman was always ahead of the vast majority of his contemporaries. But behind all of Hamilton's policies, both foreign and domestic, was a confidence that, by adopting the proper measures, the United States would rise into the ranks of the most powerful and prosperous nations on earth. At the same time, Mr. Hamilton worried that the American people, the public and its various states and demagogic politicians would defeat his plans, not only threatening his expectations but also American nationhood, as well.

American patriotism and Nationalism were central to Alexander Hamilton's political creed. An immigrant from the West Indies, he was not invested in any particular colony or state. Much of his agenda was driven by his concern that America's deep, local loyalties—which led many Americans to see their home as their state, would undermine the fragile unity that marked America during the Revolution.

This fear of the great American statesman was key to understanding his Nationalism and the view that Lawrence Kaplan was entirely correct. Mr. Hamilton doubted the ability of a loose confederation of states—often bickering with each other—would be able to acquire the sufficient political and economic strength needed for the nation as a whole. America needed to be able to defend itself in a world of emerging nation-states, one of which, Revolutionary France, was aggressively pursuing an ideological cause that Mr. Hamilton regarded as dangerous to freedom, civilization and religion in America.

In the great American statesman's view, the United States was to be a new nation, one that was to serve normative ends higher than the nation itself. Mr. Hamilton sketched out the purposes of the proposed national Constitution. He wrote in the first of *The Federalist Papers*:

> It is to preserve the purposes of the proposed national Constitution and the true principles of the republican government and to provide additional security...to the preservation of that species of government, to liberty, and to property.

Republicanism, liberty and property, of course, was the language of the late eighteenth-century Enlightenment that bound together individuals of all nations. This language is connected to what George Washington called "a growing liberality of sentiment," that he thought transcended national boundaries.[371] Mr. Hamilton hoped that the new America would embody these values and act as an example to other nations. It would be an effort to show others what humanity is capable of.

The great American statesman wanted the United States to be a great nation, a nation to be distinct from other nations, a nation able to manage its domestic and international affairs. Hamilton wanted

America to be on equal footing with powerful, modernizing countries like France and Great Britain. But unlike Mr. Jefferson, Mr. Hamilton did not believe that America's greatness depended on whether it did, or did not, follow the popular sentiment of the people. In fact, Mr. Hamilton believed that America's greatness would require making political choices that may contradict the will of the people.

This aspect of Mr. Hamilton's Nationalism does not sit well with Americans on the Left of the contemporary American political environment. On the Right, those who consider themselves now to be Nationalists would also be surprised to find out what Mr. Hamilton really believed about the rule by the majority.

Nearly all scholars agree that Alexander Hamilton's economic policies are among the great American statesman's most important accomplishments. He put the new government on a firm financial foundation. He successfully pushed the federal government to fund the national debt and to assume the war debts of the states. He advocated tariffs to bolster the manufacturing sector, and he convinced President George Washington to back the statesman's idea of a national bank. All of these ideas were part of Alexander Hamilton's overall goal of making the United States a nation as formidable as Great Britain or France.

At the close of Essay 11 of *The Federalist Papers*, Alexander Hamilton wrote this:

> Let the thirteen States, bound together in a strict and indissoluble Union, should concur in erecting one great American system, superior to the control of all transatlantic force or influence, and able to dictate the terms of the connection between the old and the new world.

Essay 11 was published on November 23, 1787. In addition to his claim to the superiority of the American system over other "transatlantic forces," an obvious Nationalistic claim, Mr. Hamilton also speaks about developing a superior navy in Essay 11. About the navy, and the consequences of not having one, the great American statesman told us:

> A nation, despicable by its weakness, forfeits even the privilege of being neutral. The utilization

of the Navy would allow protection from foreign countries' demands that would otherwise ruin the country's commerce.

In *The Federalist Papers* Essay 11, Alexander Hamilton also portrays Europeans—particularly the French and British—as arrogantly subjecting the peoples of Asia, Africa and America, to dominion and economic exploitation. He also draws on what he calls "American exceptionalism," and he calls on his fellow citizens to "vindicate the honor of the human race" by standing up to European predation.

Mr. Hamilton concludes Essay 11 by warning that, were Americans to become disunited, they would become just another victim of European imperialism. It should be clear that Alexander Hamilton was expressing aspects of eighteenth-century Nationalism in Essay 11, as he had done in Essay 1, we mentioned earlier. Historian Craig L. Symonds believes that in these two essays of *The Federalist Papers*, the great American statesman Alexander Hamilton was:

> Looking for all the accoutrements of world power, a vital domestic industry, a healthy world trade and, to protect that trade and the national integrity, a great naval fleet.[372]

It should be clear that from Mr. Hamilton's references to American superiority and American exceptionalism that great American statesman Alexander Hamilton should be considered as a believer in American Nationalism. We should answer the question raised at the beginning of this section of Chapter Nine decidedly in the affirmative.

Mr. Hamilton would not be happy, we think, with the contemporary American Left's view that America is rotten to the core, items number three of their beliefs mentioned earlier. It is clear that millennials are notably less attached to the symbols of the American nation—and less drawn to patriotic pride—than their elders. Alexander Hamilton would have viewed this as a desecration of what he had created.

This brings us to the conclusions of Chapter Nine. The major function of Chapter Ten, the final chapter, is to give a summary of the major conclusions we have made in this study on Alexander Hamilton's religion.

Conclusions to Chapter Nine

In this chapter of great American statesman Alexander Hamilton's religion, we began by making some general observations about the nature and history of the idea of Nationalism. After defining the concept of Nationalism, we moved next to a modern history of the idea from the French Revolution and Nationalism in nineteenth-century Germany to the question of when in America colonists stopped identifying themselves as British subjects and started thinking of themselves as "Americans."

By utilizing the scholarly work of Alexander Ziegler, who did a study of South Carolina newspaper articles from 1750 until 1800, Ziegler identifies the year 1775 as the tipping point, the same year that the American Revolution began.[373]

In the second section of Chapter Nine, we examined the idea of Nationalism in America from 1755 until 1800 and concentrated on the Federalists Party, the first party in American politics. We also identified Alexander Hamilton as one of the most important figures in the Federalist Party and that Thomas Jefferson was the main opposition of that party.

We also introduced a collection of core ideas that all the Founding Fathers seemed to have had in common—ideas to be found in the Founding documents of the United States in the eighteenth century. Many of these ideas, we have shown, are to be found in the first and other amendments of the US Constitution.

In the third section of Chapter Nine, we introduced the idea of Civil Religion, a view that says that a nation is bound by certain fundamental beliefs, values, holidays and rituals that constitutes a way of understanding what a nation, as well as what patriotism and Nationalism are. In this section, we also introduced the scholarship of Robert Bellah and his 1967 essay entitled "Civil Religion in America."[374]

We also employed the scholarship of sociologist Anthony Squiers who sketched out fourteen different beliefs that he maintains are the core beliefs of the American Civil Religion.[375]

Next, we introduced several comments that Alexander Hamilton wrote in Essay 11 of *The Federalist Papers*, and from these comments, we added two more beliefs to Dr. Squiers, for a total now of sixteen beliefs.

At the very end of the third section of Chapter Nine, we introduced a collection of six ideas that the American baby boomer generation grew up believing, ideas that had a nature thought to be sacrosanct. We called this collection of ideas "Supplemental Beliefs" of the American Civil Religion, beliefs that could not be questioned in the 1950s to 1970s.

In the fourth section of Chapter Nine, we began a discussion of President Donald Trump's version of Nationalism and his idea of "America First," from his inaugural address in January of 2017 until the final day of his presidency. In that section, we introduced a collection of five fundamental beliefs now held by the American Left.

We also suggested in the same section of Chapter Nine that Mr. Trump and his followers' responses to black athletes who refuse to stand for the national anthem, schools that do not begin with the Pledge of Allegiance, and that the idea that America is rotten to its core, all are beliefs that break the belief system that baby boomers were taught as children.

In the fifth and final section of Chapter Nine, we raised the question of whether great American statesman Alexander Hamilton was a Nationalist. By utilizing the scholarship of Lawrence S. Kaplan and his book, *Alexander Hamilton: Ambivalent Anglophile*, we answered our query in the affirmative.[376]

In the final section of Chapter Nine, we used *The Federalist Papers* Essays 1 and 11 as further evidence that Alexander Hamilton was, indeed, an American Nationalist. We also indicated that it is unlikely that either the contemporary Left or Right in American politics would either be political points of view about which Alexander Hamilton would be happy.

We have also shown in the final section of Chapter Nine that the two American generations that followed the baby boomers have decidedly different views than their elders about what American Nationalism is and is not. Indeed, in that discussion, we introduced the one-question survey I conducted with the 1,632 undergraduate students of whom I asked, "What is more important, diversity or freedom?" and my findings that only 549 of those undergraduate responses answered "Freedom."

This brings us to Chapter Ten, the final chapter of this study of great American statesman Alexander Hamilton's religion. Chapter Ten is a summation in which we will catalog the major conclusions made in the other nine chapters of this study.

Chapter Ten
Major Conclusions of this Study

Introduction

The main purpose of this chapter is to give a summary or a catalog of the major conclusions made in this study. We will, therefore, divide Chapter Ten into nine sections, each describing the conclusions made in each of the previous nine chapters.

Conclusions of Chapter One

The initial chapter of this study was divided into three main sections. The first of those was to provide a short survey of the life of Alexander Hamilton. Indeed, in that section, we divided the life of the great statesman into nine parts, including his birth and childhood in the Caribbean, his early education, his career in the army, his work on the Constitution and *The Federalist Papers*, Hamilton's service as the treasury secretary, his post-secretary years, his duel with Vice-President Burr, and Alexander Hamilton's death and influence.

The second goal of Chapter One has been an exploration and analysis of eight poems written in Mr. Hamilton's youth that contain many religious themes. After describing and quoting these poems, we suggested four conclusions that can be made about Mr. Hamilton's early poetic efforts.

1. That Hamilton, even early on, was a firm believer in God.
2. His early theological views were influenced by the Rev. Hugh Knox and his home library.

3. Alexander Hamilton was a firm believer in the soul and its survival after death.

4. His early poetry suggested belief in a whole host of Christian theological ideas, including the possibility of a beatific vision; that one ought to sing the praises of the Lord; that Hamilton assented to the Retributive Justice model in regard to the issues of evil and suffering, as well as the Test and Moral Qualities Perspectives.

The third goal of Chapter One was to catalog many of the ways in which Mr. Hamilton's early education was instrumental in the statesman's religious life. More specifically, we pointed to three different school experiences that contributed to Alexander Hamilton's early religious life. These were the Hebrew grammar school he attended on the island of Nevis, where he learned to read the Ten Commandments in the original Hebrew. And, his study for two terms at the Elizabethtown Academy, where he also made lifelong friendships with the Livingston and Boudinot families.[377]

Finally, we indicated in Chapter One that, although he did not graduate, his time at King's College was filled with religious services, events and prayer that surely went into the making of the earliest religious life of the great American statesman Alexander Hamilton.

Conclusions of Chapter Two

In the introduction to Chapter Two on Alexander Hamilton regarding Christianity, we suggested the chapter would unfold in four main sections. In the first of those, we explored what roles Christianity appears to have played at the end of Alexander Hamilton's life, including the statesman's overall wish to receive the sacrament of Holy Communion at the end of his life and Dr. Mason and Bishop Moore's initial responses against doing so. However, we indicated that Rev. Moore relented the following day and administered the sacrament shortly before the statesman's death.

In the first section of Chapter Two, we spoke about the accounts from Rev. Mason and Rev. Moore about the conversations the two had with Alexander Hamilton on his deathbed. Indeed, from those conversations, we showed that Mr. Hamilton expressed belief in the existence and attributes of God, belief in the soul and immortality, and belief in the saving grace of the death and resurrection of Jesus Christ.

In the second section of Chapter Two, we turned our attention to several general comments that Alexander Hamilton made about God. We indicated that Mr. Hamilton made four separate kinds of general observations regarding the Divine, which were summarized this way:

1. Very general comments like those of other Founding Fathers.
2. God and the Constitution.
3. God and American politics.
4. The value of Christian faith.

We then offered examples of each of these four types about commenting on God such as he (Hamilton) avoided the use of the word "God" in favor of more Enlightenment names for the Divine such as "Nature's God" and "the Hand of the Divine," for example.[378]

We also indicated that Alexander Hamilton was against the idea of including any language about God in the US Constitution, as well as in the other Founding documents of the United States. Mr. Hamilton's views on established religion and religious "tests" in America were other topics covered in section two of Chapter Two, where we said that the statesman was decidedly against both practices.

Regarding the value of the Christian religion for American politics, we made three conclusions about Mr. Hamilton's perspectives. First, that Hamilton believed Christianity was the finest religion ever devised by man. Second, the great American statesman believed this could be empirically verified. And finally, Hamilton thought the division of Christianity into sects is often more harmful to society because he believed, as Thomas Jefferson did, that those sects had obscured the original, natural religion of Jesus.

We devoted the third section of Chapter Two to what Alexander Hamilton believed and wrote about the person of Jesus of Nazareth.

To glean what these views were, we relied on the conversations with Mr. Hamilton and the Reverends Mason and Moore at the end of the statesman's life, several essays of Mr. Hamilton's in *The Federalist Papers*, as well as other material such as the final letter to his wife, Eliza, written a week before his death.

In the fourth section of Chapter Two, we turned our attention to an idea of Alexander Hamilton's and his friend James A. Bayard to establish something the pair called a "Christian Constitutional Society," an organization to be devoted to the establishment of Christian clubs, societies and activities all dedicated to the establishment of good "Christian living in America."[379]

We also related in section four of Chapter Two that one of Mr. Hamilton's greatest worries was the blatant atheism of many of the proponents of the French Revolution, as well as the time that Mr. Jefferson had spent in Paris as ambassador to France and Hamilton's fear that the third president had become too enamored of the French philosophers.

Conclusions of Chapter Three

Chapter Three of this study on Alexander Hamilton's religion was organized into four parts. In the first of these, we related some very general comments in which the statesman spoke of the Holy Scriptures. The second section of the chapter was devoted to Mr. Hamilton's uses and quotations of the Old Testament and the third on New Testament passages. Finally, the fourth section of Chapter Three identified and discussed several places in *The Federalist Papers* where Mr. Hamilton made particular references to God, ethics and to the Bible.

Concerning Mr. Hamilton's general comments about the Bible, it was likely that the statesman heard many of the Rev. Knox Presbyterian sermons on the island of St. Croix, and he studied many books from the minister's library devoted to the Bible. We know that the great American statesman also studied the Bible at the Hebrew School his mother had sent him to on Nevis, at the Elizabethtown Academy in New Jersey and at King's College in New York.

We also indicated several experiences in Mr. Hamilton's life when the Bible became a central concern of the great American statesman's life, including his mentorship by Elias Boudinot, the first president of the American Bible Society.[380]

The period after the death of Alexander Hamilton's son, Philip in 1801, until his death in 1804, the statesman became considerably more religious by all outward appearances. He attended church with his children, "making a sign of the cross and praying" and pointing out, "This has never happened before."[381]

In the second section of Chapter Three, we turned our attention to Mr. Hamilton's uses and quotations from the Old Testament. In that section, we indicated that the statesman quoted directly from, or made references to, passages in Micah, Zechariah, First Kings, Isaiah, Deuteronomy, Proverbs, Psalms and the Book of Job, one of Mr. Hamilton's favorites because of its discussion of innocent suffering and its beliefs in the immortality of the soul and resurrection of the body.

Favorite New Testament passages of Mr. Hamilton's was the focus of the third section of Chapter Three. In that section, we pointed to nine separate passages in the New Testament about which Mr. Hamilton was fond of or from which he quoted directly. These included two portions of the Gospels, four selections from the letters of Paul, and three passages from First and Second Peter. We also observed that Mr. Hamilton was so interested in these New Testament passages because they emphasize Moral Virtues.

We also indicated that, like some of the other Founding Fathers such as Thomas Jefferson, for example, Mr. Hamilton saw little value in certain parts of the New Testament and at the top of the list of those passages is the final book of the New Testament, the Book of Revelation.

In Chapter Three's fourth and final section, we turned our attention to several places in *The Federalist Papers* where Mr. Hamilton wrote about God, ethics and religion. As we have shown, these references can be found in the *Papers'* Essays 1, 20, 31, 37, 43, 44, 51, 56 and 57.

We also indicated that Mr. Hamilton believed the judicial branch, the court system and the Supreme Court, were the weakest part of the federal government, arguing that if Supreme Court justices are to have lifetime appointments, then there also should be some provisions in place that those justices be of the "highest of moral character."

Conclusions of Chapter Four

The fourth chapter of this study on Alexander Hamilton's religion was devoted to what the statesman thought, said and wrote about three religions other than his own. That is, Judaism, Catholicism and Islam. To that end, the chapter was divided into three sections, one each on the three faiths.

We began the first section of Chapter Four with a short review of what we already know about Mr. Hamilton and Judaism: that he went to Hebrew School as a child where he learned to read the Ten Commandments in the original classical Hebrew language, and that there was an extensive Jewish population on the island of Nevis during Mr. Hamilton's childhood.

We continued Chapter Four by discussing five other incidents in the life of Alexander Hamilton where the statesman had some contact with Jews or with Judaism. These were Mr. Hamilton's friendship with Rabbi Seixas,[382] Hamilton's many responses to anti-Semitism in his life, an article published in the *New York Daily Advertiser* about the Jews to which Mr. Hamilton responded, George Washington's treatment of the Jews and influence on Mr. Hamilton, and the accusation that Alexander Hamilton was a Jew.

In each of these five instances where Mr. Hamilton had contact with Judaism, we gave a lengthy analysis. In regard to Rabbi Seixas, we have shown that Mr. Hamilton was influential in getting the rabbi a place on the Board of Regents of Columbia University and that Hamilton was also responsible for the rabbi being invited to the inauguration of George Washington.[383]

We also indicated that the great American statesman gave a scathing denunciation of anti-Semitism in his closing remarks before the New York State Supreme Court, and that Mr. Hamilton had the sneaking suspicion that his clients, who were being sued before the court, was more because of their Jewishness than the legal merits of the case.

We have shown that when the city of New York planned a celebration that fell on a Jewish holiday, Mr. Hamilton was instrumental in getting the city to change the date so the Jewish community could participate in the events.[384]

We also introduced the scholarship of Andrew Porwancher at the University of Oklahoma and his thesis that Alexander Hamilton was, in fact, Jewish. After summarizing Dr. Porwancher's arguments, we concluded that the jury is still out on the matter.[385]

In the second section of Chapter Four, we began by suggesting that eight different pieces of information went into the making of Alexander Hamilton's views on Roman Catholicism. From these eight pieces of information, we concluded that Mr. Hamilton had ambiguous and ambivalent views on the Catholic Church.

On the one hand, Hamilton had many Catholic friends and stood up for Catholic religious liberty when the proper time came to do so. But, on the other hand, he was staunchly against the Quebec Act, mainly because the French Canadians were Roman Catholic. We also indicated that some of the reasons for being against the Quebec Act might have been his mother Rachel's anti-Catholic Huguenot faith and his father's Presbyterianism, as well as the strong anti-Catholic sentiments in the Constitutions of ten of the thirteen colonies.

In the third and final section of Chapter Four, we introduced and discussed several occasions and ways where Moslems and the Islamic faith can be seen in the life of the great American statesman. As we have indicated, among these occasions and ways were the other Founding Fathers commenting about Islam. Indeed, we pointed out that in addition to Mr. Hamilton, his mentor, George Washington, as well as John Adams, Thomas Jefferson, Richard Henry Lee, Yale President Ezra Stiles, and many other figures in the late colonial period in America said or wrote many positive things about Muslims, Al-Qur'an, the Muslim Holy Book, and the Islamic faith.

We have also shown in the third section that, at the Continental Congress in the summer of 1787, amid a discussion of whether "Mohametans and atheists were Americans," Alexander Hamilton argued forcefully in the affirmative in answering that query. In the same way that the great American statesman responded forcefully to anti-Semitism and anti-Catholic sentiments, he did precisely the same thing in his defense that Muslims and atheists could, in fact, also be Americans.

In the third section of Chapter Four, we examined the uses that Alexander Hamilton may have made of the Turkish Ottoman Empire practices for collecting taxes in their empire, which later became important for establishing the Internal Revenue Service in America.

We also observed that, at the end of Chapter Four, during the crisis known as the Barbary Wars when North African pirates confiscated American merchant ships, detained their crews and then demanded payment of tribute for their release, there were many responses in the Jefferson Administration about how to respond to the pirates.[386]

Mr. Hamilton's response was totally different from the others. As we indicated, he pointed out that the Barbary Wars showed the need for the United States to have a larger and more powerful navy. And it turns out he was entirely correct about that pronouncement.

Conclusions of Chapter Five

In the introduction to Chapter Five, we stated that this chapter would consist of four parts. These parts were the sources for Alexander Hamilton's views on ethics; a second section on Hamilton's actual references of ethics and morality; third, what the American statesman said about ethics in *The Federalist Papers*; and the final section on Mr. Hamilton's affair with Mrs. Maria Reynolds and an analysis of the moral actors in the affair.

In the initial section of Chapter Five, we suggested that the principal sources for Alexander Hamilton's views on ethics were the moral teachings of Jesus; Greco-Roman materials such as Cicero, Virgil, Julius Caesar; and philosopher Aristotle's *Nicomachean Ethics*. We also suggested that the Greek philosopher's Virtue Ethics was one that Mr. Hamilton found very attractive.

We indicated that several modern European philosophers and literary artists were also employed by Alexander Hamilton to construct his theory of ethics. Among these philosophers were Thomas Hobbes, John Locke, Edmund Burke, the Baron Montesquieu, and especially Scottish philosopher David Hume.

Among the literary figures that Alexander Hamilton found helpful in cobbling together his views on ethics were Michel Montaigne's *Essays*, the dramas of Moliere, and Joseph Addison's play *Cato: A Tragedy*.[387]

In the second section of this fifth chapter on Alexander Hamilton and ethics, we introduced and discussed thirteen separate passages of the great American statesman where he specifically speaks or wrote about morality and Moral Responsibility. Indeed, at the end of our analysis of this material, we introduced the work of contemporary scholar Dr. Kate Elizabeth Brown, who, among other things, shows how reliant Alexander Hamilton was when it came to the application of Aristotle's understanding of Moral Responsibility.[388]

In the third section of Chapter Five, we analyzed and discussed ten pieces of moral advice that Alexander Hamilton frequently gave to young people, including his own children, as we have shown. These ten pieces of advice were about genius, procrastination, debt, looking smart, spending time with one's family, embracing adversity, keeping one's promises, and forgiving one's enemies, which, in Mr. Hamilton's case, included his forgiveness of Vice-President Aaron Burr on his deathbed.

In the second section of Chapter Five, we indicated that each of these ten pieces of moral advice often had profound moral attributes, as well as moral implications to be found in them.

"Hamilton, Ethics, and *The Federalist Papers*" was the subject matter of the third section of Chapter Five. This section used an essay by former US Attorney General Edwin Meese III, who listed ten separate political and moral categories that Mr. Meese found in *The Federalist Papers*.[389]

In his analysis, we have shown that several of the items on Mr. Meese's list are addressed specifically in several of Hamilton's essays of *The Federalist Papers*. Among those essays of Hamilton's were the *Papers* numbered 31 to 35, 68 and 84, the next to the final essay of the *Papers*.

In the fourth and final section of Chapter Five on Alexander Hamilton's ethics, we discussed the moral nature and character of the persons involved in the great American statesman's affair with Mrs. Maria Reynolds in the summer of 1791 until June of 1792. In our analysis of the actors involved, we made four major conclusions about the tryst.

First, that the great American statesman was fully and morally responsible for his behavior in the affair. Secondly, we concluded that Maria Reynold's husband, James Reynolds, was also fully responsible for his untoward behavior. Thirdly, we concluded that Alexander Hamilton's behavior in the affair with Maria Reynolds was decidedly out of character when it came to the statesman's normal moral behavior throughout the rest of his life. Fourthly, Eliza Hamilton forgave her husband but certainly need not have done so. Her motivation was not entirely clear. But she outlived her husband for half a century, and in that time, she spoke no ill will of her brilliant and clever husband.

We have also shown that, in his *Reynolds Pamphlet*, the great American statesman said the entire affair might have been a "set-up" constructed by the Reynolds couple and Maria's second husband, Jacob Clingman. And given the reports of the criminal moral characters of both men related to Maria, it seems that Mr. Hamilton may have been correct about the origins of the affair.

At the very end of Chapter Five, we suggested that the forgiving action of Eliza Hamilton toward her husband's affair with Mrs. Reynolds can only be explained by what both Eliza and her husband, Alexander, could only explain as an act of Divine Grace.

Conclusions of Chapter Six

We began Chapter Six of this study on religious freedom and religious toleration in the life and works of Alexander Hamilton by suggesting that the chapter would unfold in three principal sections. The first of these was devoted to sixteen separate examples of Mr. Hamilton's where he spoke or wrote in very general terms of the phenomenon of religious liberty. Among the Hamilton texts from which we gleaned these observations were *The Farmer Refuted*, "A Full Vindication of the Measures of Congress," as well as several other tracts in his *Collected Papers*.[390]

In most of these observations about religious liberty, Mr. Hamilton either endorsed the Founding documents regarding religious liberty, or were short, pithy statements about the relations of religious liberty to civil liberty.

The second section of Chapter Six was taken up with an exploration on a dozen or so comments by Mr. Hamilton made about religious liberty made in *The Federalist Papers*. Again, as we have seen, most of these are about the relation of religious liberty to civil liberty in the United States.

The idea of religious toleration in the life and work of Alexander Hamilton was the subject matter of section three of Chapter Six. We began by providing a catalog of sorts on the sources of the great American statesman's views on the matter of religious toleration. Among those sources were philosopher Pierre Bayle; Voltaire's *Treatise on Toleration*; John Locke's 1689 *An Essay on Toleration*; comments made by Mr. Hamilton on toleration at the 1787 Constitutional Convention; the state constitutions of Pennsylvania, Massachusetts, Virginia and Delaware; as well as George Washington's influence on Mr. Hamilton's perspectives on religious toleration, both as a general and as a president.[391]

Indeed, we indicated in the fourth section of Chapter Six that the best places to look for Alexander Hamilton's views on religious toleration were the comments on other religions introduced in Chapter Four, particularly Judaism, Catholicism and Islam.

We also stated that when Washington and Hamilton were at the Constitutional Convention in the summer of 1787, on Sundays, the general and a few colleagues began attending houses of worship in Philadelphia principally to show their support of ecumenism. This included services at a Catholic mass, a Presbyterian church, and a Friends Meeting House in Philadelphia.

We also pointed out that there was no word in American English in the late eighteenth century to explain religious toleration, so the Founding Fathers adapted the French *Tolerantisme* to express the idea in the United States during that time.

We indicated that it was not until Article 1, Section 1, of the state of Florida's 1838 Constitution was built into one of the state's compacts. It was also the state of Florida, on May 19, 1947, that the Miami Beach City Council unanimously approved the one-page "Ordinance on Discrimination" that outlawed anti-Semitic signs for housing in the city.

Conclusions of Chapter Seven

The chief function of Chapter Seven of this study on Alexander Hamilton's religion is what he said, did and wrote about the idea of prayer. The chapter was divided into three sections. In the first of these parts, we introduced and discussed what a number of the other

Founding Fathers, besides Alexander Hamilton, had to say about the phenomenon of prayer.

In the first section of Chapter Seven, we introduced proclamations calling for days of prayer and thanksgiving from George Washington, John Adams, Thomas Jefferson, James Monroe and James Madison. We also indicated that only President James Madison had misgivings about doing so in a text of his called the "Detached Memorandum" from January 31, 1820.

In the second section of Chapter Seven, we explored the phenomenon of prayer as it appeared in the early life of Alexander Hamilton up to the time of entering the army in 1775, at either the age of eighteen or twenty. In that second section, we pointed to several possible influences that may or may not had influenced the young Mr. Hamilton on prayer. Among these sources include his attendance at Hebrew School on the island of Nevis; the theological influences from Presbyterian minister, the Rev. Hugh Knox; comments about Hamilton praying in college from his roommate Robert Troup; and the possible influences from Hamilton's friend Hercules Mulligan with whose family Mr. Hamilton stayed when he lived in New York and attended King's College.

In the third section of Chapter Seven, we analyzed and discussed the roles that prayer played in the life of Alexander Hamilton from the time he left the army in 1782 until his death on July 12, 1804. We related that most of the observations about Mr. Hamilton and prayer came from the statesman's son and biographer, John Church Hamilton. In fact, it is from the younger Mr. Hamilton that we garnered that the elder Hamilton sons took turns before breakfast leading the family in a Bible reading and a prayer connected to the reading.[392]

We also indicated that after the death of Mr. Hamilton's eldest son, Philip, in a duel in 1801, Alexander Hamilton returned to attending church in the final three years of his life. We also indicated from John Church Hamilton that his father had a habit of leading the family in prayer in the garden on Sunday afternoons after church at their home they called The Grange.[393]

We have shown in Chapter Seven that both Dr. Mason and Bishop Moore prayed with Mr. Hamilton in the final two days of his life, although the two ministers disagreed about what were the great American statesman's final words.

We also spoke of the prayerful hymn Mr. Hamilton wrote to his wife, Eliza, if he did not survive the duel with Vice-President Burr. In that final missive to his wife on July 4, 1804, Mr. Hamilton spoke of "redeeming grace and Divine mercy" that may lead to a "happy immortality." And that he desired his wife "return to the bosom of Abraham" in the "hope of meeting you in a better world."

Thus, the great American statesman Alexander Hamilton appears to have remained faithful and prayerful to the end. There is no record, however, about when Mrs. Hamilton opened the letter from her husband, nor what her reactions or responses were when she did so.

Conclusions of Chapter Eight

Chapter Eight of this study on Alexander Hamilton's religion, which is on the great American statesman's views on slavery, was divided into four sections. In the first of these, we outlined what we called the "traditional, scholarly view on Hamilton and slavery." This perspective is that, in general, Alexander Hamilton had a benign and abolitionist view of human captivity for most of his life.

We presented this traditional scholarly view by relying on the works of writers such as John C. Miller, Forest McDonald, Ron Chernow, Richard Brookhiser, Broadus Mitchell, Henry Cabot Lodge, James Oliver, as well as many other writers and scholars, in our description of Alexander Hamilton's traditional view on slavery.[394]

We dedicated the second section of this chapter to an analysis of what we know of the practice of slavery on the Caribbean islands of Nevis, St. Kitts and St. Croix, where Mr. Hamilton spent his earliest years. In that section, we made some very general observations about buying, selling and keeping slaves on the three islands in the late eighteenth century.

We evaluated a long-held belief by those who hold the traditional view of Hamilton on slavery that, as a small child, he learned to hate the institution of slavery. As indicated, however, there is no empirical evidence that this perspective is true. We have, however, pointed out in section two that slave revolts and slave insurrections frequently occurred in the Caribbean, and Mr. Hamilton may have heard tales about some of these rebellions, for example, a very large one took place on the island of Nevis a generation before his birth in either 1755 or 1757.[395]

In the third section of Chapter Eight, we presented a description of and then evaluated a new theory on Alexander Hamilton and slavery, which is at odds with the traditional perspective from section one of this chapter. Jessie Serfilippi developed this new theory in a study she published called "As Odious and Immoral a Thing: Alexander Hamilton's Hidden History as an Enslaver." Indeed, we have shown that Ms. Serfilippi has claimed that Alexander Hamilton was both a slave owner and a slave dealer.

After sketching out the evidence she puts forward for her thesis, we also pointed out that Harvard scholar Annette Gordon-Reed is in full agreement with the Serfilippi thesis, as evidence by an interview she did with the *Harvard Gazette* from October 7, 2016. In fact, in that interview, Dr. Gordon-Reed said of Alexander Hamilton, "He was not an abolitionist. He bought and sold slaves for his in-laws, and opposing slavery was never at the forefront of his agenda."

At the close of section three of Chapter Eight, we supplied a tentative response to the Serfilippi/Gordon-Reed thesis in which we suggested, as others like Ron Chernow have done, that neither scholar placed their evidence in the context of a larger understanding of Hamilton on slavery that includes lots of evidence that will support the traditional view that Mr. Hamilton was an abolitionist.

Among those pieces of evidence, we pointed out that the 1800 US census said nothing of slaves living at the Hamilton residence, but it does indicate four black "servants" living there. Mr. Hamilton's work for the New York Manumission Society and his support of John Laurens plans to raise black companies of soldiers from South Carolina and Georgia, whom, after their service, would be, in Mr. Hamilton's words, "Free with muskets."[396]

Another criticism we made of the Serfilippi/Gordon-Reed thesis is that there is nothing in the essay, nor in the *Harvard Gazette* interview, that discusses Alexander Hamilton's comments on slavery he wrote in *The Federalist Papers*. In fact, as we have shown, Mr. Hamilton's overarching fear about America was that slavery would be responsible for the keeping of what the great American statesman called "Unity" in America.[397]

Indeed, we have shown that in *The Federalist Papers* numbers 6, 7, 8, 11 and 12, Mr. Hamilton expressed the view that what will keep American from retaining its unity would be the issue of slavery. And the statesman's concerns about that fact were some of the earliest presages of what will come to pass later in the century from 1861 to 1865, the American Civil War.

Surely, for Mr. Hamilton the specter of slavery was forever in the background of the issue of unity. He feared we would become "Two Americas," and he was entirely correct about that judgment in a lot of ways.[398]

We have shown in section four of Chapter Eight that James Madison, another author of some of *The Federalist Papers*, also wrote about the phenomenon of slavery in Essays 38, 42, 49 and 54, in which Mr. Madison related that "Slaves are property as well as people."

The bottom-line conclusion made in Chapter Eight is that we see no good reason for not believing or promoting the traditional scholarly view of Alexander Hamilton on slavery that we described in the first section of Chapter Eight of the study on Alexander Hamilton's religion. That is, Alexander Hamilton was a stalwart abolitionist when it came to his views on slavery.

Mr. Hamilton held a more progressive view on slavery than most of the other Founding Fathers concerning the equality of race. In 1774, he published his first major political essay, "A Full Vindication of the Measures of Congress," where he drew a direct comparison between American slaves and the yoke that held American colonists being oppressed by the British.[399] In the essay, the great American statesman asserted that both varieties of "enslavement" were immoral by their very natures.

When defending Mr. Laurens plan to recruit black companies into the Continental Army, Mr. Hamilton wrote the following to the Continental Congress:

> I have not the least doubt that the negroes
> will make very excellent soldiers, with proper

> management. Their natural faculties are probably
> as good as ours.

Mr. Hamilton's lobbying for Mr. Laurens' plan failed to win the support that was needed, and the South Carolinian's plan was soon abandoned. Interestingly enough, however, George Washington was against the plan from the very beginning.

In the same 1774 essay, Alexander Hamilton clearly stated his bottom-line view on race and slavery when he wrote,

> All men have one common origin. They par-
> ticipate in one common nature and consequently
> have one common right.

Conclusions of Chapter Nine

In the ninth chapter of this study of great American statesman Alexander Hamilton's religion, we began by making some general observations about the nature and history of the idea of Nationalism. After defining the concept of Nationalism, we moved our attention to a modern history of the idea of Nationalism from the French Revolution and Nationalism to nineteenth-century Germany. And then to the question of when American colonists stopped identifying themselves as British subjects and began to think of themselves as Americans. By utilizing the scholarly work of Alexander Ziegler, who did a study of South Carolina newspaper articles from 1750 to 1800, Mr. Ziegler identified the year 1775 as the "tipping point," the same year that the American Revolutionary War began.[400]

In the second section of Chapter Nine, we examined the idea of Nationalism in the American context from 1755 until 1800, and we concentrated our efforts on the Federalist Party, the first party in American politics. We also identified Mr. Hamilton as one of the leading figures of that party.[401]

We also identified a collection of core ideas that all of the Founders seemed to have had in common—ideas to be found in the Founding documents of the United States in the late eighteenth century. As we have shown, many of these ideas are to be found in the first and other amendments of the US Constitution.

In the third section of Chapter Nine, we introduced the idea of Civil Religion, a view that says a nation is bound up by certain fundamental beliefs, values, holidays and rituals that constitute a way of understanding what a nation is, as well as what patriotism and Nationalism are.

In this section, we introduced the scholarship of Sociologist Robert Bellah and his 1967 essay entitled "Civil Religion in America."[402] We also employed the work of Sociologist Anthony Squiers, who sketched out fourteen different beliefs that he thought are the core tenets of the American Civil Religion.[403]

Next, we introduced several comments Alexander Hamilton wrote in Essay 11 of *The Federalist Papers*, and from these comments, we added two more beliefs to Dr. Squire's list, for a total now of sixteen beliefs.[404]

At the very end of the third section of Chapter Nine, we introduced a collection of six ideas that American baby boomers were taught in American schools in the 1850s and 1960s. We called this collection the "Supplemental Beliefs" of the American Civil Religion, beliefs that could not be questioned during that time.[405]

In the fourth section of Chapter Nine, we began a discussion about one of those American baby boomers, President Donald J. Trump, and his version of American Nationalism, as well as his idea "America First," from his inauguration address in January of 2017 until the final days of his presidency.[406]

In that section, we introduced a collection of five fundamental beliefs currently held by the American Left that constitute their view of what counts as the core American beliefs, a set of beliefs in stark contrast to the perspectives of Robert Bellah and Anthony Squiers.

We also suggested in the same section of Chapter Nine that the responses of Mr. Trump and his followers to black athletes refusing to stand for the national anthem, schools that do not begin the day with the Pledge of Allegiance, and the idea that America is rotten to the core, are all beliefs that break the belief system that the baby boomer generation was taught as children.

On July 5, 2020, President Trump delivered an address at the annual Salute to America celebration in Washington, DC, in which he said that "The United States is the greatest, most exceptional, and most virtuous nation in the history of the world." In those words, he was going back to the set of beliefs that American schoolchildren learned when he was a grammar school student. And one of those beliefs was that the United States is the greatest nation on earth—a postulate of the modern American version of American Nationalism.

The last task of Chapter Nine was to ask the question of whether great American statesman Alexander Hamilton should be considered to have been a Nationalist. Indeed, in the fifth and final section of the chapter, we again used *The Federalist Papers* Essays 1 and 11 to establish an affirmative answer to our query.

We indicated that it is unlikely that the contemporary American Left or Right in American politics would either be political points of view with which Alexander Hamilton would be comfortable. Despite this fact, conservatives like Senator Marco Rubio invoke Alexander Hamilton's economic policies often. At the same time, Liberals such as scholar Jonathan Dan Hartog, in works like his essay, "Religion, the Federalists, and American Nationalism," also argue for Mr. Hamilton's economic policies and banking principles in putting forth his Leftist agenda.[407]

In the final section of Chapter Nine, we have shown that the two American generations that followed the baby-boomers, have decidedly different views than their elders about what American Nationalism is and is not. Indeed, in that discussion, we introduced a one-question survey conducted with 1,632 American undergraduate students, of whom we asked, "What is more important in American Society, diversity or freedom?" In the results of that survey, we pointed out that only 549 of the 1,632 students surveyed answered the query as "freedom." The other 1,183 undergraduates answered "diversity."

Many conclusions may be drawn from the results of the survey of undergraduates, but one conclusion seems to be undeniable—that in the time of one generation in America, or perhaps in two generations—the United States has gone from one set of core beliefs among the baby boomer generation to an entirely different set of core beliefs.

Perhaps another conclusion that can be made about the findings of the one-question survey is that the American culture that is still in the process of that transformation and transition from one world view to another, the resulting squabbles between the American Right and American Left, have begun to look more and more like a second Civil War in the United States.

Appendix
Foreign Words and Phrases

Over the course of this study of Hamilton's religion, we made reference to the following foreign words and phrases in the following languages: classical Hebrew, classical Arabic, Latin, and Modern French.

Ahl al-Kitab - "People of the Book" (Arabic)
Am Ha-Sefer - "People of the Book" (Hebrew)
Coda Duello - "The Code of Dueling" (Latin)
De Officiis - "On Obligation" (Latin)
Dictionaire de France - "The Dictionary of France" (French)
Essais - "Essay" (French)
Lettres philosophique - "philosophical letters" (French)
Musa - Islamic name for "Moses" (Arabic)
Al-Qur'an - The Holy Book of Islam (Arabic)
Tolerantisme - "toleration" (French)
Torah - "Law" or First five books of Moses (Hebrew)
Virtus - "Virtue" (Latin)

Bibliography

Ames, Fisher. *A Sketch of the Character of Alexander Hamilton.* Boston: Repertory Office, 1804.

Anderson, Benedict. *Imagined Communities.* (New York: Verso Books, 2016).

Anonymous. *Dictionaire de France.* Paris: n. p., 1762.

Anonymous. Editorial "On Duelling." *New York Evening Post.* (November 21, 1801).

Anonymous. "The Inhabitants of Nevis and St. Kitts, 1678." *Caribbean* 4 (1914): 68–77.

——. *Royal Africa Company.*

Appleby, Joyce. *Liberalism and Republicanism: In the Historical Imagination.* Cambridge: Harvard University Press, 1991.

Aristotle. *Nicomachean Ethics.* New York: Hackett Books, 2019.

Bailyn, Bernard. *Ambiguities of the American Founders.* New York: Alfred A. Knopf, 2003.

Ball, Ankeet. "Ambition and Bondage: An Inquiry into Alexander Hamilton and Slavery." https://bit.ly/3vGRF82.

Bayle, Pierre. *Philosophical Commentary on the Gospels of Jesus Christ.* Washington: Liberty Fund, 2005.

Bellah, Robert. "Civil Religion in America." *Daedalus* 96, no 1 (Winter 1967): 1–21.

Broadus, Mitchell. "Hamilton's Quarrel with Washington." *The William and Mary Quarterly* 12, no 2 (April 1955).

Brookhiser, Richard. *Alexander Hamilton.* New York: Free Press, 1999.

Brooks, Robin. "Alexander Hamilton, Melancton, Smith, and the Ratification of the Constitution in New York," *The William and*

Mary Quarterly 24, no 3 (July 1967).

Brown, Kate Elizabeth. "Alexander Hamilton and the Development of American Law." Address at the Alexander Hamilton Awareness Society. The Grange National Memorial. January 21, 2019.

Bruchy, Stuart. "Alexander Hamilton and the State Banks." *The William and Mary Quarterly* 27, no. 3 (July 1970).

Burr, Aaron. *Political Correspondence and Public Papers*. 2 vols. Princeton: Princeton University Press, 1983.

Butler, Nicholas. "Address at the Unveiling of the Statue of Alexander Hamilton in the City of Paterson" (May 30, 1907).

Callahan, North. *Henry Knox: General Washington's General*. New York: Rinehart, 1958.

Callender, Tom. *Letters to Alexander Hamilton*. New York: Richard Reynolds, 1802.

Chan, Michael D. *Aristotle and Hamilton*. Columbia: University of Missouri Press, 2006.

Charles, Joseph. "Hamilton and Washington: The Origins of the American Party System." *The William and Mary Quarterly* 12, no. 2 (April 1955).

Chernow, Ron. *Alexander Hamilton*. New York: Penguin Books, 2005.

Cicero. *On Obligation*. Oxford: Oxford University Press, 2008.

Collins, Peter. "Procession." *The New York Daily Advertiser* (July 23, 1786).

Cooke, Jacob. *Alexander Hamilton: A Profile*. New York: Hill and Wang, 1967.

Cooper, Samuel. "Sermon on the Hebrew Republic." October 26, 1780.

Cunningham, Anna K. *The Schuyler Mansion*. Albany: New York State Education Department, 1955.

Domett, Henry. *A History of the Bank of New York, 1784–1884*. New York: Greenwood Books, 1884.

Dreisbach, Daniel. "The Vine and Fig Tree." https://bit.ly/3pl5GWD.

Edwards, Jonathan. "On the Great Awakening." Sermon (1738).

Elkins, Stanley and Eric McKintrick. *The Age of Federalism: The Early American Republic*. New York: Oxford University Press, 1995.

Emery, Noemie. *Alexander Hamilton*. New York: Putnam, 1982.

Ferro, Shaunacy. "Eleven Lessons from Alexander Hamilton." (March

31, 2017). https://bit.ly/3uLAsJt.

Fleming, Thomas. *Duel: Alexander Hamilton, Aaron Burr, and the Future of America*. New York: Basic Books, 1999.

Flexner, James. *The Young Hamilton: A Biography*. Boston: Back Bay Books, 1974.

Gaddis, David Lewis. *The Cold War: A New History*. New York: Penguin Books, 2006.

Goebel, Julius, ed. *The Law Practice of Alexander Hamilton*. 5 vols. New York: Columbia University Press, 1964–1981.

——. *The Papers of Alexander Hamilton*. 27 vols. New York: Columbia University Press,1961–1987.

Gordon-Reed, Annette. "Interview with *Harvard Gazette*. (October 7, 2016).

Greenfield, Liah. *Nationalism: Five Steps to Modernity*. Cambridge: Harvard University Press, 1993.

Hamilton, John Church. *Life of Alexander Hamilton*. 7 vols. Boston: Houghton Osgood, 1947.

——. *The Federalist: A Commentary on the Constitution of the United States*. Washington: Regnery, 1947.

Hamilton, Philo. "The Alexander Hamilton Slavery Smear." *New York Daily News* (January 16, 2021).

Herder, Johann. *Abhadlung uber den Orsrung der Sprache*. Berlin, 1770.

Hibri, Azizah Al-. "How Alexander Hamilton borrowed constitutional ideas from the Ottoman Empire." https://bit.ly/3yS4cYt.

Hickey, Donald F. *Citizen Hamilton*. New York: Rowman and Littlefield, 2006.

Hroch, Miroslav. *The Sociology of Nationalism*. Oxford: Clarendon, 1998.

Hume, David. *Political Discourses*. North Shore, New Zealand: Sagwan Press, 2015.

Jaffa, Harry. *Crisis of a House Divided*. Chicago: University of Chicago Press, 2009.

Jefferson, Thomas. *Autobiography*. New York: Dover Books, 2017.

Kay, Julia. "Synagogue in the Sand." *The Forward* (March 2, 2012). https://bit.ly/3uLBHID.

Kaplan, Lawrence S. "Alexander Hamilton: Ambivalent Anglophile." *Scholarly Resources* (2002).

Kent, James. *Commentaries on American Law*. (Chicago: University of Chicago Press, 1826).

Larson, Harold. "The Last Hours of Alexander Hamilton." *Columbia University Quarterly* 29, no. 1 (March 1937).

——. "Alexander Hamilton: Fact and Fiction of His Early Life." *The William and Mary Quarterly* 9, no. 2 (April 1952).

——. "The Birth and Parentage of Alexander Hamilton." *The American Genealogist* 21, no. 3 (January 1945).

Lind, Michael, ed. *Hamilton's Republic: Readings in the American Democratic Nationalist Tradition*. New York: Free Press, 1997.

Livingston, John. "Alexander Hamilton and the American Tradition." *Midwest Journal of Political Science* 1, no. 3 (November 1957).

Locke, John. *An Essay on Toleration*. Oxford: Clarendon, 2006.

Lodge, Henry Cabot. *Alexander Hamilton*. New York: Lume Books, 2016.

Lomask, Milton. *Aaron Burr: The Conspiracy Years*. New York: Farrar, Straus, and Giroux, 1982.

Lowry, Rick. *The Case for Nationalism*. New York: Harper Collins, 2019.

Marsh, Philip. "Hamilton and Monroe." *Mississippi Historical Review* 34, no. 3 (December 1947).

McDonald, Forest. *Alexander Hamilton: A Biography*. New York: Norton, 1982.

Meese, Edwin. "The Moral Foundations of Republican Government." *Imprimus* 15, no. 9 (September 1986).

Miller, John C. *Alexander Hamilton: Portrait of a Paradox*.

Miscencik, Paul. *The Original American Spies*. Washington: McFarland Books, 2014.

Moliere. *The Misanthrope and Tartuffe*. Translated by Richard Wilbur. New York: Mariner Books, 1965.

Morse, Anson. "Alexander Hamilton." *Political Science Quarterly* 5, no. 1 (March 1890).

O'Brien, Michael. *Hercules Mulligan*. New York: Kennedy and Sons, 1937.

Ogden, David. *Four Letters on the Death of Alexander Hamilton.* Portland, Maine: Anthoensen Press, 1980.

Oliver, Vere. *Caribbean.* 6 vols. London: Mitchell Hughes and Clarke, 1910–1919.

Paley, William. *Natural Theology.* Oxford: Oxford University Press, 2008.

——. *A View of the Evidence of Christianity.* London: Suzeteo Books, 2012.

——. *Principles of Morals and Political Philosophy.* Washington: Liberty Fund, 2003.

Parker, Cortland. *Alexander Hamilton and William Paterson.* Philadelphia: E. C. Markley and Sons, 1880.

Pisale, Gene. "Living History Part Two: Hamilton and Washington Were Brothers in Arms." *21ˢᵗ Century Media* (July 21, 2016).

Porwacher, Andrew. "A Jewish Founding Father: Alexander Hamilton's Hidden Life." Lecture and talk, January 11, 2021.

Rasmus, Jack. *Alexander Hamilton and the Origins of the Fed.* New York: Rowman and Littlefield, 2019.

Renwick, James. *Lives of John Jay and Alexander Hamilton.* New York: Harper, 1840.

Rieger, Michael. "Islam, Tolerance, and Thomas Jefferson." In *Libertarianism.* June 29, 2017.

Rossignol, Bernadette. "Census on the Island of Nevis."

Rossiter, Clinton. *The Federalist Papers.* New York: Signet Books, 2003.

Rousseau, Jean-Jacques. *Discourse on Inequality.* New York: Penguin Books, 1987.

Sabine, Lorenzo. *Notes on Duels and Duelling.* Boston: Crosby and Nichols, 1855.

Schuessler, Jennifer. "Alexander Hamilton, Enslaver? New Research Says Yes," *New York Times* (November 9, 2020).

Sedgewick, Theodore. *A Memoir of the Life of William Livingston.* New York: Harpers, 1833.

Serfilippi, Jessie. "As Odious and Immoral a Thing: Alexander Hamilton's Hidden History as an Enslaver." https://on.ny.gov/3fLOTsO.

Squiers, Anthony. *The Politics of the Sacred in America*.

Stern, Malcolm. "Some Notes on the Jews of Nevis." https://bit. ly/3vMtQLZ.

Stern-Taeubler, Selma. "The Jews in the Economic Policy of Frederick the Great." *Jewish School Studies* 11, no 2 (1949): 129–152.

Swanson, Donald. "Alexander Hamilton's Hidden Sinking Fund." *The William and Mary Quarterly* 49, no 1 (January 1992).

Steinberg, Mark. *Alexander Hamilton: Founding Father*. New York: Create Space, 2016.

Stevens, John Austin. *Colonial Records of the New York Chamber of Commerce*. New York: John Trow, 1867.

Stiles, Ezra. "The United States Elevated to Glory and Honor." Sermon. New Haven, 1783.

Torrey, Raymond. "Hamilton's Grange." *Scenic and Historic America* 3, no. 3 (April 1934).

Tugwell, Rexford. "Alexander Hamilton: Nation Maker." *Columbia University Quarterly* 29, no. 4 (December 1937).

Vicchio, Stephen. "The Origins and Development of Anti-Catholicism in America." *Perspectives on the American Catholic Church*. Edited by Stephen Vicchio and Sister Virginia Geiger. (Westminster: Christian Classics,1989): 85–103.

——. "What is More Important, Diversity or Freedom?" Study of Undergraduate Opinions, 2010–2015.

Vidal, Gore. *Burr*. New York: Vintage Books, 2000.

Voltaire. *Treatise on Toleration*. New York: Penguin Books, 2017.

——. "Reflections on Religion." In *Philosophical Works*. London: Art Now, 2016.

——. *Philosophical Dictionary*. New York: Hackett Books, 2020.

Wadsworth, Eliot. "Alexander Hamilton: First Secretary of the Treasury." *Columbia Alumni News* 16, no. 12 (December 19, 1924).

Webb, James. "The Fateful Encounter." *American Heritage* 26, no. 5 (August 1975).

West, Thomas G. *Alexander Hamilton*. New York: Independently Published, 2021.

——. *Vindicating the Fathers*. New York: Rowman and Littlefield, 1997.

Westergard, Waldemar. *The Danish West Indies Under Company Rule.* New York: Macmillan, 1917.

Wetterau, James. "New Light on the First Bank of the United States." *Pennsylvania Magazine* 61, no. 3.

Wills, Garry. *Explaining America: The Federalist.* New York: Penguin Books, 1982.

Wilson, Jackson. "The Founding Father." *The New Republic* 188, no. 23 (June 13, 1983).

Wood, Gordon S. *The American Revolution.* New York: Modern Library, 1982).

——. "The Revenge of Aaron Burr." *New York Review of Books* (February 2, 1984).

Ziegler, Alexander. "From Colonies to Nation: The Emergence of Nationalism." *Chrestomathy* 5 (2006): 347–375.

Endnotes

1   Ron Chernow, *Alexander Hamilton* (New York: Penguin Books, 2005), 16–17.

2   Ibid., 21–22.

3   Ibid.

4   James Hamilton (1753–1786) was the son of James Alexander Hamilton and Rachel Faucette and the brother of Alexander Hamilton. He was also the husband of Anna Hamilton and made his living as a carpenter.

5   James Hamilton Sr. (1718–1799), father of Alexander Hamilton, was born in Scotland. He made his living as a merchant.

6   John Adams letter to Benjamin Rush, April 21, 1806.

7   Michael E. Newton, *Discovering Hamilton* (London: Eleftheria Books, 2019), 217–220.

8   Cherno, 47–54.

9   Ibid.

10   Battles of Long Island and Trenton were fought on August 27, 1776, and December 26, 1776. The Second Battle of Trenton occurred on January 2, 1777. Hamilton served under the leadership of General Washington.

11   Gene Pisale, "Living History Part Two: Hamilton and Washington Were Brothers in Arms," *21st Century Media* (July 21, 2016).

12   Newton, 471–486.

13   The "Conway Cabal" was a group of Continental Army officers in late 1777 and early 1778 who wished to have George Washington replaced as the commander-in-chief. The movement was named after General Thomas Conway, the organizer of the group.

14   Alexander and Eliza's eight children were: Philip, Angelica, Alexander, James, John Church, William Stephen, Eliza and Philip.

15   *Hamilton Papers*, vol. 2, 178.

16 Ibid.

17 When Hamilton retired from the army in 1782, he declined to receive an army pension. After his untimely death on July 12, 1804, his wife Eliza presented a petition to the House of Representatives asking Congress to restore the pension. Her petition was denied, but in 1816, Congress passed a bill granting five years' pay as a pension for the years Hamilton was actually in combat.

18 This provision for a pension of 50 percent pay for Continental Army soldiers was passed by Congress in May of 1778.

19 Hamilton was a New York delegate of the Constitutional Convention in 1787. He sketched out what he saw as the weaknesses of the Articles of Confederation in *The Federalist Papers*, Essay 21. He suggested the articles had three difficulties. That the government does not have enough power to enforce its laws, that states do not have a guarantee of their rights, and states can ignore tax quotas set by the national government.

20 *Hamilton Papers*, vol. 17, 99–101.

21 The New York ratification process took place in Poughkeepsie, New York, in June and July 1788. July 26, 1788, the US Constitution was ratified in New York by a majority vote of 30 to 27.

22 Hamilton was secretary of the Treasury from 1789 until 1795.

23 *Hamilton Papers*, vol. 17, 112–124.

24 Ibid., 123.

25 Alexander Hamilton used a variety of pseudonyms over the years, including Junius, Publius, American Farmer, Camillus, Philo Camillus and many others, some in *The Federalist Papers* and others elsewhere.

26 Hamilton was inspector general from July 19, 1798, until February of 1800.

27 Alexander Hamilton founded the *New York Evening Post* in January of 1800. The first editor was William Coleman, who was replaced in 1829 by William Cullen Bryant.

28 *Hamilton Papers*, vol. 1, 227.

29 Chernow, *Alexander Hamilton*, 680–709.

30 Ibid., 682–683.

31 Ibid., 650–655.

32 Rev. Hugh Knox (1733–1790) was a Scottish Presbyterian minister at odds with the mainstream of his tradition, mostly because of his

firm belief in free will over and against the Calvinist doctrine of predestination. Knox was one of the mentors that contributed money to send the young Mr. Hamilton to New York.

33 Hamilton was at King's College from the Fall of 1774 until the Fall of 1776. He was also a trustee at King's from 1784 until 1804, when he died.

34 The doctrine of predestination is a view that all that happens is a result of the Will of God. In addition to Calvin, the doctrine was also held by Huldrych Zwingli and even earlier by Augustine of Hippo.

35 John Harris Cruger (1738–1807) was a mentor to Alexander Hamilton along with the Rev. Knox. Two letters from Hamilton to Cruger survive from October 31, 1771, and February 24, 1772.

36 It is likely that Alexander Hamilton learned to speak French from his mother, Rachel Fawcett, whose father was a French Huguenot physician, Johann Michael Fawcett.

37 *The Royal Danish American Gazette* was a semi-weekly newspaper published on the island of St. Croix between 1770 and 1797 in the city of Christiansted.

38 Alexander Hamilton, "In Yonder Mead My Love I Found," *Royal Danish American Gazette*, April 10, 1771.

39 Alexander Hamilton, "Celia's an Artful Little Slut," *Royal Danish American Gazette*, September 25, 1772.

40 Alexander Hamilton, "Response to the Hurricane," *Royal Danish American Gazette*, October 14, 1772.

41 Alexander Hamilton, "An Answer to the Inquiry of Why I Sighed," *Royal Danish American Gazette*, September 19, 1771.

42 Alexander Hamilton, "Christiansted: A Character," *Royal Danish American Gazette*, October 23, 1772.

43 *Hamilton Papers*, vol. 1, 119–122.

44 Hamilton attended the Elizabethtown Academy, which was located at 42 Broad Street in Elizabeth, New Jersey, from the Fall and Winter of 1771 until the Spring of 1772.

45 Chernow, 42.

46 Henry Brockholst Livingston (1757–1823) was a captain in the Continental Army and a New York Court of Appeals judge.

47 Rev. James Caldwell (1734–1781) was a Virginia-born Presbyterian minister and patriot during the American Revolutionary War.

48 Caldwell's First Presbyterian Church was across the square from the Academy in Elizabeth, New Jersey.

49   John Church Hamilton, *Life of Alexander Hamilton*, vol. 2, 143.

50   Ibid.

51   Chernow, 63.

52   Ibid.

53   Ibid., 51–54.

54   Ibid., 53–54.

55   Clinton Rossiter, ed., *The Federalist Papers* (New York: Signet Classics, 2003).

56   Alexander Hamilton, "Essay on the Hurricane," *Royal Danish American Gazette*, September 6, 1772.

57   Chernow, 582.

58   Ibid.

59   Ibid.

60   Ibid., 583.

61   Ibid.

62   Ibid., 706–707.

63   Ibid.

64   Ibid., 708.

65   Ibid., 713.

66   Alexander Hamilton, *The Farmer Refuted*, National Archive, Founders Online, February 23, 1775, https://bit.ly/3dQtVYd.

67   The US Declaration of Independence, 1776. Second Continental Congress.

68   Altogether, we have counted ten names for God in the works of Alexander Hamilton, but he rarely uses the word "God." The names he did use were Creator, Supreme Judge, Supreme King, Providence, the Great Designer, the Great Judge, a Finger of the Almighty Hand, the Hand of the Divine, Nature's God, and the Good and Just Creator.

69   *The Federalist Papers*, no. 22.

70   James Monroe at the Constitutional Convention, July 1787.

71   Ibid.

72   Alexander Hamilton at the Constitutional Convention.

73   Alexander Hamilton, "Fragment on the French Revolution," *Hamilton Papers*, 17:165–166.

74   George Washington to the Newport Hebrew Congregation, August 18, 1790.

75   Alexander Hamilton, *The History of the Republic of the United States*, vol. 7, 790.

76   Ron Chernow, *Alexander Hamilton* (New York: Penguin Books, 2005), 583.

77   Chernow, 707.

78   Ibid.

79   Ibid., 713.

80   Ibid.

81   Gospel of Luke 22:16. *See also* Mark 14:22–25 and Corinthians 11:23–25.

82   Ibid.

83   Alexander Hamilton to Elizabeth Schuyler, August 8, 1780.

84   William Paley, *A View of the Evidence of Christianity* (London: Suzeteo Enterprises, 2012). John Church Hamilton tells us his father was very fond of his copy of Paley's work.

85   Hamilton to William Bradford, November 9, 1803.

86   William Paley, *Natural Theology* (Oxford: Oxford World Classics, 2008).

87   Paley, *Principles of Morals and Political Philosophy* (Washington: Liberty Fund, 2003).

88   Paley, *Natural Theology* (Nursia: Benedictine Classics, 2017).

89   Voltaire, "Reflections on Religion," in the *Philosophical Works* (London: E-Art now, 2016).

90   John Church Hamilton, *The Life of Alexander Hamilton*, vol. 7, 333. *See also* letter to Bayard, April 16, 1802.

91   Ibid., Bayard letter.

92   Ibid.

93   Chernow, 275.

94   Bayard letter.

95   Ibid.

96   Chernow, 717.

97   Ibid., 661.

98   "Fragment on the French Revolution."

99   Ibid.

100   Ibid.

101   After being expelled from Brazil in the seventeenth century, Jews began to settle on Nevis and St. Kitts. They were mostly Sephardic Jews. These Jews brought with them the secrets of crystalizing sugar, making Nevis the Queen of the Caribbean. The Jewish community there built a synagogue in the city of Charlestown in 1684. Remains

of a Jewish cemetery are still there. It includes nineteen grave markers that date from 1679 to 1768. *See* Julie Kay, "Synagogues in the Sand," *The Forward*, February 27, 2012, https://bit.ly/3fWhH1F.

102 The Rev. Hugh Knox (1733–1790) visited the island of St. Croix in 1771 and was received warmly by the Presbyterian community there. He became a pastor at the Scots Presbyterian Church in 1772.

103 Elias Boudinot (1740–1821) was a lawyer and statesman from Elizabeth, New Jersey, and a delegate to the Continental Congress. He was also appointed by President George Washington as director of the US Mint. He was Hamilton's mentor when he attended the Elizabethtown Academy.

104 Mr. Boudinot made this comment when he accepted the job as head of the American Bible Society in 1816.

105 Ibid.

106 John Church Hamilton, *The Life of Alexander Hamilton*, vol. 6, 321.

107 Chernow, 706.

108 Ibid., 707.

109 Hamilton to John Dickinson, November 30, 1801.

110 Hamilton, quoted in Shaunacy Ferro, "Eleven Lessons from Alexander Hamilton," March 31, 2017. https://bit.ly/3ggY8jI.

111 Micah 4:4 (New International Version).

112 Zechariah 3:10 (NIV).

113 First Kings 4:25 (NIV).

114 Isaiah 36:16 (NIV).

115 George Tsakiridis, Ph.D., "Vine and the Fig Tree," https://bit.ly/2SaCPs7.

116 See Note 101.

117 The prophet *Musa* appears in the Muslim Holy Book Al-Qur'an more often than any other prophet of Islam. He is called *Kalimullah*, which means "to whom Allah has spoken."

118 John Lyde Wilson, *The Code of Honor*, https://bit.ly/3ctNOno.

119 Aristotle, *Nicomachean Ethics*, book 6, question 58.

120 Book of Job 19:25–27 (NIV).

121 Psalm 41:12 (NIV).

122 Psalm 112:3 and 7 (NIV).

123 These were all found in the *Hamilton Papers*, particularly volumes 1-10.

124 "Sitting at the right hand of the Father" is mentioned in all of these New Testament passages.

125 Luke 6:20–26 (NIV).

126 Romans 12:9–21 (NIV).

127 Colossians 3:10 (NIV).

128 First Corinthians 13:4–8 and 13 (NIV).

129 Ephesians 4:25 and 5:1–2 (NIV).

130 Judges 4:1–17.

131 Chernow, 685, 695 and 706–708.

132 The general view today is that Hamilton wrote fifty-one; Madison, twenty-nine; and Jay, five essays.

133 Ibid.

134 *The Federalist Papers*, Essay 2.

135 Ibid.

136 Ibid.

137 Ibid., Essay 15.

138 Ibid.

139 Ibid.

140 Ibid.

141 See Note 132.

142 John Church Hamilton, *The Life of Alexander Hamilton*, vol. 1, 119.

143 Ibid.

144 Chernow, 706.

145 Ibid., 254 and 296.

146 Mr. Hamilton took up the issue of the moral character of judges in *The Federalist Papers*, Essay 84.

147 Chernow, 17.

148 Simon Israel's grave marker is one of the nineteen markers in the Jewish cemetery on Nevis. *See* Julie Kay, "Synagogue in the Sand," *The Forward*, March 2, 2012. An archeological dig was conducted in Nevis of the Jewish cemetery in 2012–2018. *See* NHCS http://www.nevisheritage.org/.

149 Rabbi Gershom Seixas (1746–1816) was appointed to the Board of Regents of Columbia Univ. in 1787 and served in that capacity until 1802.

150 All these men were board members of the SUNY system.

151 George Washington's second inauguration was on March 4, 1793. The Rabbi Seixas marched in a procession that included clergymen from many different denominations and sects.

152 Congregation Shearith was established in New York City in 1654. It was the first synagogue in North America.

153 This case was called The People of the State of New York v. Croswell (1804).

154 Many of these clients of Hamilton's were board members of Rabbi Seixas' congregation.

155 People v. Croswell.

156 James Kent, "Commentaries on American Law," 2:12–22 (Chicago: University of Chicago Press, 1826).

157 Frederick II of Prussia limited the number of Jews in Breslau. *See* Selma Stern-Taeubler, "The Jews in the Economic Policy of Frederick the Great," *Jewish School Studies*, vol. 11, no. 2 (1949), 129–152.

158 In 1772, the Russian Orthodox Church forbade Jews from entering the "interior portions of Russia."

159 Voltaire, *Candide* (New York: Hackett Books, 2007); *Philosophical Dictionary* (New York: Penguin Books, 1984); *Philosophical Letters* (New York: Hackett Books, 2020).

160 Rev. Johannes Megapolensis (1603–1670) was a Dutch Reform minister. He is best known for his *An Account of the Mohawk Indians*.

161 Peter Stuyvesant (1592–1672) was known as the "New Amsterdam Jewish Crusader," https://bit.ly/3vyujAN.

162 Ibid.

163 Ibid.

164 Peter Collin, "Procession," *The Daily Advertiser* (New York, NY), July 23, 1788.

165 George Washington, Farewell Address, September 19, 1796.

166 Ibid.

167 Ibid.

168 Andrew Porwancher, *A Jewish Founding Father: Alexander Hamilton's Hidden Life*, (forthcoming).

169 Ibid.

170 Ibid.

171 Ibid.

172 Ibid.

173 Malcolm Stern, "Some Notes on the Jews of Nevis," *American Jewish Archives* (October 1958).

174 Stephen Vicchio, "The Origins and Development of Anti-Catholicism in America," in *Perspectives on the American Catholic Church 1789–1989*, ed. Stephen Vicchio and Sister Virgina Geiger (Westminster: Christian Classics, 1989), 85–103.

175 John Tracy Ellis, quoted in ibid.

176 Vicchio, "The Origins and Development of Anti-Catholicism in America."

177 Ibid.

178 Ibid.

179 Alexander Hamilton, "Remarks on the Quebec Bill," June 21, 1775.

180 Fitzsimons was an Irish-born immigrant to Philadelphia, where he became a merchant. He also was a Pennsylvania Delegate to the Constitutional Convention.

181 John Locke, *A Letter Concerning Toleration* (Oxford: Clarendon, 2006).

182 Michael Rieger, "Islam, Tolerance, and Thomas Jefferson," *Libertarianism* (June 29, 2017), https://bit.ly/3vHSf4B.

183 Thomas Jefferson, *Autobiography* (New York: Dover Books, 2017), 196.

184 George Washington, letter to the Virginia Assembly on May 17, 1790.

185 Sambo Anderson (1760–1845) was a carpenter from northwest Africa. He worked on Washington's Mount Vernon farms and retired to one of his properties in Arlington.

186 George Washington to Tench Tilghman, March 24, 1784.

187 Constitution of the State of Massachusetts, 1780.

188 Theophilus Parsons (1750–1813) was the first Chief Justice of the US Supreme Court.

189 Ezra Stiles quoted in James Hutson, "Founding Fathers and Islam," *Library of Congress* (February 2005), https://bit.ly/3jc91Xd.

190 Ibid.

191 Ibid.

192 Ibid.

193 Ibid.

194 Azizah Al-Hibri, "How Alexander Hamilton Borrowed Constitutional Ideas from the Ottoman Empire," *Islam Founding Fathers*, May 9, 2013, https://bit.ly/2Secycc.

195 John Adams, "Treaty of Tripoli," (1797).

196 Ibid.

197 Alexander Hamilton, *The Federalist Papers*, Essay 11.

198 Moliere, *The Misanthrope and Tartuffe*, ed. Richard Wilbur (New York: Mariner Books, 1965).

199 Aristotle, *Nicomachean Ethics* (New York: Hackett Books, 2019),

Book 6.

200 Alexander Hamilton's copy of Aristotle's *Nicomachean Ethics* can be found in the Rare Book and Manuscript Library of Columbia University Libraries.

201 Aristotle, Book 6.

202 Ibid.

203 Some of Hamilton's books are now owned by the Irving Public Library in Texas.

204 College of New Jersey, Admission Standards. *See* Ron Chernow, *Alexander Hamilton*, 35 and 42.

205 Alexander Hamilton's college notebook, Columbia University, New York City. *See* Chernow, 34 and 45.

206 Hamilton's visit to Monticello, April 4, 1791.

207 Chernow, 659.

208 Exchange between William Ketelas and Alexander Hamilton, May 21, 1789. *See* Chernow, 571.

209 Cicero, *On Obligations* (Oxford: Oxford University Press, 2008), 9–21.

210 Ibid., 21–30.

211 Chernow, 52.

212 David Hume, *Political Discourses* (North Shore, NZ: Sagwan Press, 2015). *See* Chernow, 296.

213 Chernow, 614 and 619.

214 Hume, *Political Discourses*.

215 Hume, 93.

216 Chernow, 296.

217 Jean-Jacques Rousseau, *Discourse on Inequality* (New York: Penguin Books, 1985).

218 Joseph Addison, *Cato: A Tragedy* (Washington: Liberty Fund, 2004). *See also* Chernow, 107 and 206.

219 Chernow, 107.

220 Ibid., 206.

221 Chernow, p. 581.

222 Alexander Hamilton, *The Federalist Papers*, Essay 1.

223 Cicero, 19. *See also* Chernow, 42 and 110.

224 Aristotle, *Ethics*, 1104b 20–26.

225 Hamilton, *The Federalist Papers*, Essay 1.

226 Hamilton made this statement in a pronouncement written between June 27 and July 4, 1804, a week to ten days before his death.

227 *New York Evening Post*, November 21, 1801.

228 Kate Elizabeth Brown, *Alexander Hamilton and the Development of American Law* (University Press of Kansas, 2017). The Alexander Hamilton Awareness Society. Hamilton Grange National Memorial.

229 Hamilton made this statement in a letter. *See* https://bit.ly/2TYmVl0.

230 Hamilton's authorship of fifty-one of *The Federalist Papers* is now the standard scholarly view.

231 Alexander Hamilton, "The Defense of the Funding System," July 1795.

232 Ibid.

233 Shaunacy Ferro, "11 Life Lessons from Alexander Hamilton," *Mental Floss*, March 31, 2017, https://bit.ly/3zP6V5n.

234 Jeff Wilser, "How Alexander Hamilton Can Help You Get Promoted," *Time*, October 7, 2016. *See also* Ferro, https://bit.ly/3zP6V5n.

235 John Church Hamilton, *The Life of Alexander Hamilton*, vol. 2, 115.

236 Letter from Alexander Hamilton to George Washington, May 17, 1795, quoted in Walter Lippmann, *The Public Philosophy* (Boston: Little Brown, 1955), 20 and 27.

237 Alexander Hamilton, *The Federalist Papers*, Essay 36.

238 Stephen Vicchio, *Theodicy in the Christian Tradition: A History* (Pittsburgh: Rose Dog Books, 2020), 19–26.

239 Mr. Hamilton made a similar statement in a letter to Mr. Burr on June 20, 1804, a few weeks before the duel.

240 Ron Chernow, *Alexander Hamilton* (New York: Penguin Books, 2005), 713 and 722.

241 This is now the standard view of the authorship of *The Federalist Papers*.

242 Edwin Meese III, "The Moral Foundations of Republican Government," *Imprimis*, vol. 15, no 9, September 1986, https://bit.ly/35Ssxjn.

243 Personal observation of the author on President Biden.

244 Chernow, 409–418.

245 Ibid.

246 Ibid.

247 Ibid.

248 Ibid.

249 Ibid.

250 Ibid.

251 Ibid.

252 Lyrics of the song "Reynolds Pamphlet" from the musical *Hamilton*.

253 Alexander Hamilton, *The Federalist Papers*, Essay 8.

254 John Church Hamilton, *The Life of Alexander Hamilton*, vol. 2, 203.

255 Ibid., 204.

256 *The Federalist Papers*, Essay 8.

257 Alexander Hamilton, "Tully," *Founders Online*, no. 3, August 28, 1794, https://bit.ly/3y2P49e.

258 Alexander Hamilton to George Washington, April 18, 1793.

259 Alexander Hamilton, *The Federalist Papers*, Essay 70.

260 Ibid., Essay 33.

261 *The Federalist Papers*, Essays 8 and 70.

262 Aristotle makes this distinction in 1104b of the *Ethics*.

263 Dr. John Faucett (1680–1745) was born in Saintonge, France, and was a French Huguenot who fled to Nevis around 1658, sometime after the Edict of Nantes. He became a physician and gentleman farmer and was married twice.

264 The Edict of Nantes was signed in April of 1598 by King Henry IV of France and granted Protestants of France substantial rights not previously held. The Edict separated civil and religious liberties for the first time.

265 *A Dictionary of the English Language* by Samuel Johnson did not list the American English word "toleration" until 1783.

266 Chernow, 544.

267 Hamilton wrote throughout his *Collected Works* on the issue of religious toleration, including *The Federalist Papers*, Essays 1, 2, 10, 23, 47, 51, 52, 55, and 84.

268 Shelly v. Kraemer (1948) was a landmark Supreme Court decision that struck down racially restrictive housing covenants. Chief Justice Fred Vinson wrote the majority opinion. He said private parties could abide by the terms of a racially restrictive covenant, but that judicial enforcement qualified as a state action and was thus prohibited by the Equal Protection Clause.

269 Boston Port Act issued on March 7, 1774, was passed by the British Parliament on March 31, 1774. It was designed to punish the residents of Boston for the incident that would later be known as the "Boston Tea Party."

270 The Apollo Room of the Raleigh Tavern was the meeting place for the

radical members of the House of Burgesses when Governor Dunmore disbanded the House. The tavern had been built in 1717 and served as a colonial meeting place. The original structure survived until 1859, when it burned down. It was later rebuilt and is now a museum and gives tours of the facilities.

271   George Washington at Valley Forge, https://bit.ly/3w7s5IN.

272   Ibid.

273   Engel v. Vitale, 370 US 421 (1962). Abingdon School District v. Schemp (1963).

274   John Adams to Abigail Adams, November 2, 1798.

275   Thomas Jefferson, "A National Prayer Day of Peace," November 11, 1779.

276   Benjamin Franklin on George Whitefield, 1739. National Humanities Center, Washington, DC.

277   James Madison, "Detached Memorandum," January 31, 1820. For more on Madison's "Detached Memorandum," see *William and Mary Quarterly* 3 (1946): 554–560.

278   Chernow, 42–43.

279   Chernow, 102.

280   Hercules Mulligan (1740–1825) was an Irish-American tailor and spy during the American Revolution. He was also a founding member of the Sons of Liberty. Mulligan's slave, Cato, was one of the first black American patriots.

281   Paul R. Misencik, *The Original American Spies: Seven Covert Agents of the Revolutionary War* (Washington: McFarland Books, 2014).

282   Ibid.

283   Ibid.

284   Ibid.

285   Ibid.

286   John Church Hamilton, *The Life of Alexander Hamilton*, vol. 7, 119–120.

287   Alexander Hamilton to James Bayard on April 21, 1802. Bayard's response was dated May 15, 1802. The subject of these letters was the establishment of the Christian Constitutional Society.

288   Hamilton, *The Life of Alexander Hamilton*, vol. 7, 342–342.

289   Chernow, 726–727.

290   Alexander Hamilton to Eliza Hamilton, July 4, 1804. *The Papers of Alexander Hamilton*, vol. 26, May 1, 1802, to October 23, 1804, ed.

Harold C. Syrett (New York: Columbia University Press, 1979), 293.

291 John C. Miller, *Alexander Hamilton: Portrait in Paradox* (Old Saybrook: Konecky and Konecky, 1959).

292 Forest McDonald, *Alexander Hamilton: A Biography* (New York: Norton, 1982).

293 Ron Chernow, *Alexander Hamilton* (New York: Penguin Books, 2004).

294 Richard Brookhiser, *Alexander Hamilton, American* (New York: Free Press, 1999).

295 Thomas G. West, *Vindicating the Founders* (New York: Rowman and Littlefield, 1997).

296 Jacob Ernest Cooke, *Alexander Hamilton: A Profile* (New York: Hill and Wang, 1967).

297 Harry V. Jaffa, *Crisis of the House Divided* (Chicago: University of Chicago Press, 2009).

298 Michael D. Chan, *Aristotle and Hamilton* (Columbia: University of Missouri Press, 2006).

299 Miller, 47.

300 McDonald, 149.

301 Chernow, 6.

302 Ibid., 215.

303 Brookhiser, 111.

304 Broadus Mitchell, *Alexander Hamilton: Youth to Maturity* (New York: Macmillan, 1957).

305 Henry Cabot Lodge, *Alexander Hamilton* (Edinburgh: n.p., 1886).

306 James Oliver, *Alexander Hamilton* (New York: Columbia University Press, 1961).

307 Chernow, 581.

308 Ibid.

309 The New York African Free School was created in 1787. The purpose of the school was to educate black children for something other than slavery before manumission in New York in 1827.

310 New York Manumission Society Charter (1785).

311 John Henry Laurens' proposal was first made on February 2, 1778. Laurens was president of the Continental Congress from 1777 to 1778 and was a lieutenant colonel in the Continental Army. He was George Washington's aide-de-camp before Alexander Hamilton.

312 Alexander Hamilton to John Jay, March 14, 1779.

313 Chernow, 94–97.

314 Philo Hamilton, "Alexander Hamilton: Slavery Smear," *New York Daily News*, January 16, 2021.

315 Anonymous, "Hamilton and Slavery," *Huffington Post*, July 7, 2020.

316 Jaffa, 73.

317 Chan, 7–8.

318 Spain was in the West Indies from 1492 until 1550. The Spanish called the area the *Hispanophone Caribbean*, which referred mostly to Cuba, the Dominican Republic and Puerto Rico.

319 The six Dutch Caribbean islands were Eustatius, Saba, Bonaire, Saint Maarten, Curacao and Aruba.

320 The Portuguese established sugar production in the Caribbean off the coast of Brazil in the 1550s, followed by the Dutch and the French. The French established sugar production in Jamaica and Saint Domingue in the 1740s.

321 "Census" of Island of Nevis, 1671. Bernadette Rossignol, *Recensement de l'Ile de Saint-Christophe: année 1671*.

322 "Inhabitants of Nevis and St. Kitts, 1678," *Caribbeana* 4 (1914): 68–77.

323 Royal Africa Company records (1695–1743). These records are kept by the British National Archives in London, as well as in Liverpool.

324 Slavery records on St. Kitts and Nevis, National Museums Liverpool. These records have essays on sugar, slaver, diet and food, slave villages and many other topics.

325 Ibid.

326 Ibid.

327 The word "Maroon" comes from a French word that means "chestnut." It was first used in English, according to the *Oxford English Dictionary* in 1791 to refer to "a fugitive black slave living in wilder parts."

328 Alexander Hamilton letter, September 6, 1772.

329 Ibid.

330 Ankeet Ball, "Ambition and Bondage: An Inquiry on Alexander Hamilton and Slavery," https://bit.ly/2UrIgDK.

331 Jessie Serfilippi, "An Odious and Immoral a Thing: Alexander Hamilton's Hidden History as an Enslaver," https://on.ny.gov/3hA1Vt3.

332 Alexander Hamilton to George Clinton (June 1, 1783).

333 Jennifer Schuessler, "Alexander Hamilton, Enslaver? New Research Says Yes," *New York Times*, November 9, 2020.

334 Philo Hamilton, "The Alexander Hamilton Slavery Smear," *The New York Daily News*, January 16, 2021.

335 Benedict Anderson, *Imagined Communities* (Brooklyn: Verso Books, 2016), 121.

336 Liah Greenfeld, *Nationalism and the Mind: Essays on Modern Culture* (New York: Oneworld Publications, 2006).

337 Donald Trump rally, October 23, 2018, Houston, Texas.

338 See, for example, Deuteronomy 14 and Genesis 15, which both imply the Jews are a "Chosen People" by the God Yahweh.

339 Christianity was established as the religion of the Roman Empire under the reign of Theodosius in 392.

340 Johann Gottfried von Herder (1744–1803) and Johann Gottlieb von Fichte (1762–1814) were two early German nationalists.

341 Johann Gottfried von Herder, *Abhandlung über den Ursprung der Sprache* (Berlin, 1770), 47.

342 Alexander Ziegler, "From Colonies to Nation: The Emergence of American Nationalism, 1750–1800," *Chrestomathy* 5, (2006): 347–375.

343 Ibid., 350.

344 Ibid., 361–362.

345 Ibid., 364.

346 Ibid., 365–366.

347 Ibid., 366–367.

348 Ibid., 368–371.

349 Miroslav Hroch, *The Sociology of Nationalism* (Oxford: Clarendon, 1998), 53.

350 Ibid.

351 Ibid., 54–55.

352 Jonathan Edwards, "On the Great Awakening" sermon, 1738.

353 Samuel Cooper, "Sermon on Hebrew Republic," October 26, 1780, Massachusetts Bay Colony.

354 Ezra Stiles, "The United States Elevated to Glory and Honor," New Haven, Connecticut, 1783.

355 The 1794 Jay Treaty between the United States and Britain was signed to settle several issues still in dispute between the two countries.

356 Alexander Hamilton established the National Bank on December 15, 1790.

357 Among many other issues, both domestic and international, there was also the role of France and the wealth in the economy.

358 Jack Rasmus, *Alexander Hamilton and the Origins of the Fed* (New York: Rowman and Litttlefield, 2019), 200–201.

359 Ibid.

360 Ibid., 256.

361 Ibid.

362 Hamilton quoted in Donald R. Hickey, *Citizen Hamilton* (New York: Rowman and Littlefield, 2006), 108.

363 Robert Bellah, "Civil Religion in America," *Daedalus* 96, no. 1 (Winter, 1967): 1–21, https://bit.ly/3dKFzDN.

364 Anthony Squiers, *The Politics of the Sacred in America* (Fort Worth: Springer, 2019).

365 David Lewis Gaddis, *The Cold War: A New History* (New York: Penguin Books, 2006).

366 Squiers, 17.

367 Author's personal experiences.

368 Personal reflections of author.

369 Bret Stephens, Kim Holmes and Elan Journo quoted in Yoram Hazony, "American Nationalists," *The American Conservative*, June 22, 2020, https://bit.ly/3dNJ24S.

370 Lawrence Kaplan, *Alexander Hamilton: Ambivalent Anglophile* (New York: Rowman and Littlefield, 2001).

371 George Washington, "Circular," June 21, 1783.

372 Craig L. Symonds quoted in Rich Lowry, *The Case For Nationalism* (New York: HarperCollins, 2019), 61.

373 Alexander Ziegler, "From Colonies to Nation: The Emergence of American Nationalism, 1750–1800," *Chrestomathy* 5, (2006): 374–375.

374 Bellah, 11–12.

375 Squiers, 67–68.

376 Kaplan, 27.

377 Ron Chernow, *Alexander Hamilton* (New York: Penguin Books, 2005), 43–46 and 280–281; and 183–184 and 285–286.

378 This same technique was employed by most of the other Founding Fathers. Washington, for example, used over ninety different terms to avoid using the word God.

379 James A. Bayard (1767–1815) was an American attorney and politician from Wilmington, Delaware.

380 Chernow, 280–281.

381 Philip Hamilton (1782–1801), Alexander's eldest son, died at the age
     of nineteen in a duel with George Eacker, defending his father's honor.
382 Rabbi Gershom Seixas (1745–1816) was the first native-born Jewish
     religious leader in America.
383 Ibid.
384 Ibid.
385 Andrew Porwancher, *The Jewish World of Alexander Hamilton*
     (Princeton: Princeton University Press, 2021).
386 For more on the Barbary Wars, see Frank Lambert, *The Barbary Wars*
     (New York: Hill and Wand, 2007).
387 Joseph Addison, *Cato: A Tragedy* (Washington: Liberty Fund, 2004).
388 Aristotle, *Nicomachean Ethics* (New York: Hackett Books, 2019),
     sections 1110a to 1111b.
389 Edwin Meese III, "The Moral Foundations of Republican
     Government," *Imprimis*, vol. 15, no. 9, September 1986, https://bit.
     ly/35Ssxjn.
390 Alexander Hamilton, *The Farmer Refuted*, National Archive, Founders
     Online, February 23, 1775, https://bit.ly/3dQtVYd.
391 John Locke, *An Essay on Toleration* (Oxford: Clarendon, 2006);
     Voltaire, *Treatise on Toleration* (New York: Penguin Books, 2017).
392 John Church Hamilton, *The Life of Alexander Hamilton*, vol. 1, 46–47.
393 Ibid., 47.
394 See Bibliography entries from Anson Morse, John Livingston and
     Jackson Wilson, for examples.
395 The first two slave rebellions on Nevis and St. Kitts were in 1639
     and 1740. We were referring to the one in 1740, fifteen years before
     Hamilton's birth.
396 Alexander Hamilton to John Jay, March 14, 1779.
397 Alexander Hamilton, *The Federalist Papers*, Essays 11 and 12.
398 *The Federalist Papers*, Essay 11.
399 Alexander Hamilton, "A Full Vindication of the Measures of
     Congress" (New York: Palala Press, 2017).
400 Alexander Ziegler, "From Colonies to Nation: The Emergence
     of American Nationalism, 1750–1800," *Chrestomathy* 5, (2006):
     347–375.
401 Ibid.
402 Robert Bellah, "Civil Religion in America," *Daedalus* 96, no. 1
     (Winter, 1967): 1–21, https://bit.ly/3dKFzDN.

403   Ibid.
404   Anthony Squiers, *The Politics of the Sacred in America* (Forth Worth: Springer, 2019).
405   Personal experience of the author.
406   Ibid.
407   Jonathan Den Hartog, "Religion, the Federalist, and American Nationalism," *Religions* 8, no 5 (2017).

Index

About the Author

Before his retirement in 2016, Stephen Vicchio taught for more than forty years at the University of Maryland, Johns Hopkins, St. Mary's Seminary in Baltimore, and other universities in Britain and the United States. He has authored over three dozen books, as well as essays and plays, mostly about the Bible, philosophy and theology. Among his books since 2000 is his interpretation of the Book of Job, *The Antichrist: A History*; *Biblical Figures in the Islamic Faith* and books about the religions of American presidents George Washington, Thomas Jefferson, Abraham Lincoln and Alexander Hamilton, including *Ronald Reagan's Religious Beliefs*.

Made in the USA
Middletown, DE
27 September 2021